ASGARDIANS OF THE GALAXY

THE INFINITY ARMADA

CULLEN BUNN
WRITER

MATTEO LOLLI
WITH ANDRÉ LIMA ARAÚJO (#3), JILL THOMPSON (#3), MIKE DEL MUNDO (#3),
NATACHA BUSTOS (#4), LUCA MARESCA (#4-5) & STEPHANIE HANS (#5)
ARTISTS

FEDERICO BLEE
WITH ERICK ARCINIEGA (#3), JILL THOMPSON (#3), MIKE DEL MUNDO (#3) & STEPHANIE HANS (#5)
COLOR ARTISTS

VC's CORY PETIT
LETTERER

DALE KEOWN & JASON KEITH
COVER ART

SARAH BRUNSTAD
EDITOR

WIL MOSS
SUPERVISING EDITOR

TOM BREVOORT
EXECUTIVE EDITOR

ANGELA CO-CREATED BY
TODD McFARLANE & NEIL GAIMAN

COLLECTION EDITOR **JENNIFER GRÜNWALD**
ASSISTANT EDITOR **CAITLIN O'CONNELL**
ASSOCIATE MANAGING EDITOR **KATERI WOODY**
EDITOR, SPECIAL PROJECTS **MARK D. BEAZLEY**
VP PRODUCTION & SPECIAL PROJECTS **JEFF YOUNGQUIST**
SVP PRINT, SALES & MARKETING **DAVID GABRIEL**

BOOK DESIGNER **ADAM DEL RE**

EDITOR IN CHIEF **C.B. CEBULSKI**
CHIEF CREATIVE OFFICER **JOE QUESADA**
PRESIDENT **DAN BUCKLEY**
EXECUTIVE PRODUCER **ALAN FINE**

ASGARDIANS OF THE GALAXY VOL. 1: THE INFINITY ARMADA. Contains material originally published in magazine form as ASGARDIANS OF THE GALAXY #1-5. First printing 2019. ISBN 978-1-302-91471-4. Published by MARVEL WORLDWIDE, INC., a subsidiary of MARVEL ENTERTAINMENT, LLC. OFFICE OF PUBLICATION: 135 West 50th Street, New York, NY 10020. © 2019 MARVEL No similarity between any of the names, characters, persons, and/or institutions in this magazine with those of any living or dead person or institution is intended, and any such similarity which may exist is purely coincidental. **Printed in Canada.** DAN BUCKLEY, President, Marvel Entertainment; JOHN NEE, Publisher; JOE QUESADA, Chief Creative Officer; TOM BREVOORT, SVP of Publishing; DAVID BOGART, Associate Publisher & SVP of Talent Affairs; DAVID GABRIEL, SVP of Sales & Marketing, Publishing; JEFF YOUNGQUIST, VP of Production & Special Projects; DAN CARR, Executive Director of Publishing Technology; ALEX MORALES, Director of Publishing Operations; DAN EDINGTON, Managing Editor; SUSAN CRESPI, Production Manager; STAN LEE, Chairman Emeritus. For information regarding advertising in Marvel Comics or on Marvel.com, please contact Vit DeBellis, Custom Solutions & Integrated Advertising Manager, at vdebellis@marvel.com. For Marvel subscription inquiries, please call 888-511-5480. **Manufactured between 2/1/2019 and 3/5/2019 by SOLISCO PRINTERS, SCOTT, QC, CANADA.**

10 9 8 7 6 5 4 3 2 1

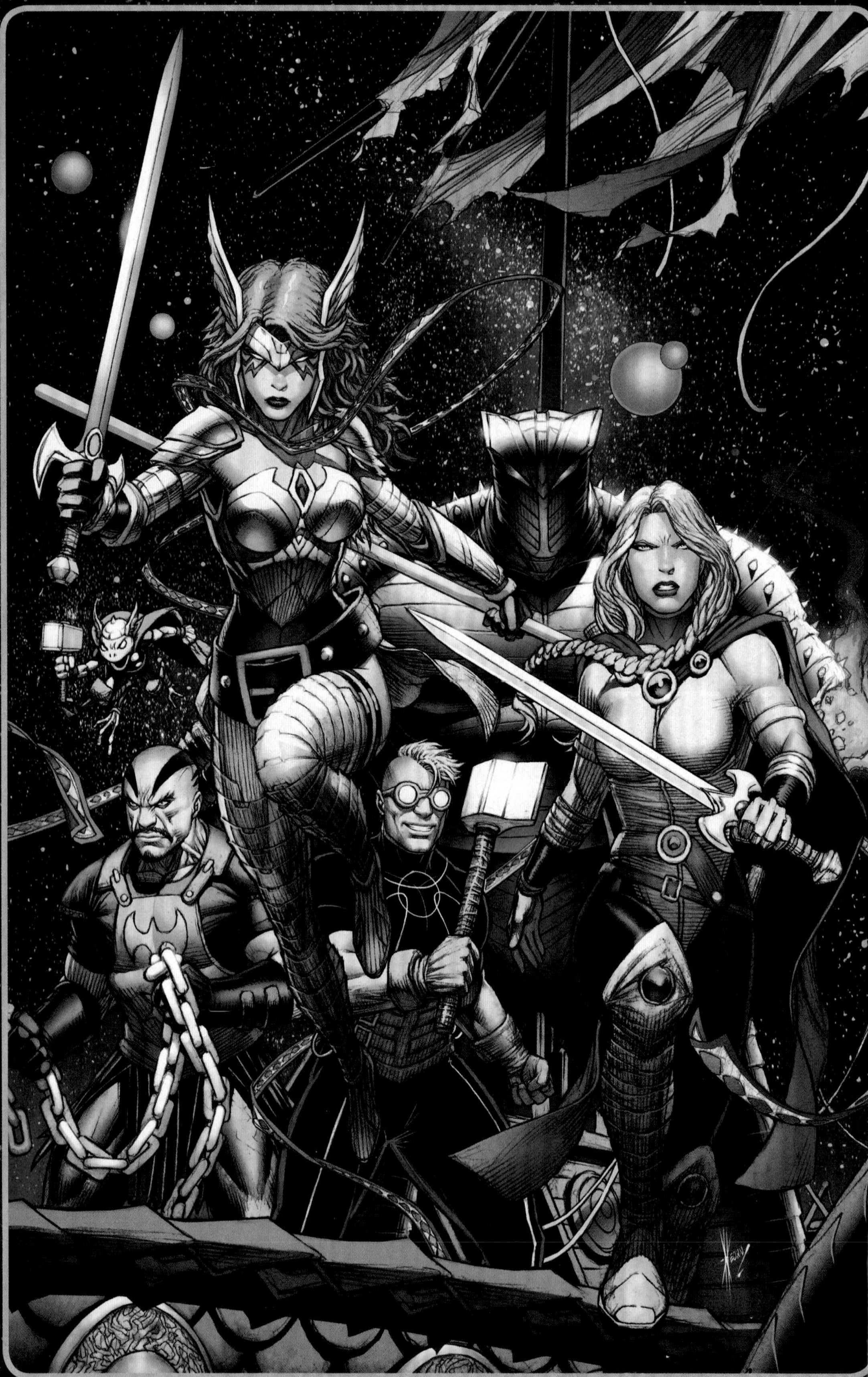

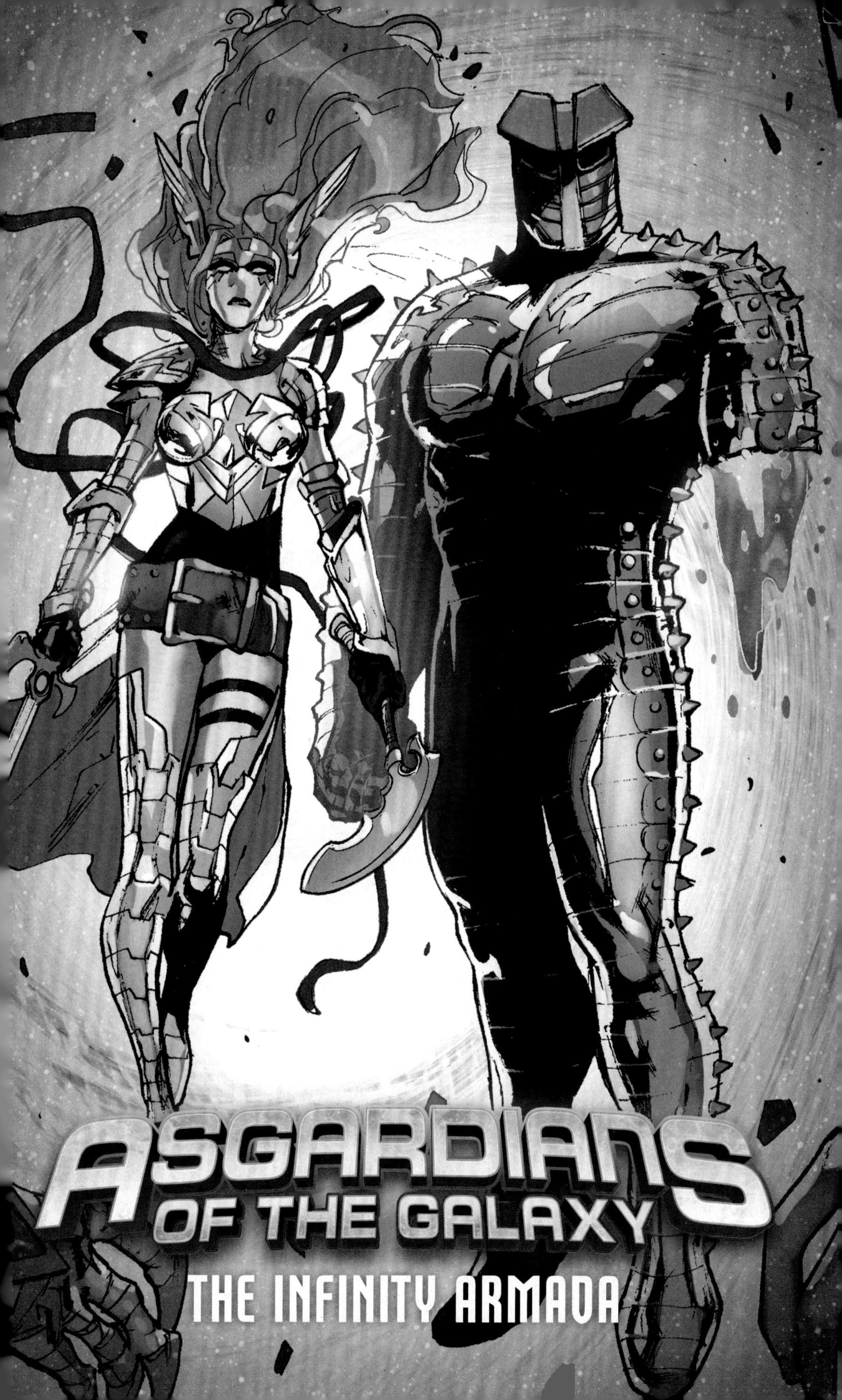
ASGARDIANS
OF THE GALAXY
THE INFINITY ARMADA

ANGELA

The firstborn child of Odin and Freyja, Angela was kidnapped and believed slain by the Queen of Angels, but a handmaiden rescued her. When Heven was reopened to the other realms years later, Angela's heritage was revealed. Branded a traitor by both Asgard and Heven, she now lives by her own code: Nothing for nothing — everything has its price.

VALKYRIE

Brunnhilde served Asgard for centuries as the leader of the Valkyrior, warrior goddesses who usher the worthy fallen to Valhalla. More recently, she led the Fearless Defenders, a group of women selected to be the shield maidens of Midgard.

ANNABELLE RIGGS

Archaeologist Annabelle Riggs joined the Fearless Defenders and died saving Valkyrie from the power of the Doom Maidens. Unwilling to accept her sacrifice, Brunnhilde journeyed to Valhalla and brought Annabelle back by merging their life forces, so they now share one body.

THE DESTROYER

The Destroyer is a mystical suit of armor built to contain enough energy to fight off a Celestial. It was nearly destroyed in a fight with the Mangog that tore apart Asgardia, and it still bears the wound of a missing arm. Without a spirit of its own, the armor requires a bearer or controller.

SKURGE THE EXECUTIONER

One of Asgard's greatest warriors, Skurge fell in love with Amora the Enchantress and has often fought fellow Asgardians in her name. He was redeemed when he died holding the bridge Gjallerbru against Hela with nothing but a pair of Midgardian M16s. Since then, he has wandered Hel in search of a purpose.

THUNDERSTRIKE

When Eric Masterson proved himself a true hero, he was granted the enchanted mace Thunderstrike by Odin. After Eric died in battle, Captain America gave the mace to Eric's son, Kevin, who soon proved himself worthy of the title and the weapon.

THROG

After his wife's death, Simon Walterson sought help from a witch, who turned him into a frog. When Loki turned his brother Thor into a frog, the two human-amphibians found themselves allies. Thor was soon restored, but Simon grabbed a fragment of Mjolnir and was transformed into Throg, the Frog of Thunder.

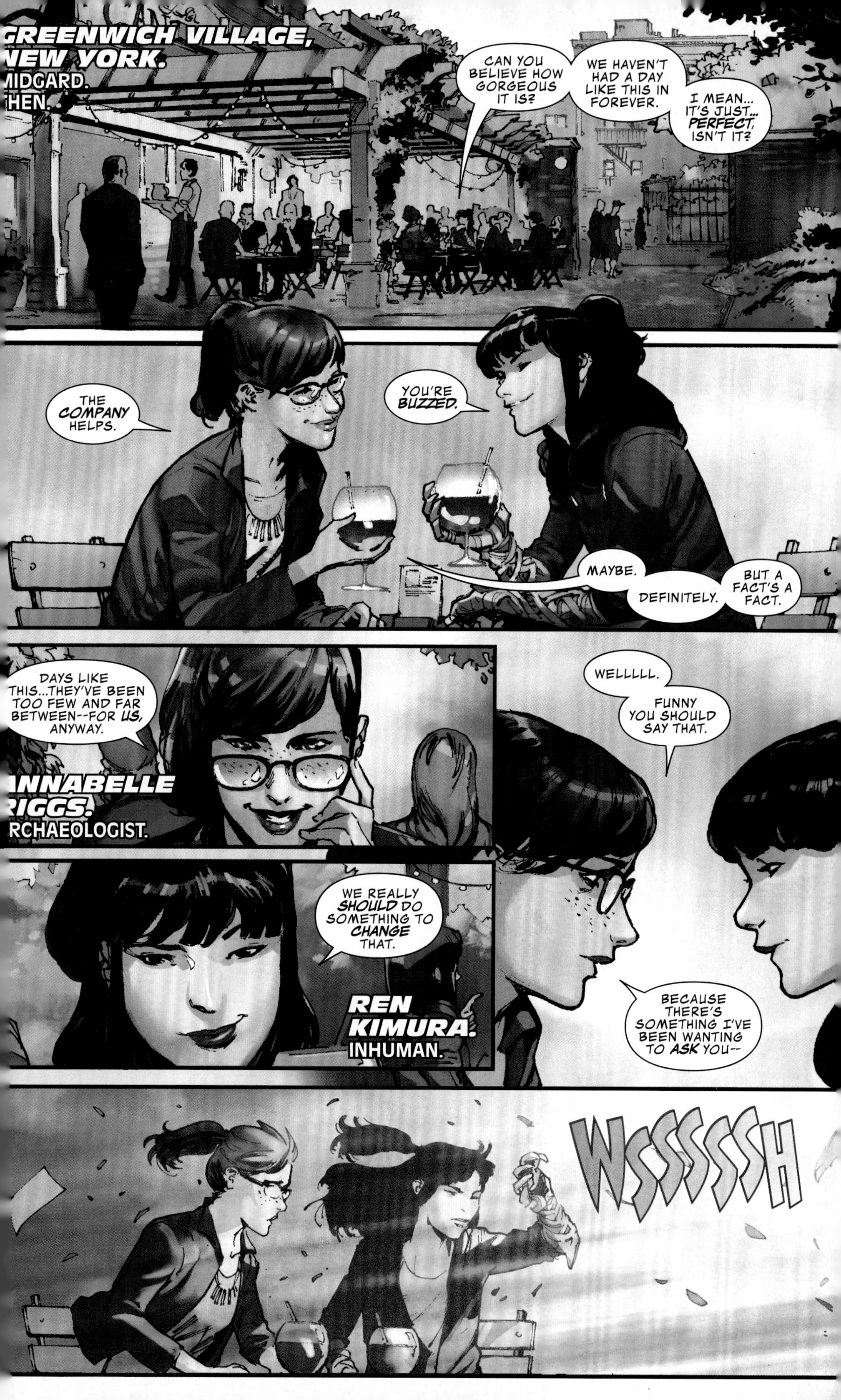

GREENWICH VILLAGE, NEW YORK.
MIDGARD.
THEN.
CAN YOU BELIEVE HOW GORGEOUS IT IS?
WE HAVEN'T HAD A DAY LIKE THIS IN FOREVER.
I MEAN... IT'S JUST... PERFECT, ISN'T IT?
THE COMPANY HELPS.
YOU'RE BUZZED.
MAYBE.
DEFINITELY.
BUT A FACT'S A FACT.
DAYS LIKE THIS...THEY'VE BEEN TOO FEW AND FAR BETWEEN--FOR US, ANYWAY.
ANNABELLE RIGGS.
ARCHAEOLOGIST.
WELLLLL.
FUNNY YOU SHOULD SAY THAT.
WE REALLY SHOULD DO SOMETHING TO CHANGE THAT.
REN KIMURA.
INHUMAN.
BECAUSE THERE'S SOMETHING I'VE BEEN WANTING TO ASK YOU--
WSSSSSH

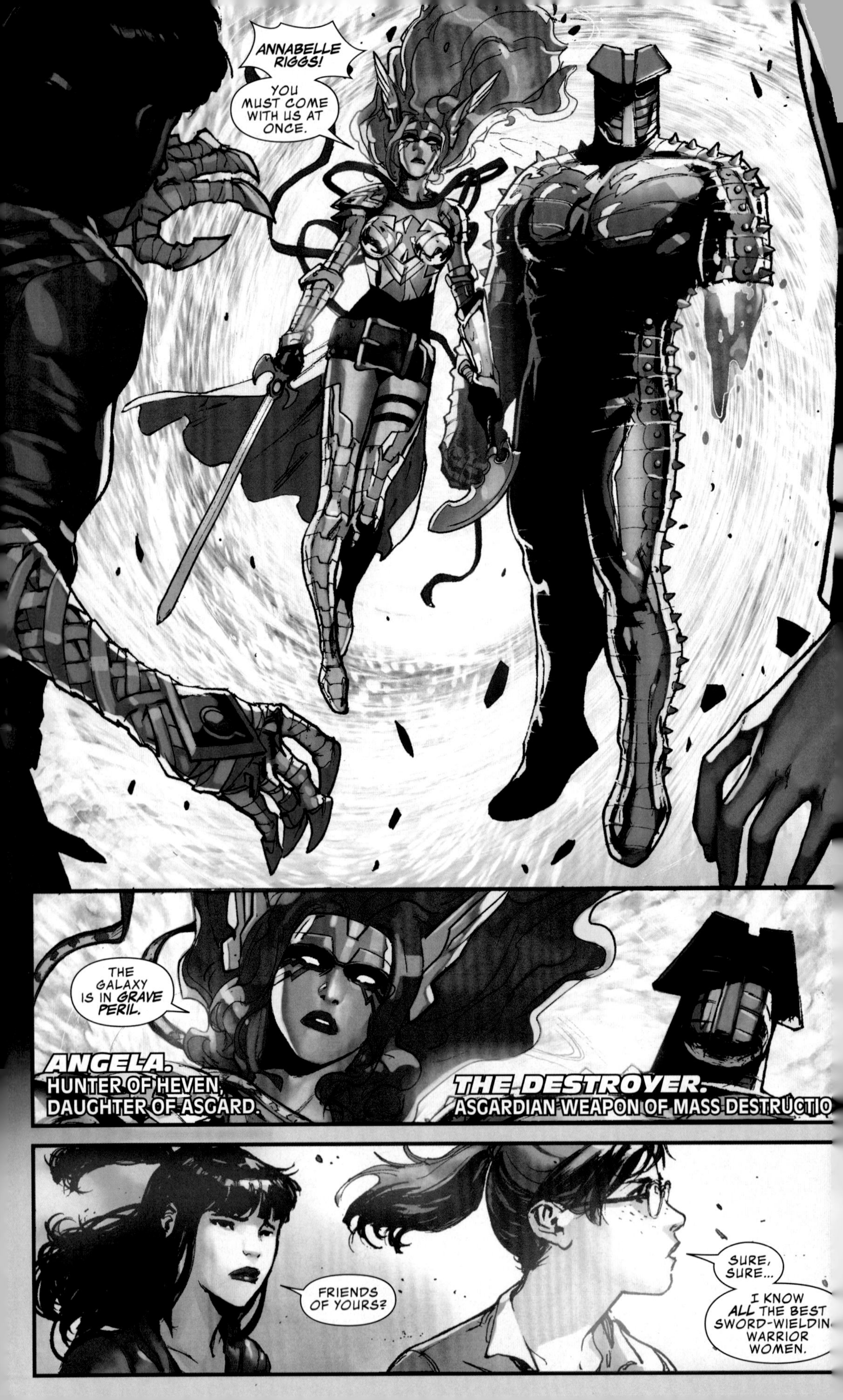
ANNABELLE RIGGS!
YOU MUST COME WITH US AT ONCE.
THE GALAXY IS IN GRAVE PERIL.
ANGELA.
HUNTER OF HEVEN, DAUGHTER OF ASGARD.
THE DESTROYER.
ASGARDIAN WEAPON OF MASS DESTRUCTIO
FRIENDS OF YOURS?
SURE, SURE...
I KNOW ALL THE BEST SWORD-WIELDIN WARRIOR WOMEN.

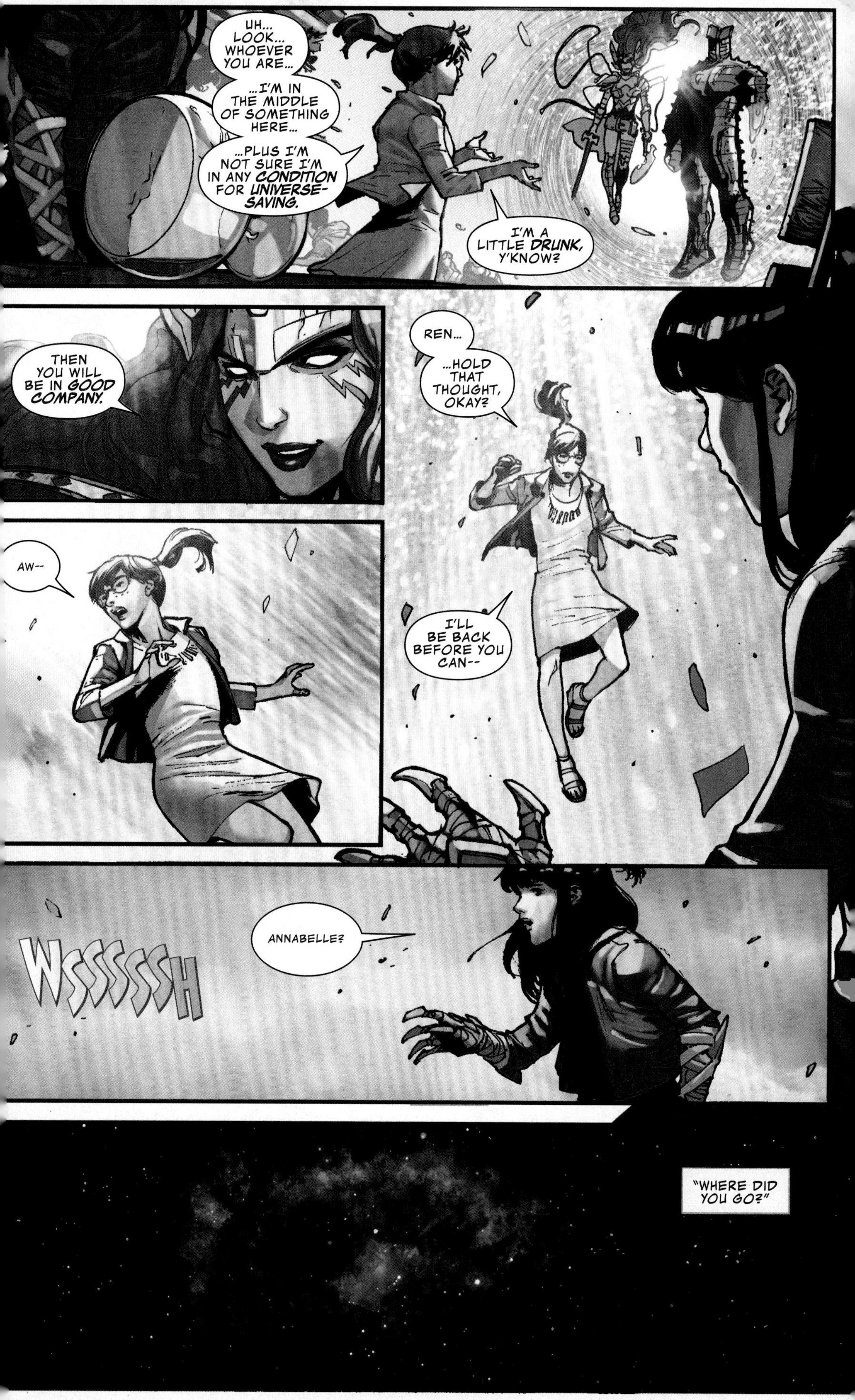
UH... LOOK... WHOEVER YOU ARE...
...I'M IN THE MIDDLE OF SOMETHING HERE...
...PLUS I'M NOT SURE I'M IN ANY CONDITION FOR UNIVERSE-SAVING.
I'M A LITTLE DRUNK, Y'KNOW?
THEN YOU WILL BE IN GOOD COMPANY.
REN...
...HOLD THAT THOUGHT, OKAY?
I'LL BE BACK BEFORE YOU CAN--
AW--
WSSSSSH
ANNABELLE?
"WHERE DID YOU GO?"

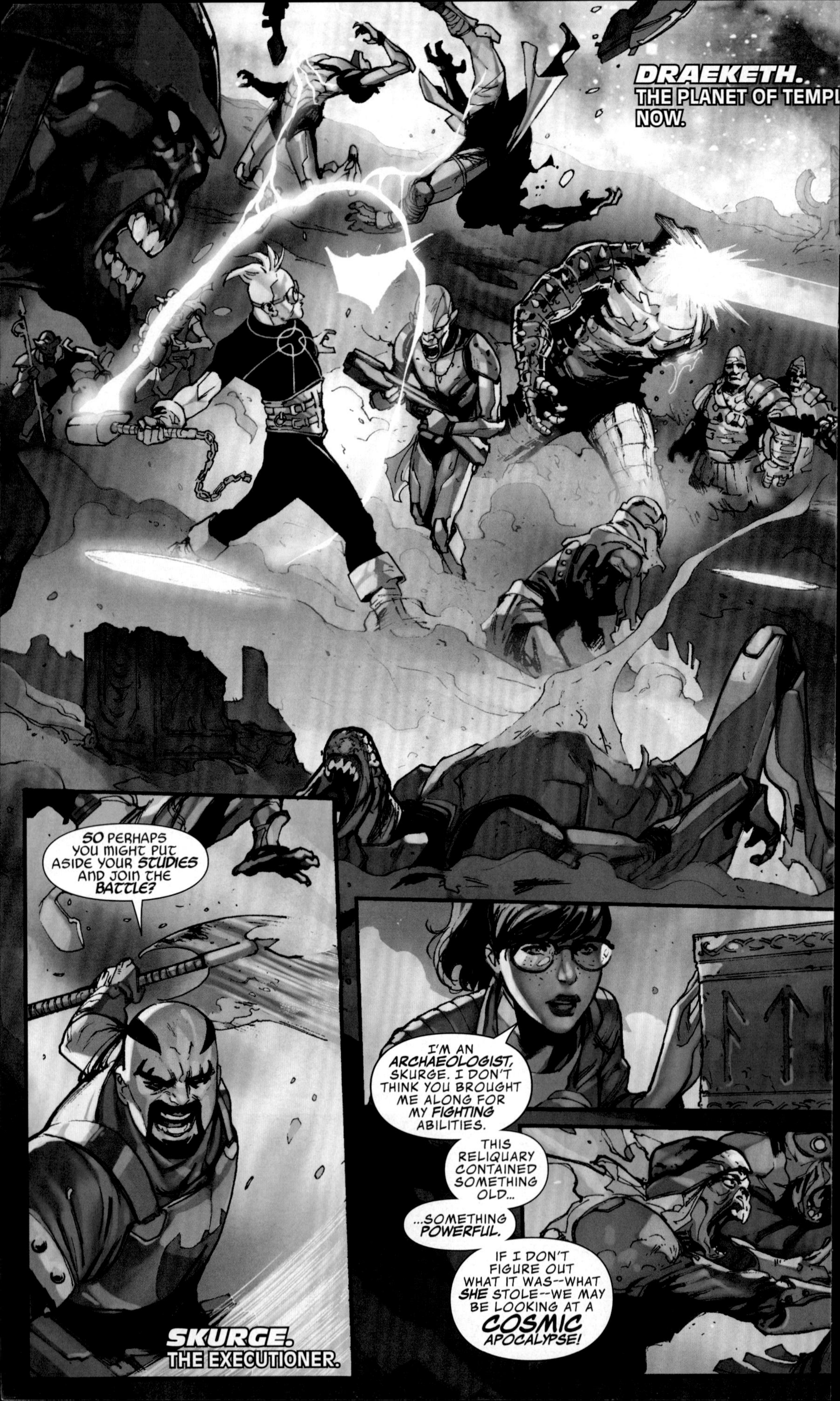
DRAEKETH.
THE PLANET OF TEMPL
NOW.
SO PERHAPS YOU MIGHT PUT ASIDE YOUR STUDIES AND JOIN THE BATTLE?
I'M AN ARCHAEOLOGIST, SKURGE. I DON'T THINK YOU BROUGHT ME ALONG FOR MY FIGHTING ABILITIES.
THIS RELIQUARY CONTAINED SOMETHING OLD...
...SOMETHING POWERFUL.
IF I DON'T FIGURE OUT WHAT IT WAS--WHAT SHE STOLE--WE MAY BE LOOKING AT A COSMIC APOCALYPSE!
SKURGE.
THE EXECUTIONER.

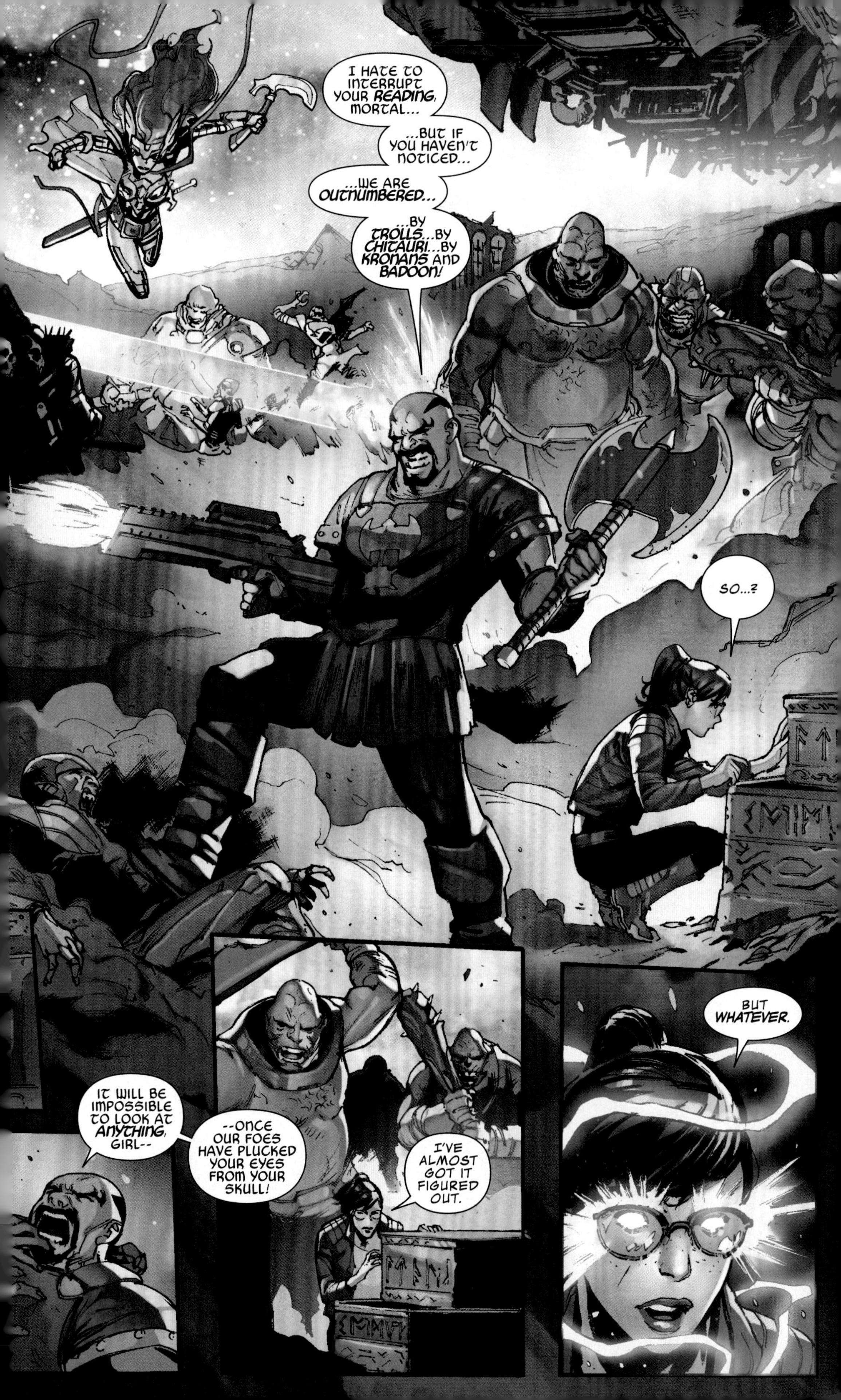

I HATE TO INTERRUPT YOUR READING, MORTAL...
...BUT IF YOU HAVEN'T NOTICED...
...WE ARE OUTNUMBERED...
...BY TROLLS...BY CHITAURI...BY KRONANS AND BADOON!
SO...?
IT WILL BE IMPOSSIBLE TO LOOK AT ANYTHING, GIRL--
--ONCE OUR FOES HAVE PLUCKED YOUR EYES FROM YOUR SKULL!
I'VE ALMOST GOT IT FIGURED OUT.
BUT WHATEVER.

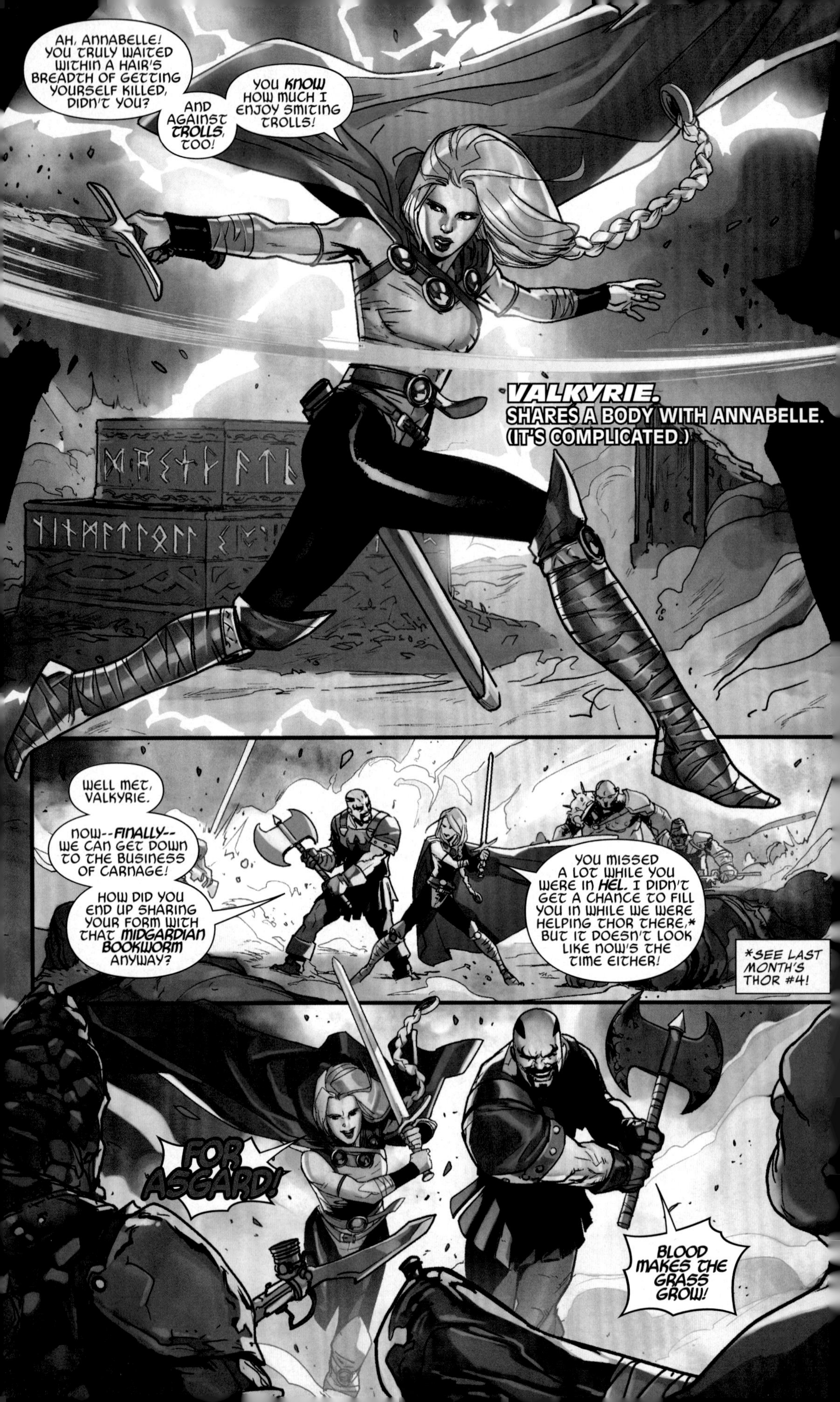
AH, ANNABELLE! YOU TRULY WAITED WITHIN A HAIR'S BREADTH OF GETTING YOURSELF KILLED, DIDN'T YOU?
AND AGAINST TROLLS, TOO!
YOU KNOW HOW MUCH I ENJOY SMITING TROLLS!
VALKYRIE.
SHARES A BODY WITH ANNABELLE. (IT'S COMPLICATED.)
WELL MET, VALKYRIE.
NOW--FINALLY--WE CAN GET DOWN TO THE BUSINESS OF CARNAGE!
HOW DID YOU END UP SHARING YOUR FORM WITH THAT MIDGARDIAN BOOKWORM ANYWAY?
YOU MISSED A LOT WHILE YOU WERE IN HEL. I DIDN'T GET A CHANCE TO FILL YOU IN WHILE WE WERE HELPING THOR THERE,* BUT IT DOESN'T LOOK LIKE NOW'S THE TIME EITHER!
*SEE LAST MONTH'S THOR #4!
FOR ASGARD!
BLOOD MAKES THE GRASS GROW!

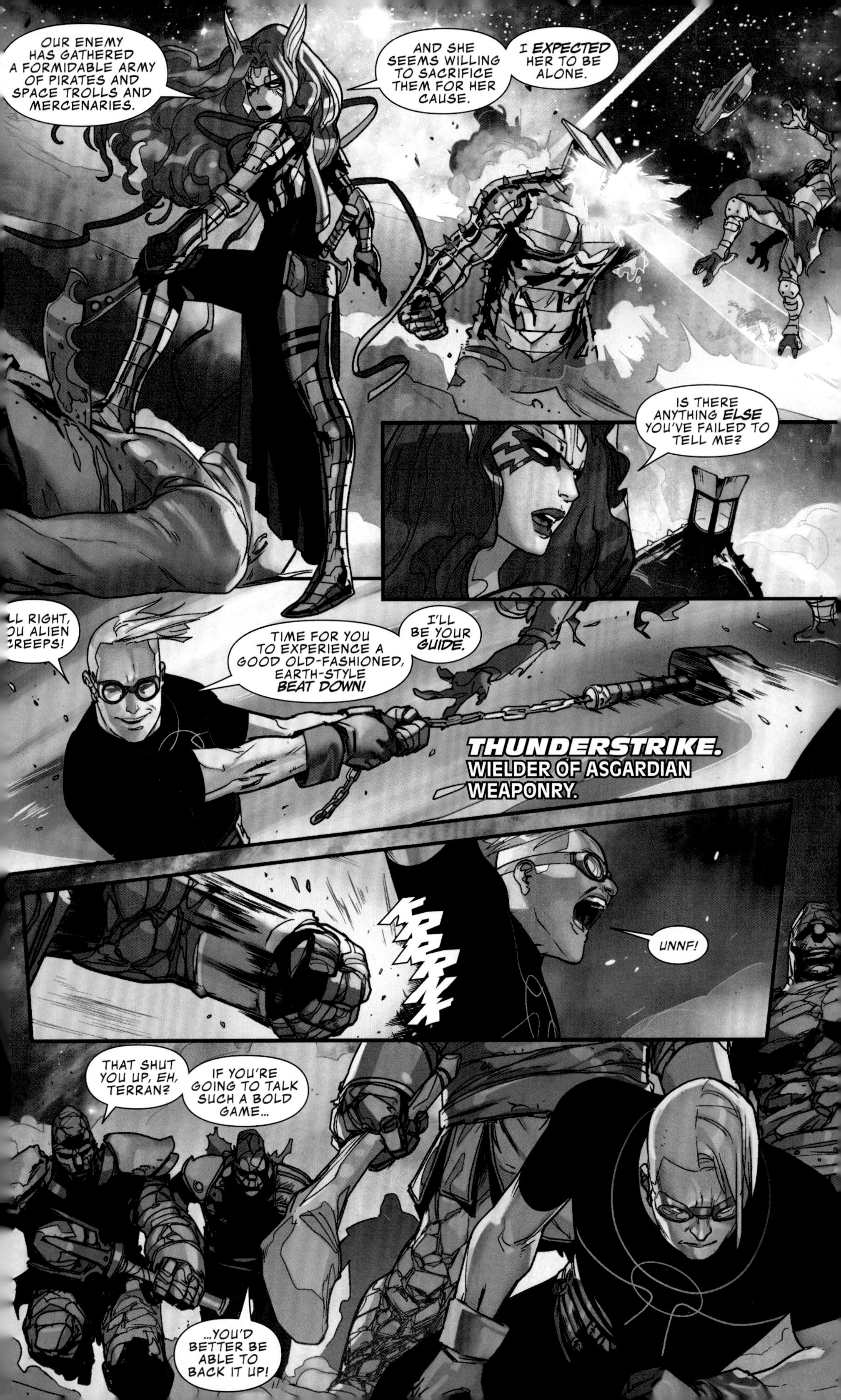
OUR ENEMY HAS GATHERED A FORMIDABLE ARMY OF PIRATES AND SPACE TROLLS AND MERCENARIES.
AND SHE SEEMS WILLING TO SACRIFICE THEM FOR HER CAUSE.
I EXPECTED HER TO BE ALONE.
IS THERE ANYTHING ELSE YOU'VE FAILED TO TELL ME?
LL RIGHT, OU ALIEN CREEPS!
TIME FOR YOU TO EXPERIENCE A GOOD OLD-FASHIONED, EARTH-STYLE BEAT DOWN!
I'LL BE YOUR GUIDE.
THUNDERSTRIKE.
WIELDER OF ASGARDIAN WEAPONRY.
KRRRK
UNNF!
THAT SHUT YOU UP, EH, TERRAN?
IF YOU'RE GOING TO TALK SUCH A BOLD GAME...
...YOU'D BETTER BE ABLE TO BACK IT UP!

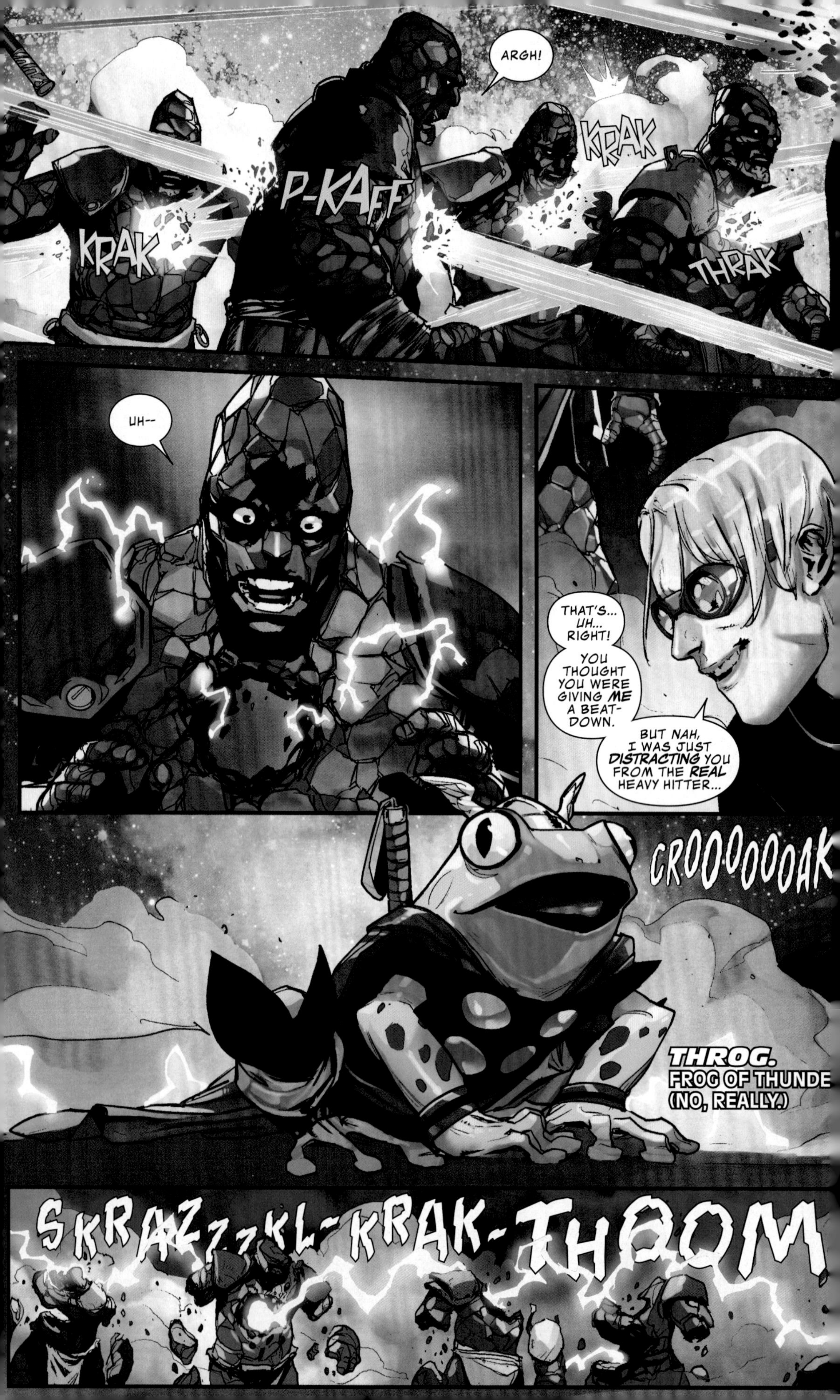

ARGH!
KRAK
P-KAFF
KRAK
THRAK
UH--
THAT'S... UH... RIGHT!
YOU THOUGHT YOU WERE GIVING ME A BEAT-DOWN.
BUT NAH, I WAS JUST DISTRACTING YOU FROM THE REAL HEAVY HITTER...
CROOOOOOOAK
THROG.
FROG OF THUNDE
(NO, REALLY.)
SKRAZZZKL-KRAK-THOOM

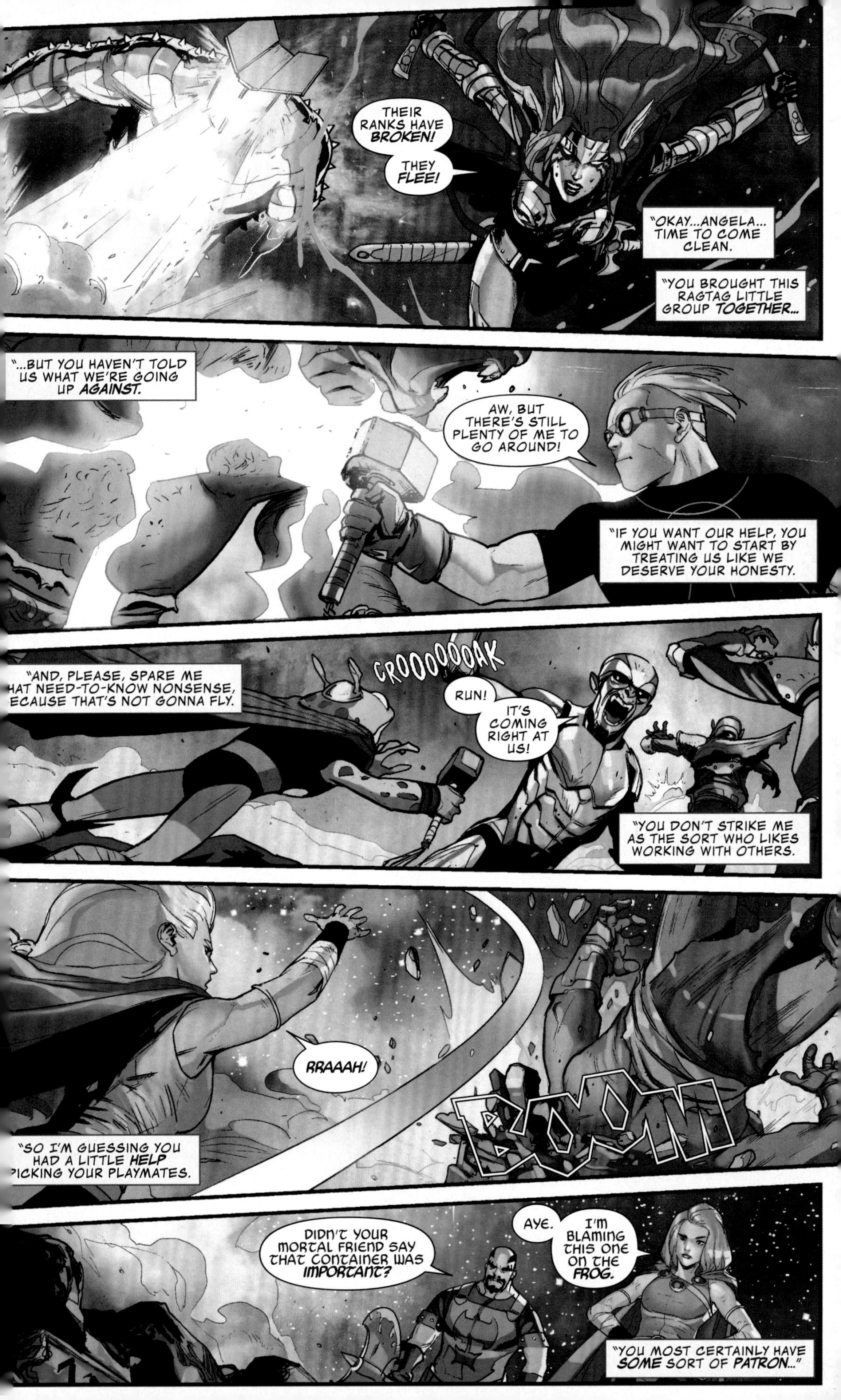
THEIR RANKS HAVE BROKEN!
THEY FLEE!
"OKAY...ANGELA... TIME TO COME CLEAN.
"YOU BROUGHT THIS RAGTAG LITTLE GROUP TOGETHER...
"...BUT YOU HAVEN'T TOLD US WHAT WE'RE GOING UP AGAINST.
AW, BUT THERE'S STILL PLENTY OF ME TO GO AROUND!
"IF YOU WANT OUR HELP, YOU MIGHT WANT TO START BY TREATING US LIKE WE DESERVE YOUR HONESTY.
"AND, PLEASE, SPARE ME THAT NEED-TO-KNOW NONSENSE, BECAUSE THAT'S NOT GONNA FLY.
CROOOOOOAK
RUN!
IT'S COMING RIGHT AT US!
"YOU DON'T STRIKE ME AS THE SORT WHO LIKES WORKING WITH OTHERS.
BRAAAH!
BOOM
"SO I'M GUESSING YOU HAD A LITTLE HELP PICKING YOUR PLAYMATES.
DIDN'T YOUR MORTAL FRIEND SAY THAT CONTAINER WAS IMPORTANT?
AYE.
I'M BLAMING THIS ONE ON THE FROG.
"YOU MOST CERTAINLY HAVE SOME SORT OF PATRON..."

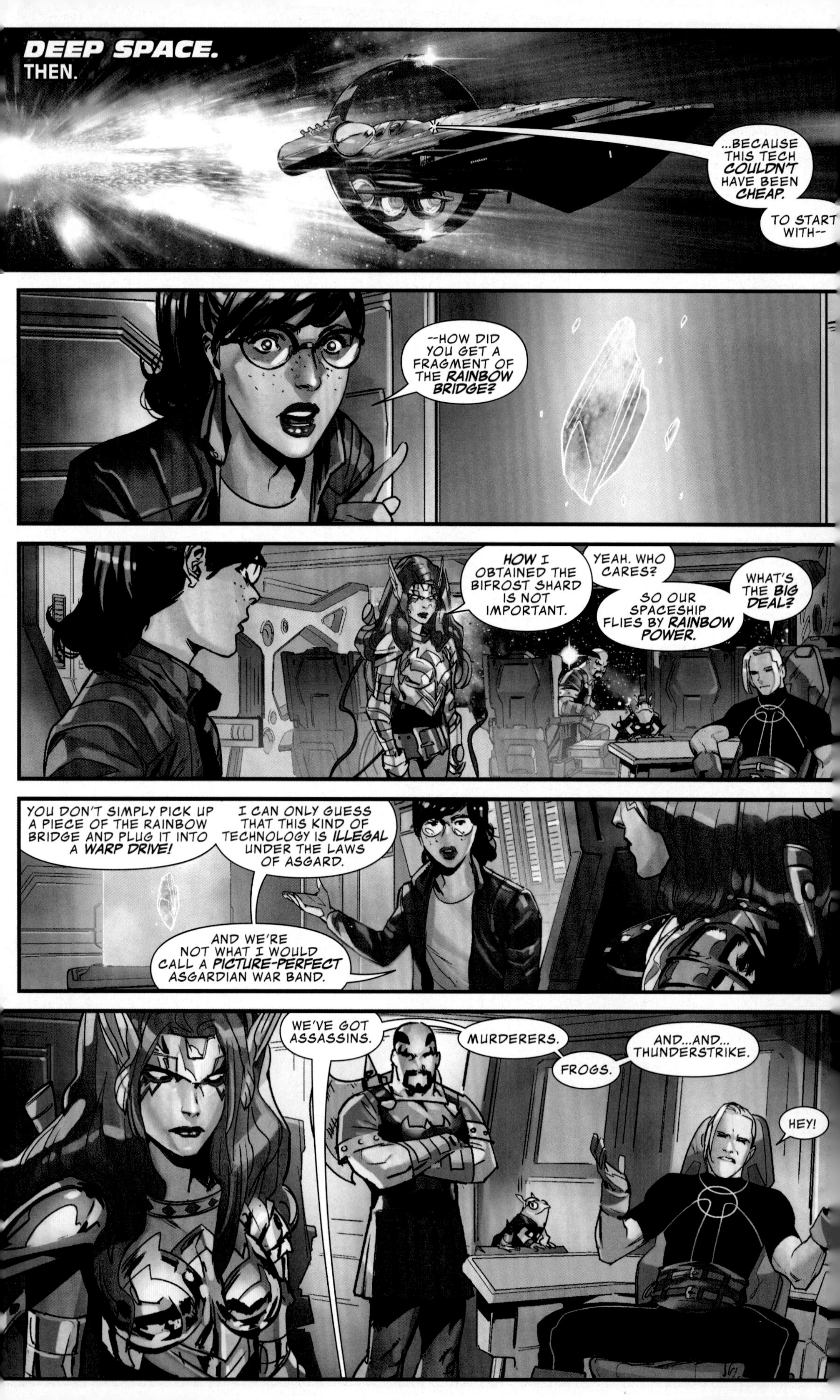

DEEP SPACE. THEN.
...BECAUSE THIS TECH COULDN'T HAVE BEEN CHEAP.
TO START WITH--
--HOW DID YOU GET A FRAGMENT OF THE RAINBOW BRIDGE?
HOW I OBTAINED THE BIFROST SHARD IS NOT IMPORTANT.
YEAH. WHO CARES?
SO OUR SPACESHIP FLIES BY RAINBOW POWER.
WHAT'S THE BIG DEAL?
YOU DON'T SIMPLY PICK UP A PIECE OF THE RAINBOW BRIDGE AND PLUG IT INTO A WARP DRIVE!
I CAN ONLY GUESS THAT THIS KIND OF TECHNOLOGY IS ILLEGAL UNDER THE LAWS OF ASGARD.
AND WE'RE NOT WHAT I WOULD CALL A PICTURE-PERFECT ASGARDIAN WAR BAND.
WE'VE GOT ASSASSINS.
MURDERERS.
FROGS.
AND...AND... THUNDERSTRIKE.
HEY!

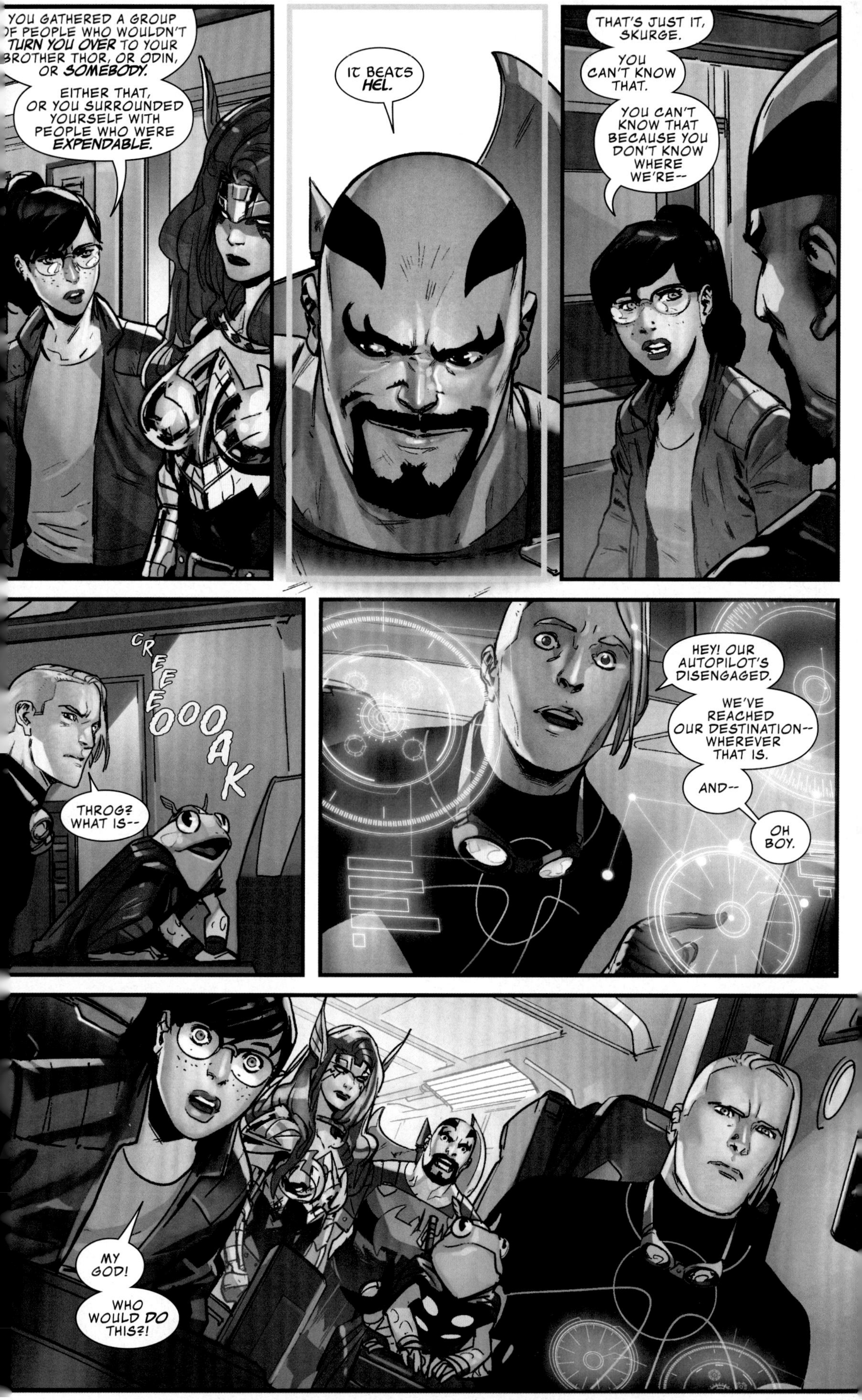
YOU GATHERED A GROUP OF PEOPLE WHO WOULDN'T TURN YOU OVER TO YOUR BROTHER THOR, OR ODIN, OR SOMEBODY.
EITHER THAT, OR YOU SURROUNDED YOURSELF WITH PEOPLE WHO WERE EXPENDABLE.
IT BEATS HEL.
THAT'S JUST IT, SKURGE.
YOU CAN'T KNOW THAT.
YOU CAN'T KNOW THAT BECAUSE YOU DON'T KNOW WHERE WE'RE--
CREEEOOOAK
THROG? WHAT IS--
HEY! OUR AUTOPILOT'S DISENGAGED.
WE'VE REACHED OUR DESTINATION-- WHEREVER THAT IS.
AND--
OH BOY.
MY GOD!
WHO WOULD DO THIS?!

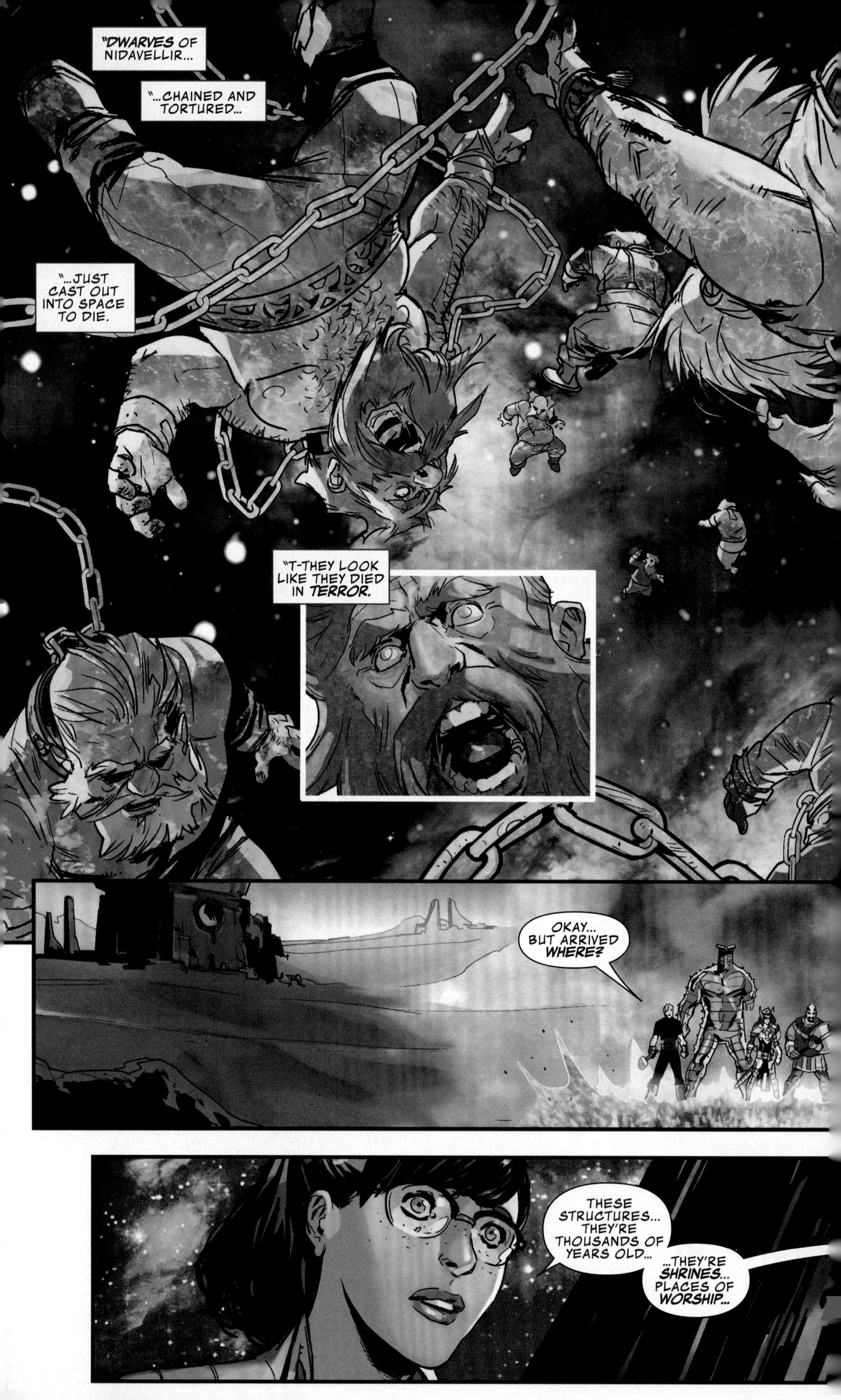
"DWARVES OF NIDAVELLIR...
"...CHAINED AND TORTURED...
"...JUST CAST OUT INTO SPACE TO DIE.
"T-THEY LOOK LIKE THEY DIED IN TERROR.
OKAY... BUT ARRIVED WHERE?
THESE STRUCTURES... THEY'RE THOUSANDS OF YEARS OLD...
...THEY'RE SHRINES... PLACES OF WORSHIP...

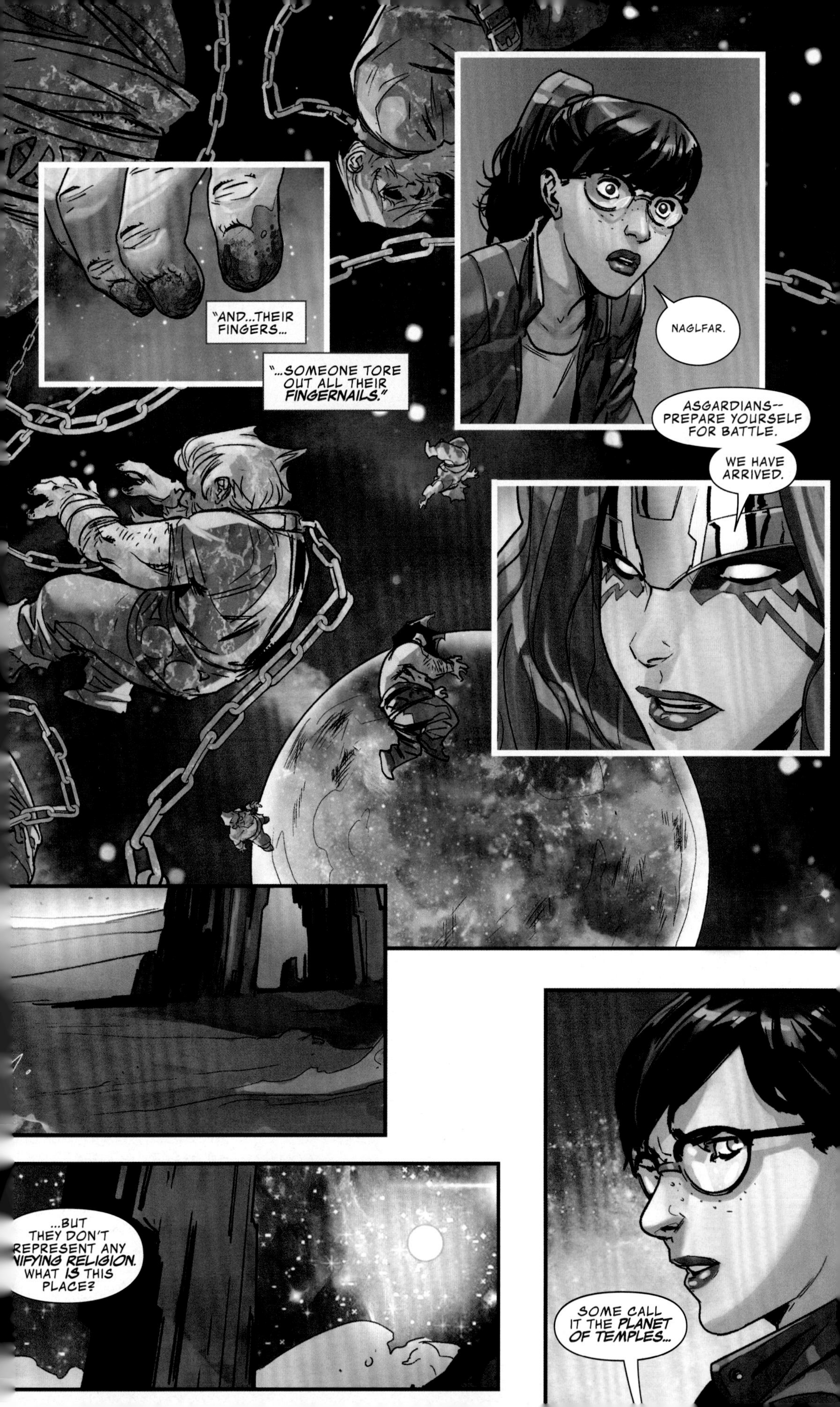
"AND...THEIR FINGERS...
"...SOMEONE TORE OUT ALL THEIR FINGERNAILS."
NAGLFAR.
ASGARDIANS-- PREPARE YOURSELF FOR BATTLE.
WE HAVE ARRIVED.
...BUT THEY DON'T REPRESENT ANY UNIFYING RELIGION. WHAT IS THIS PLACE?
SOME CALL IT THE PLANET OF TEMPLES...

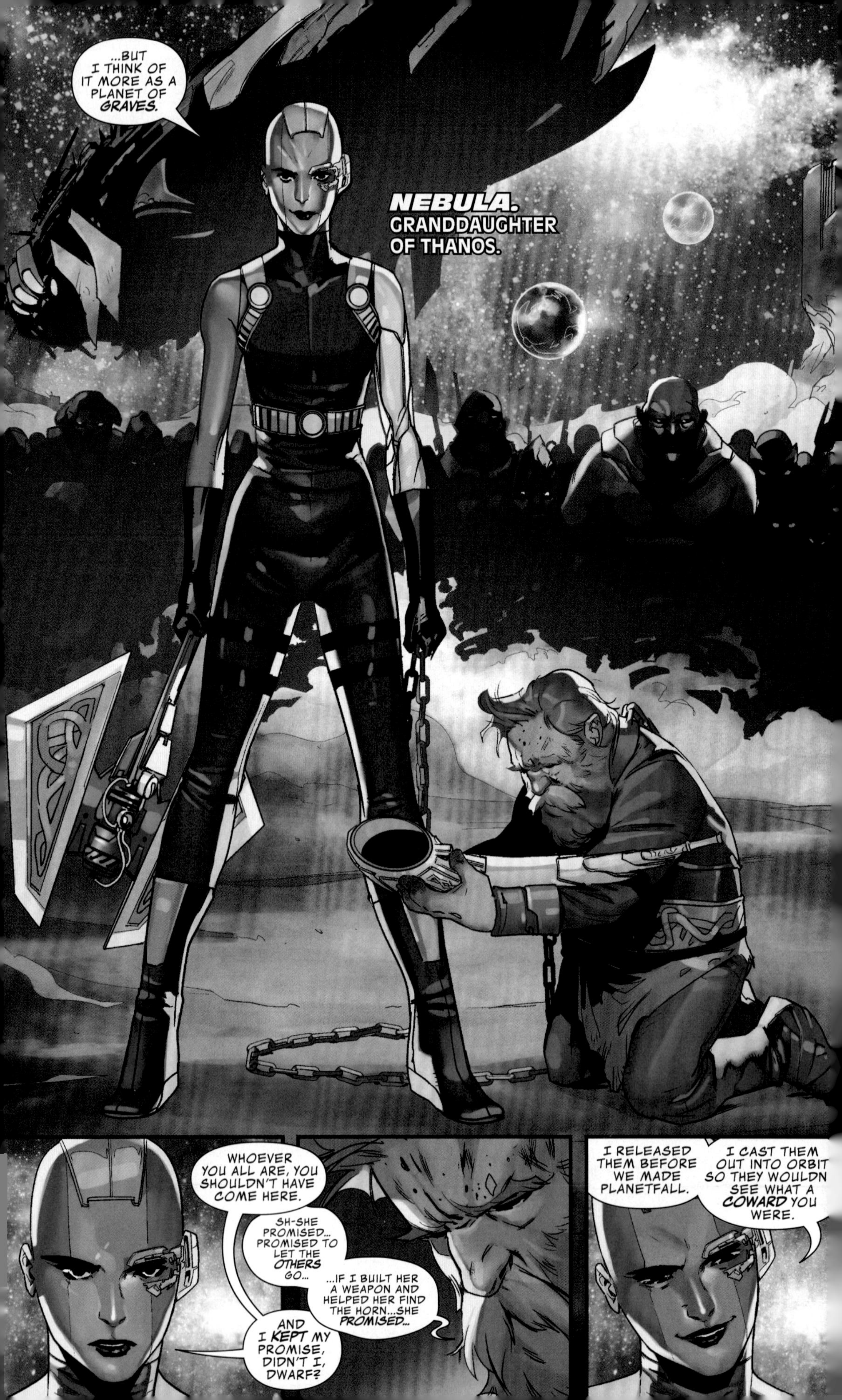

...BUT I THINK OF IT MORE AS A PLANET OF GRAVES.
NEBULA. GRANDDAUGHTER OF THANOS.
WHOEVER YOU ALL ARE, YOU SHOULDN'T HAVE COME HERE.
SH-SHE PROMISED... PROMISED TO LET THE OTHERS GO...
...IF I BUILT HER A WEAPON AND HELPED HER FIND THE HORN...SHE PROMISED...
AND I KEPT MY PROMISE, DIDN'T I, DWARF?
I RELEASED THEM BEFORE WE MADE PLANETFALL.
I CAST THEM OUT INTO ORBIT SO THEY WOULDN SEE WHAT A COWARD YOU WERE.

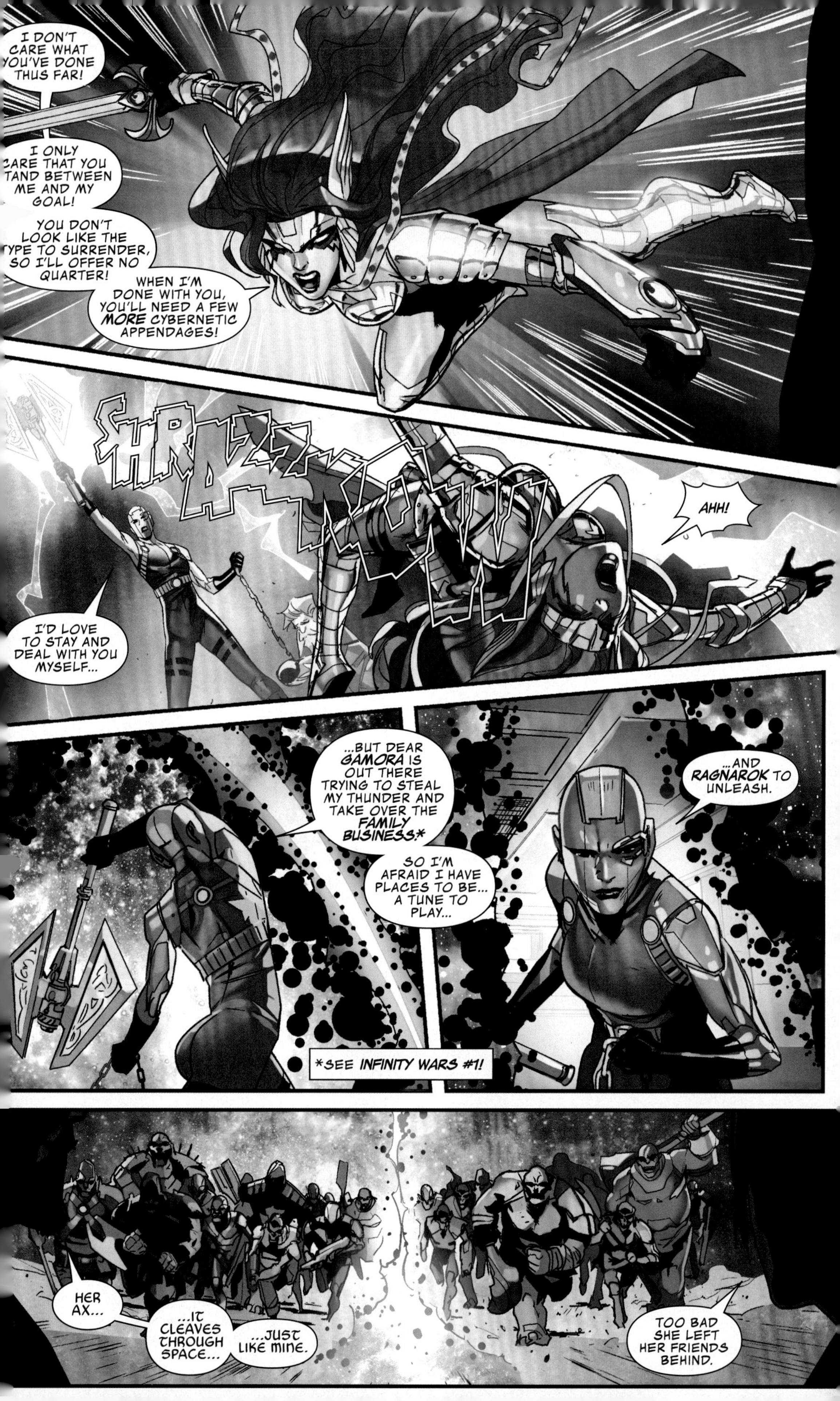

I DON'T CARE WHAT YOU'VE DONE THUS FAR!
I ONLY CARE THAT YOU STAND BETWEEN ME AND MY GOAL!
YOU DON'T LOOK LIKE THE TYPE TO SURRENDER, SO I'LL OFFER NO QUARTER!
WHEN I'M DONE WITH YOU, YOU'LL NEED A FEW MORE CYBERNETIC APPENDAGES!
AHH!
I'D LOVE TO STAY AND DEAL WITH YOU MYSELF...
...BUT DEAR GAMORA IS OUT THERE TRYING TO STEAL MY THUNDER AND TAKE OVER THE FAMILY BUSINESS.*
SO I'M AFRAID I HAVE PLACES TO BE... A TUNE TO PLAY...
...AND RAGNAROK TO UNLEASH.
*SEE INFINITY WARS #1!
HER AX...
...IT CLEAVES THROUGH SPACE...
...JUST LIKE MINE.
TOO BAD SHE LEFT HER FRIENDS BEHIND.

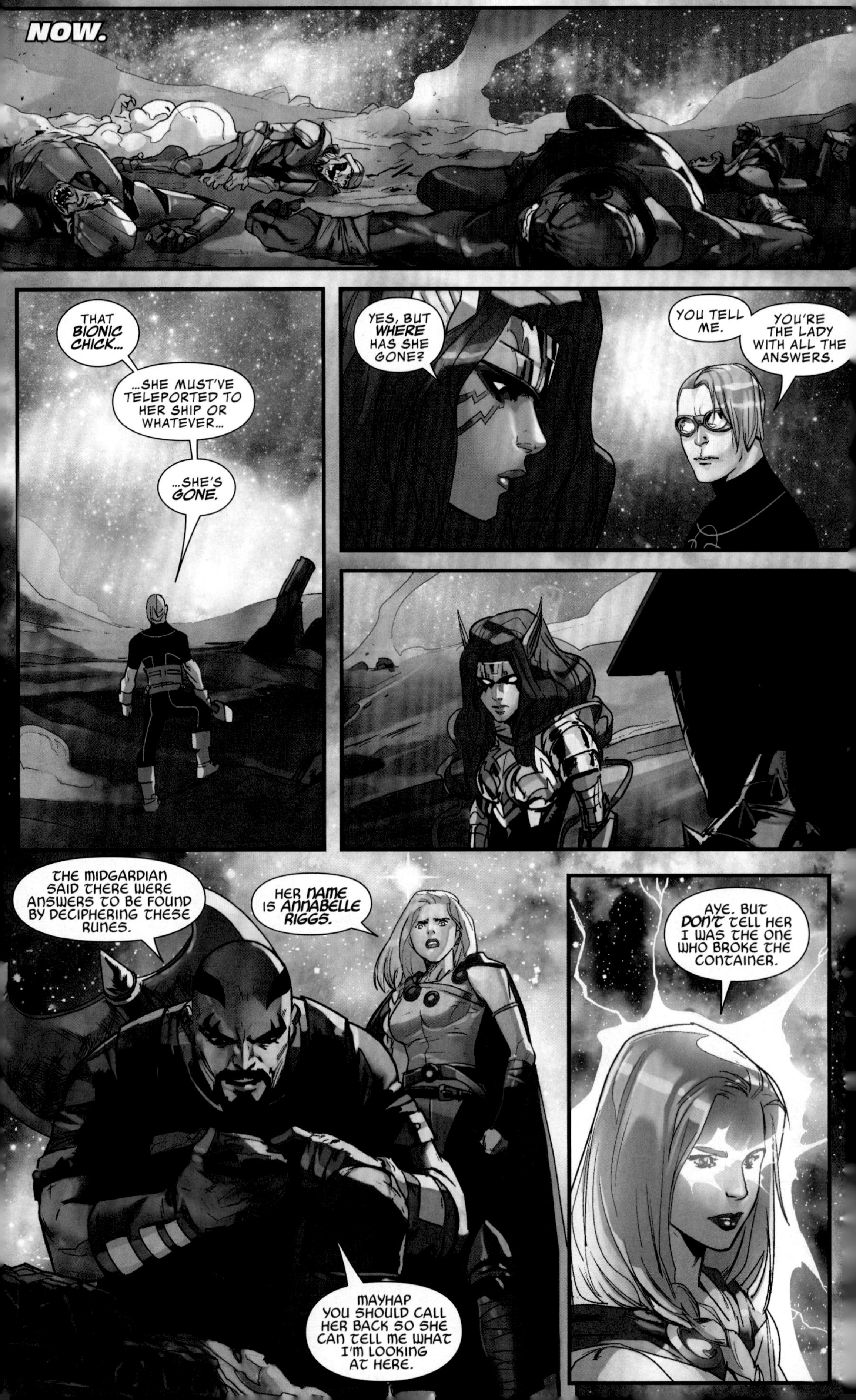
NOW.
THAT BIONIC CHICK...
...SHE MUST'VE TELEPORTED TO HER SHIP OR WHATEVER...
...SHE'S GONE.
YES, BUT WHERE HAS SHE GONE?
YOU TELL ME.
YOU'RE THE LADY WITH ALL THE ANSWERS.
THE MIDGARDIAN SAID THERE WERE ANSWERS TO BE FOUND BY DECIPHERING THESE RUNES.
HER NAME IS ANNABELLE RIGGS.
MAYHAP YOU SHOULD CALL HER BACK SO SHE CAN TELL ME WHAT I'M LOOKING AT HERE.
AYE. BUT DON'T TELL HER I WAS THE ONE WHO BROKE THE CONTAINER.

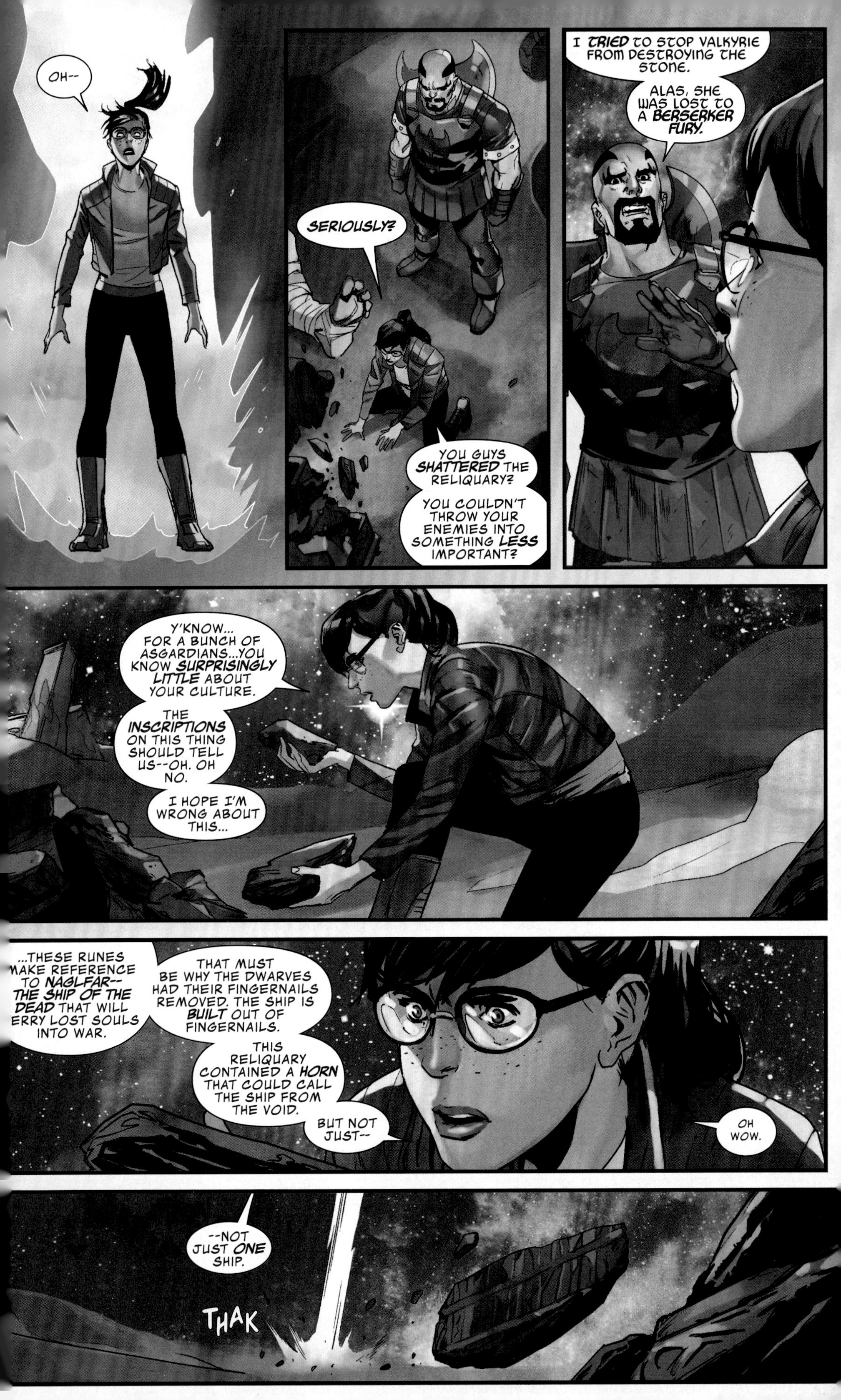
OH--
SERIOUSLY?
YOU GUYS SHATTERED THE RELIQUARY?
YOU COULDN'T THROW YOUR ENEMIES INTO SOMETHING LESS IMPORTANT?
I TRIED TO STOP VALKYRIE FROM DESTROYING THE STONE.
ALAS, SHE WAS LOST TO A BERSERKER FURY.
Y'KNOW... FOR A BUNCH OF ASGARDIANS...YOU KNOW SURPRISINGLY LITTLE ABOUT YOUR CULTURE.
THE INSCRIPTIONS ON THIS THING SHOULD TELL US--OH. OH NO.
I HOPE I'M WRONG ABOUT THIS...
...THESE RUNES MAKE REFERENCE TO NAGLFAR--THE SHIP OF THE DEAD THAT WILL ERRY LOST SOULS INTO WAR.
THAT MUST BE WHY THE DWARVES HAD THEIR FINGERNAILS REMOVED. THE SHIP IS BUILT OUT OF FINGERNAILS.
THIS RELIQUARY CONTAINED A HORN THAT COULD CALL THE SHIP FROM THE VOID.
BUT NOT JUST--
OH WOW.
--NOT JUST ONE SHIP.
THAK

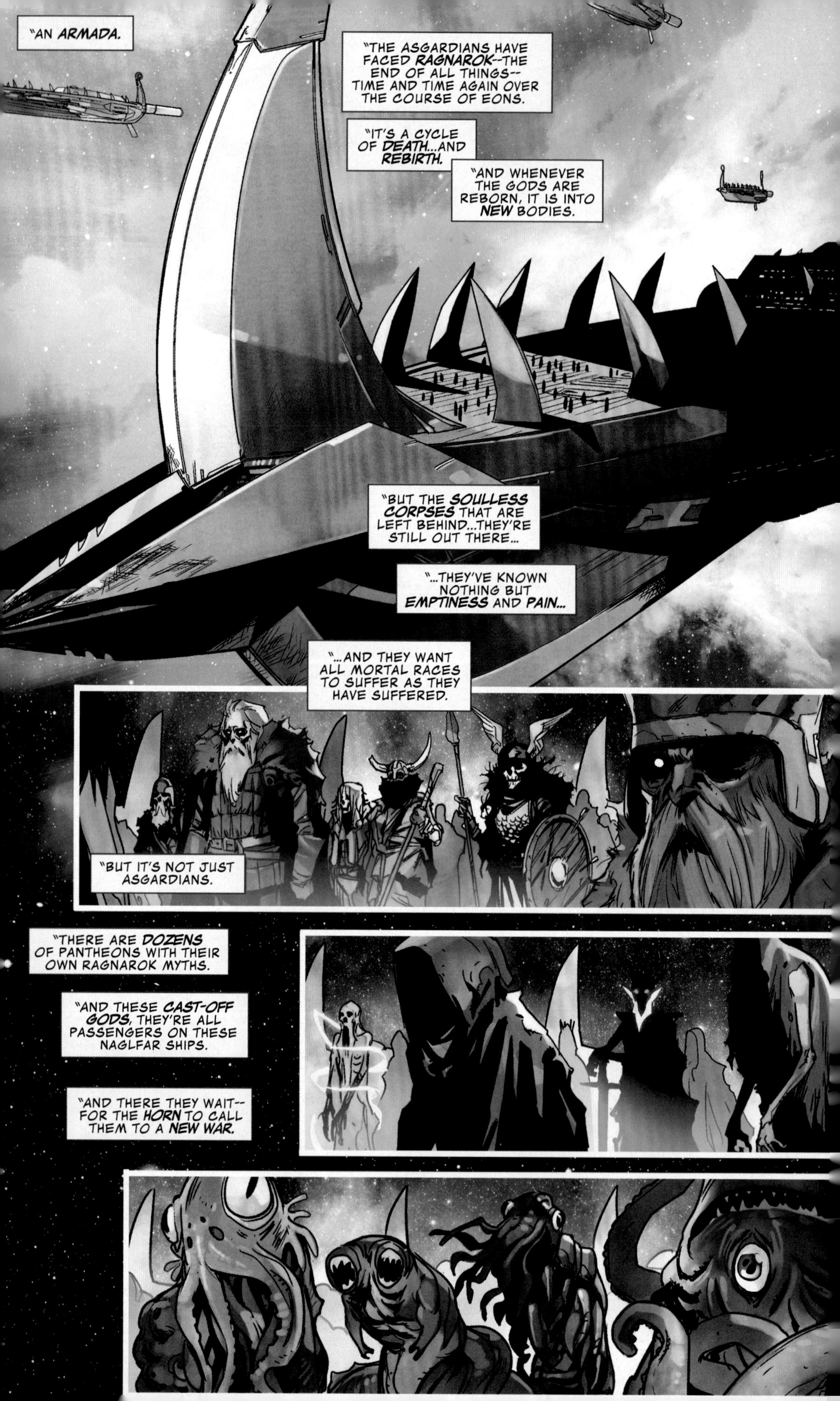

"AN ARMADA.
"THE ASGARDIANS HAVE FACED RAGNAROK--THE END OF ALL THINGS--TIME AND TIME AGAIN OVER THE COURSE OF EONS.
"IT'S A CYCLE OF DEATH...AND REBIRTH.
"AND WHENEVER THE GODS ARE REBORN, IT IS INTO NEW BODIES.
"BUT THE SOULLESS CORPSES THAT ARE LEFT BEHIND...THEY'RE STILL OUT THERE...
"...THEY'VE KNOWN NOTHING BUT EMPTINESS AND PAIN...
"...AND THEY WANT ALL MORTAL RACES TO SUFFER AS THEY HAVE SUFFERED.
"BUT IT'S NOT JUST ASGARDIANS.
"THERE ARE DOZENS OF PANTHEONS WITH THEIR OWN RAGNAROK MYTHS.
"AND THESE CAST-OFF GODS, THEY'RE ALL PASSENGERS ON THESE NAGLFAR SHIPS.
"AND THERE THEY WAIT--FOR THE HORN TO CALL THEM TO A NEW WAR.

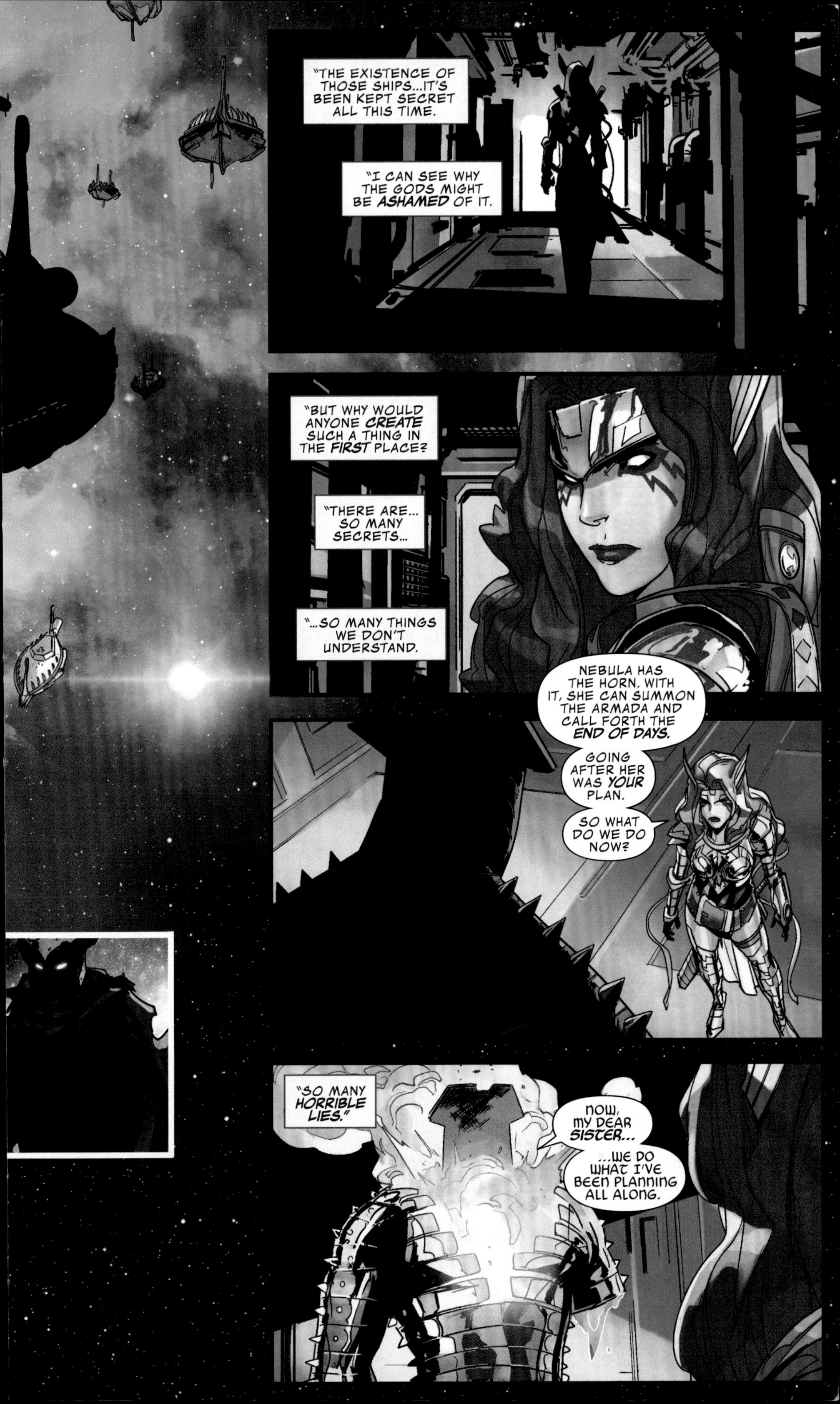
"THE EXISTENCE OF THOSE SHIPS...IT'S BEEN KEPT SECRET ALL THIS TIME.
"I CAN SEE WHY THE GODS MIGHT BE ASHAMED OF IT.
"BUT WHY WOULD ANYONE CREATE SUCH A THING IN THE FIRST PLACE?
"THERE ARE... SO MANY SECRETS...
"...SO MANY THINGS WE DON'T UNDERSTAND.
NEBULA HAS THE HORN. WITH IT, SHE CAN SUMMON THE ARMADA AND CALL FORTH THE END OF DAYS.
GOING AFTER HER WAS YOUR PLAN.
SO WHAT DO WE DO NOW?
"SO MANY HORRIBLE LIES."
NOW, MY DEAR SISTER...
...WE DO WHAT I'VE BEEN PLANNING ALL ALONG.

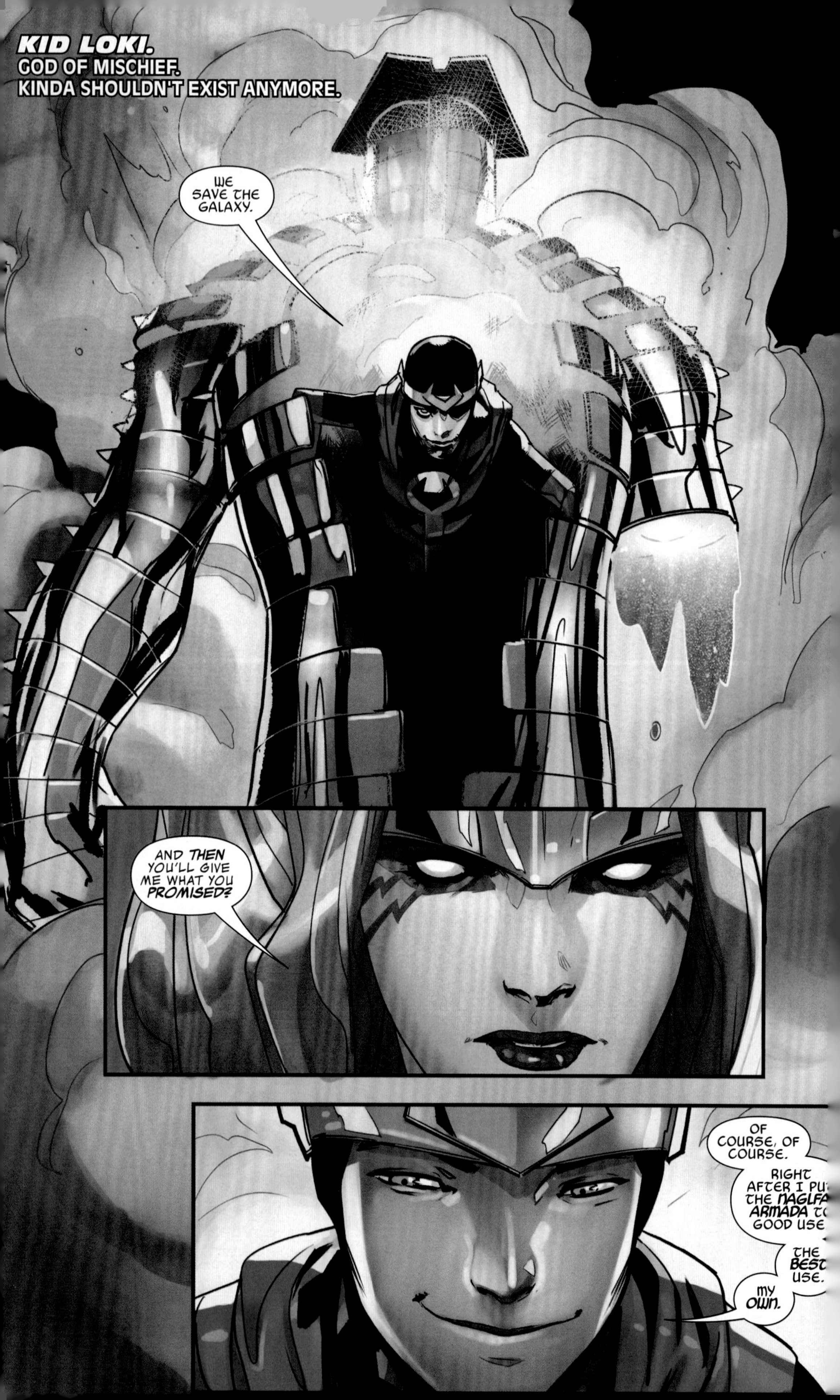
KID LOKI.
GOD OF MISCHIEF.
KINDA SHOULDN'T EXIST ANYMORE.
WE SAVE THE GALAXY.
AND THEN YOU'LL GIVE ME WHAT YOU PROMISED?
OF COURSE, OF COURSE.
RIGHT AFTER I PU THE NAGLFA ARMADA TO GOOD USE.
THE BEST USE.
MY OWN.

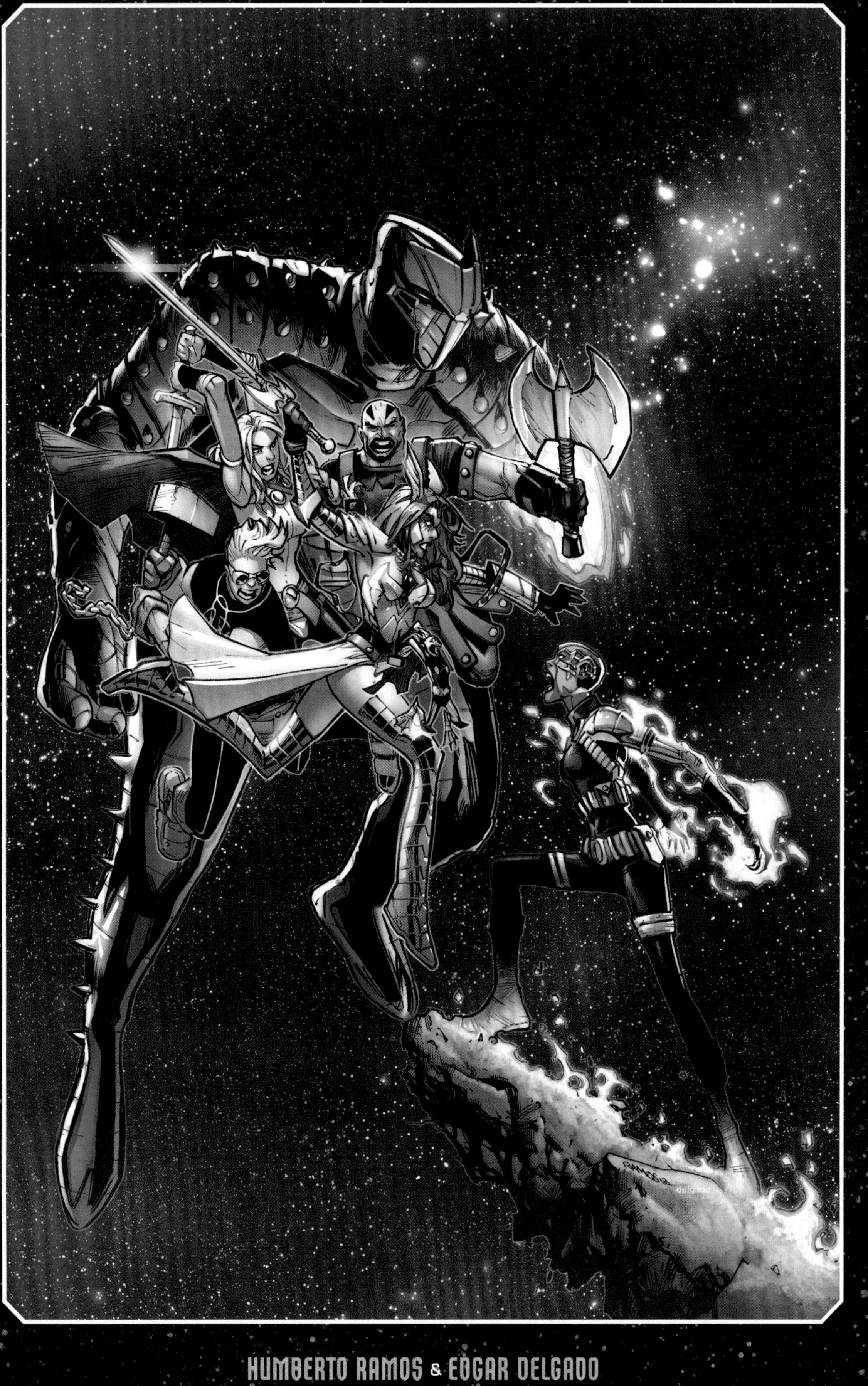

HUMBERTO RAMOS & EDGAR DELGADO
#1 VARIANT

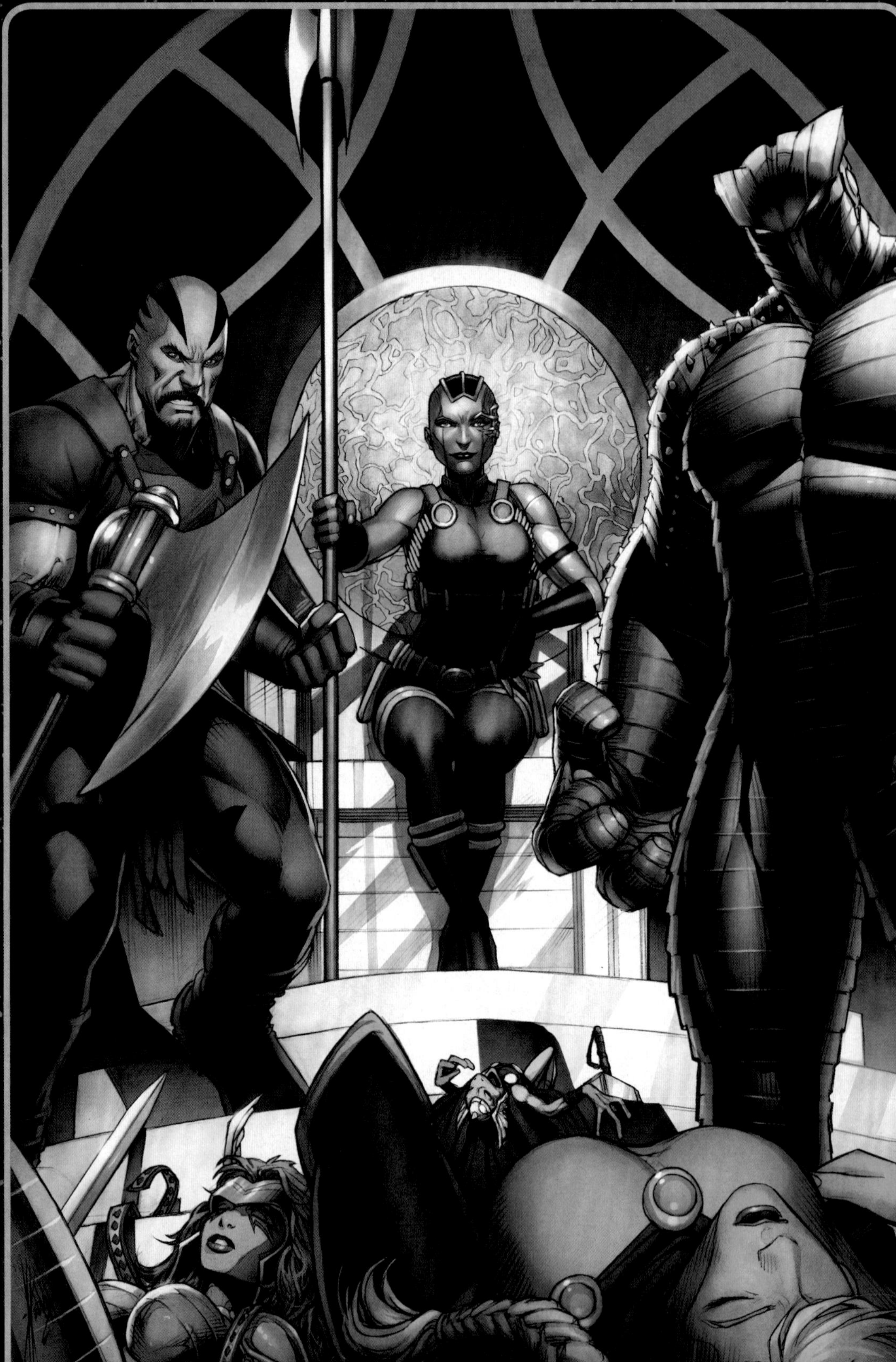

2

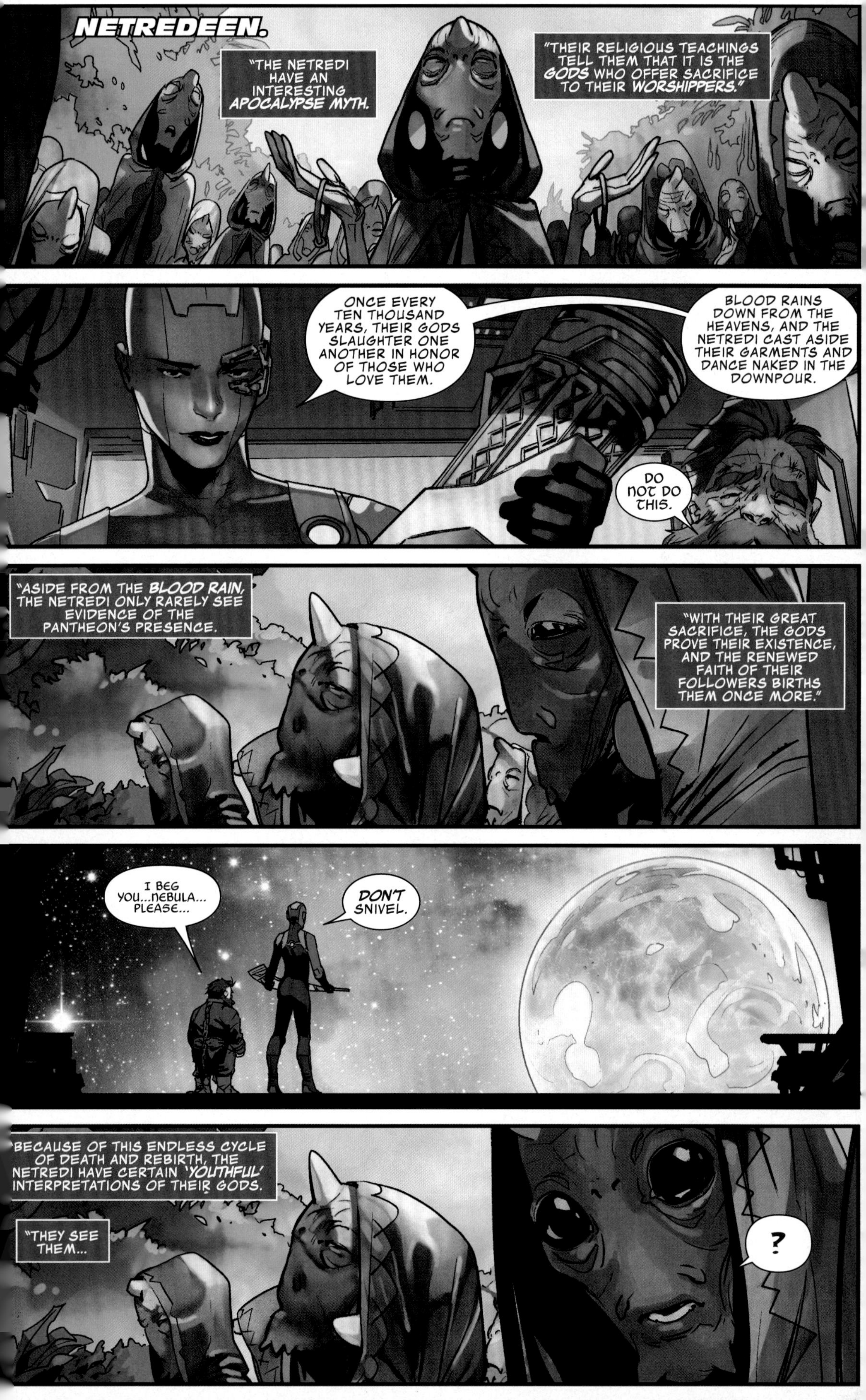
NETREDEEN.
"THE NETREDI HAVE AN INTERESTING APOCALYPSE MYTH.
"THEIR RELIGIOUS TEACHINGS TELL THEM THAT IT IS THE GODS WHO OFFER SACRIFICE TO THEIR WORSHIPPERS."
ONCE EVERY TEN THOUSAND YEARS, THEIR GODS SLAUGHTER ONE ANOTHER IN HONOR OF THOSE WHO LOVE THEM.
BLOOD RAINS DOWN FROM THE HEAVENS, AND THE NETREDI CAST ASIDE THEIR GARMENTS AND DANCE NAKED IN THE DOWNPOUR.
DO NOT DO THIS.
"ASIDE FROM THE BLOOD RAIN, THE NETREDI ONLY RARELY SEE EVIDENCE OF THE PANTHEON'S PRESENCE.
"WITH THEIR GREAT SACRIFICE, THE GODS PROVE THEIR EXISTENCE, AND THE RENEWED FAITH OF THEIR FOLLOWERS BIRTHS THEM ONCE MORE."
I BEG YOU...NEBULA... PLEASE...
DON'T SNIVEL.
"BECAUSE OF THIS ENDLESS CYCLE OF DEATH AND REBIRTH, THE NETREDI HAVE CERTAIN 'YOUTHFUL' INTERPRETATIONS OF THEIR GODS.
"THEY SEE THEM...
?

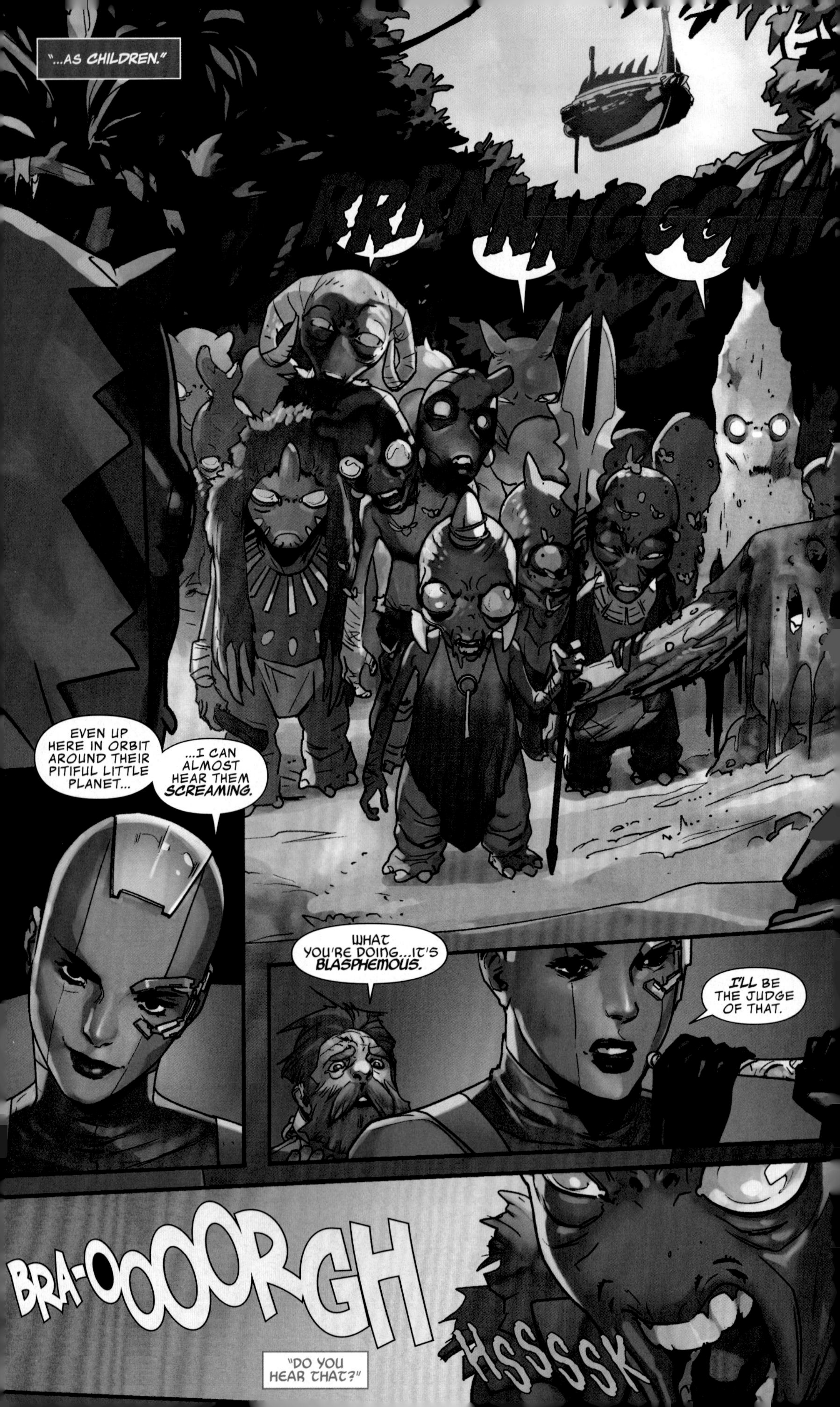

"...AS CHILDREN."
KRRNNNGGCHH
EVEN UP HERE IN ORBIT AROUND THEIR PITIFUL LITTLE PLANET...
...I CAN ALMOST HEAR THEM SCREAMING.
WHAT YOU'RE DOING...IT'S BLASPHEMOUS.
I'LL BE THE JUDGE OF THAT.
BRA-OOOORGH
HSSSSK
"DO YOU HEAR THAT?"

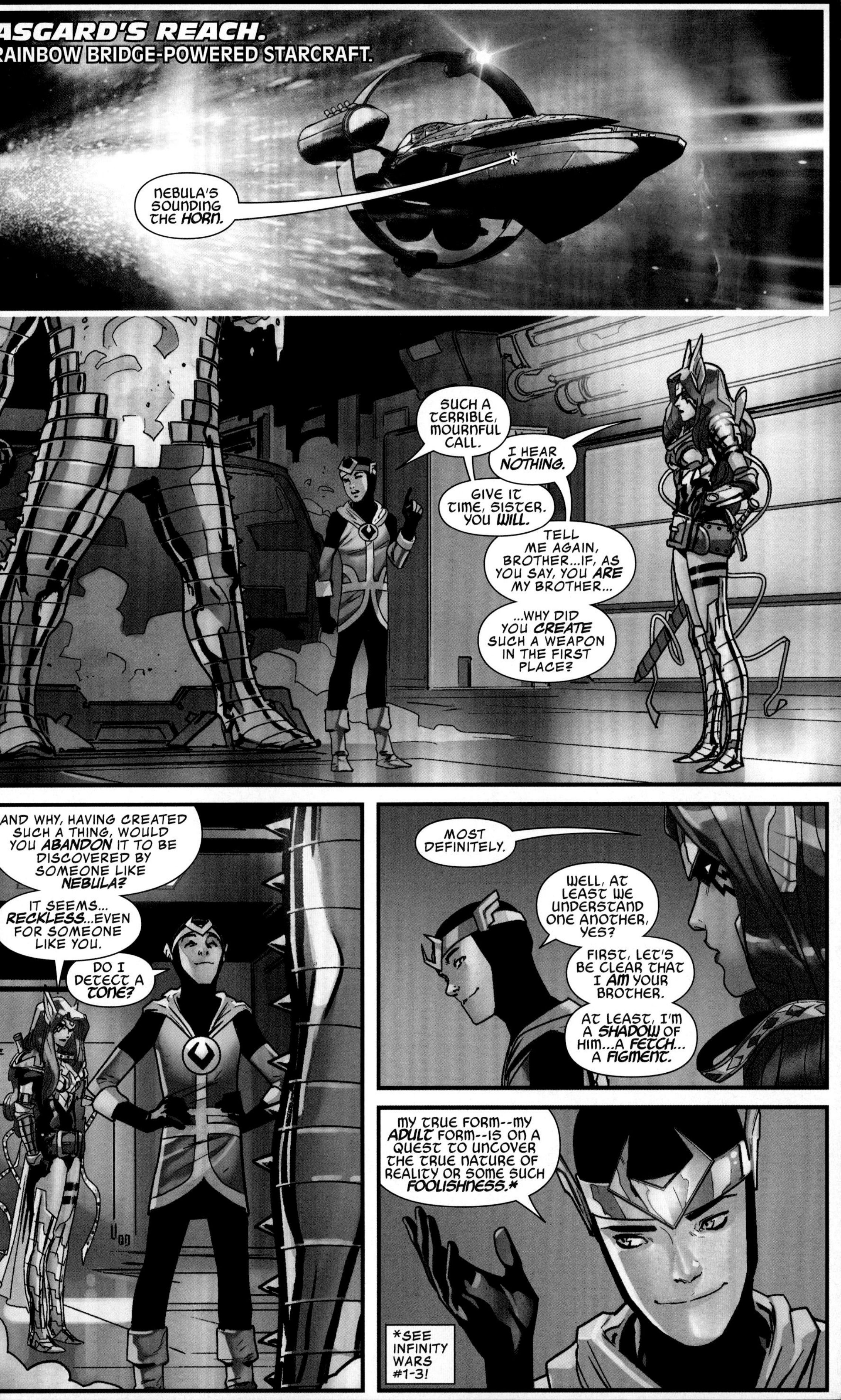

ASGARD'S REACH.
RAINBOW BRIDGE-POWERED STARCRAFT.
NEBULA'S SOUNDING THE HORN.
SUCH A TERRIBLE, MOURNFUL CALL.
I HEAR NOTHING.
GIVE IT TIME, SISTER. YOU WILL.
TELL ME AGAIN, BROTHER...IF, AS YOU SAY, YOU ARE MY BROTHER...
...WHY DID YOU CREATE SUCH A WEAPON IN THE FIRST PLACE?
AND WHY, HAVING CREATED SUCH A THING, WOULD YOU ABANDON IT TO BE DISCOVERED BY SOMEONE LIKE NEBULA?
IT SEEMS... RECKLESS...EVEN FOR SOMEONE LIKE YOU.
DO I DETECT A TONE?
MOST DEFINITELY.
WELL, AT LEAST WE UNDERSTAND ONE ANOTHER, YES?
FIRST, LET'S BE CLEAR THAT I AM YOUR BROTHER.
AT LEAST, I'M A SHADOW OF HIM...A FETCH... A FIGMENT.
MY TRUE FORM--MY ADULT FORM--IS ON A QUEST TO UNCOVER THE TRUE NATURE OF REALITY OR SOME SUCH FOOLISHNESS.*
*SEE INFINITY WARS #1-3!

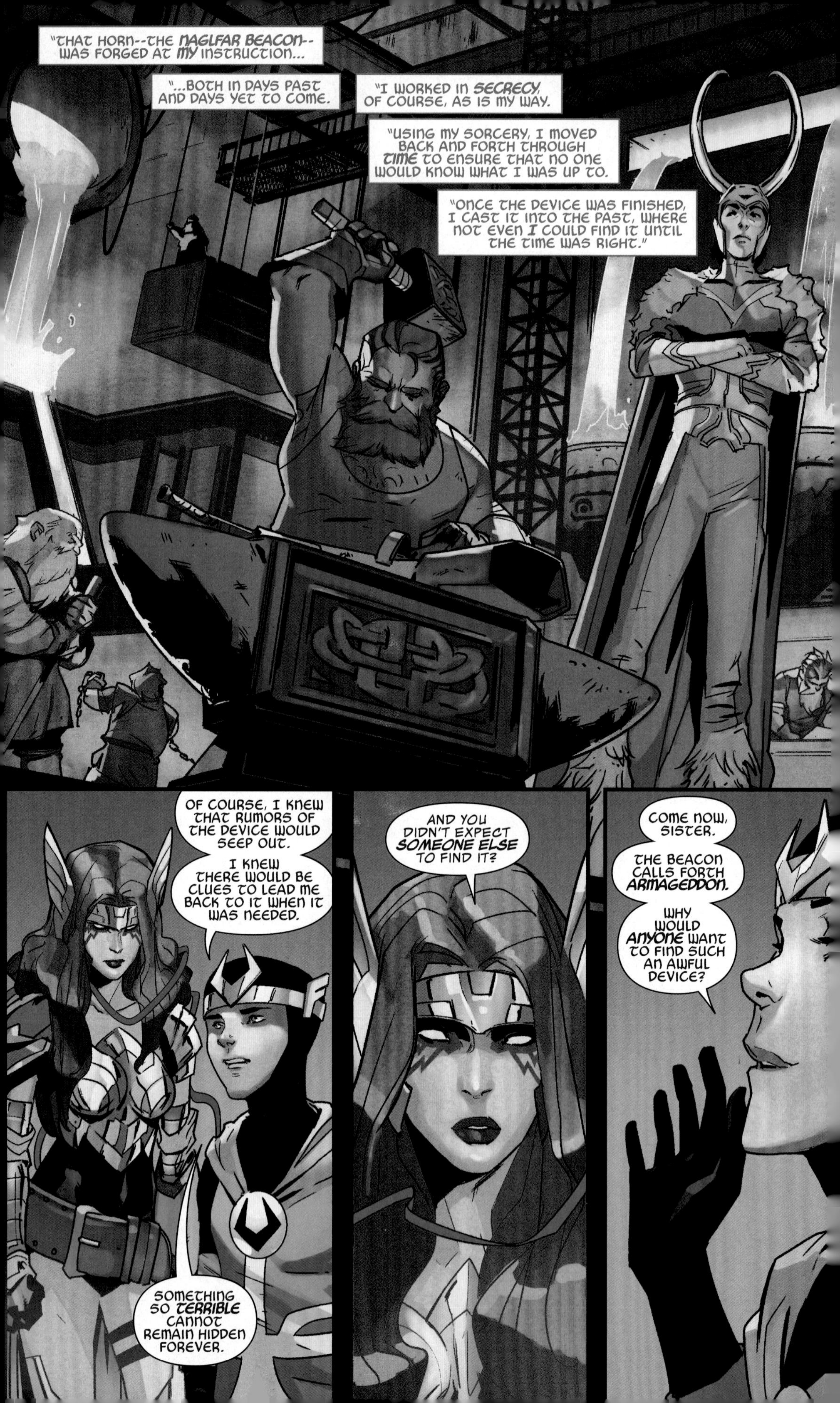

"THAT HORN--THE NAGLFAR BEACON--WAS FORGED AT MY INSTRUCTION...
"...BOTH IN DAYS PAST AND DAYS YET TO COME.
"I WORKED IN SECRECY, OF COURSE, AS IS MY WAY.
"USING MY SORCERY, I MOVED BACK AND FORTH THROUGH TIME TO ENSURE THAT NO ONE WOULD KNOW WHAT I WAS UP TO.
"ONCE THE DEVICE WAS FINISHED, I CAST IT INTO THE PAST, WHERE NOT EVEN I COULD FIND IT UNTIL THE TIME WAS RIGHT."
OF COURSE, I KNEW THAT RUMORS OF THE DEVICE WOULD SEEP OUT.
I KNEW THERE WOULD BE CLUES TO LEAD ME BACK TO IT WHEN IT WAS NEEDED.
SOMETHING SO TERRIBLE CANNOT REMAIN HIDDEN FOREVER.
AND YOU DIDN'T EXPECT SOMEONE ELSE TO FIND IT?
COME NOW, SISTER.
THE BEACON CALLS FORTH ARMAGEDDON.
WHY WOULD ANYONE WANT TO FIND SUCH AN AWFUL DEVICE?

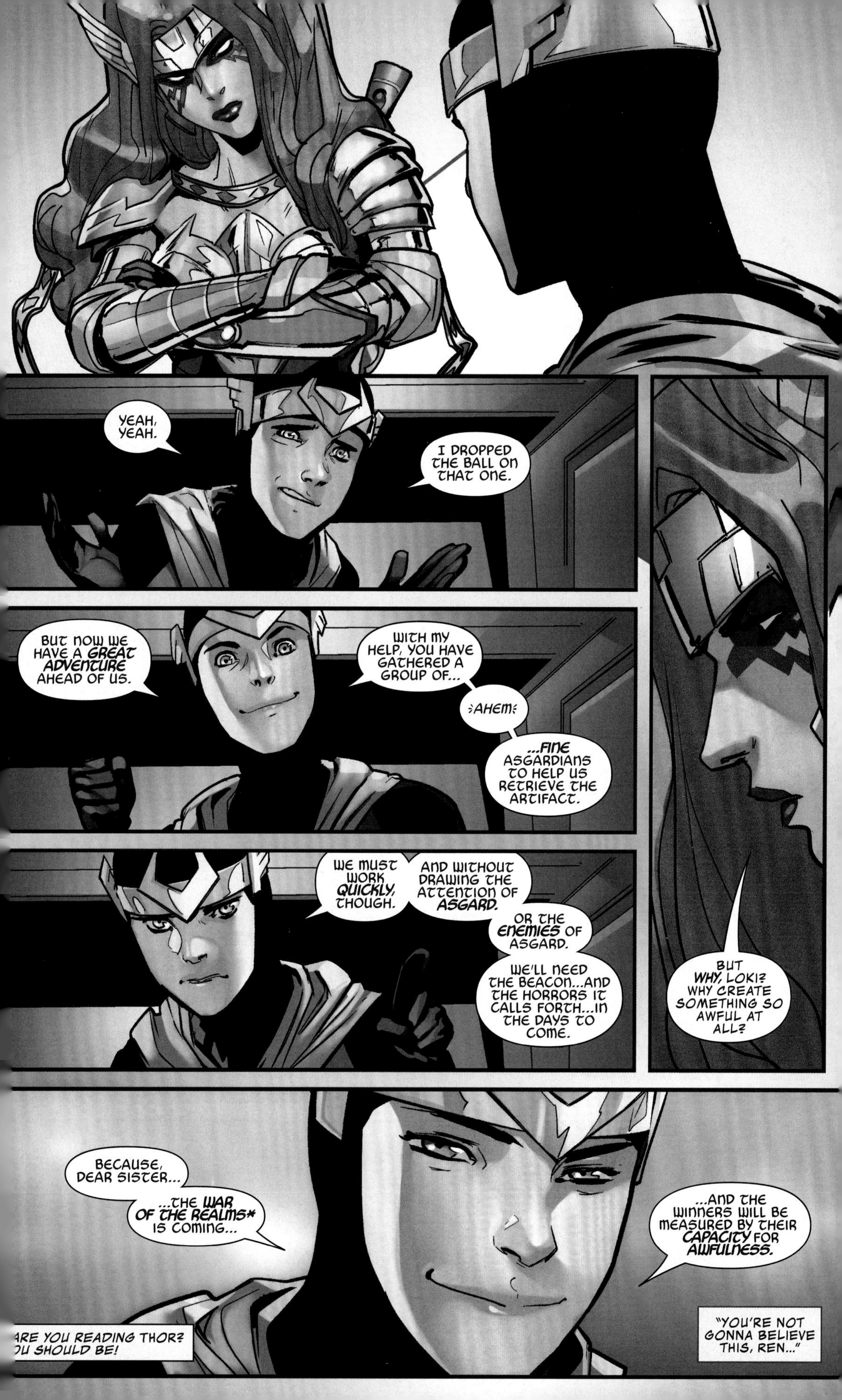
YEAH, YEAH.
I DROPPED THE BALL ON THAT ONE.
BUT NOW WE HAVE A GREAT ADVENTURE AHEAD OF US.
WITH MY HELP, YOU HAVE GATHERED A GROUP OF...
AHEM
...FINE ASGARDIANS TO HELP US RETRIEVE THE ARTIFACT.
WE MUST WORK QUICKLY, THOUGH.
AND WITHOUT DRAWING THE ATTENTION OF ASGARD.
OR THE ENEMIES OF ASGARD.
WE'LL NEED THE BEACON...AND THE HORRORS IT CALLS FORTH...IN THE DAYS TO COME.
BUT WHY, LOKI? WHY CREATE SOMETHING SO AWFUL AT ALL?
BECAUSE, DEAR SISTER...
...THE WAR OF THE REALMS* IS COMING...
...AND THE WINNERS WILL BE MEASURED BY THEIR CAPACITY FOR AWFULNESS.
ARE YOU READING THOR? OU SHOULD BE!
"YOU'RE NOT GONNA BELIEVE THIS, REN..."

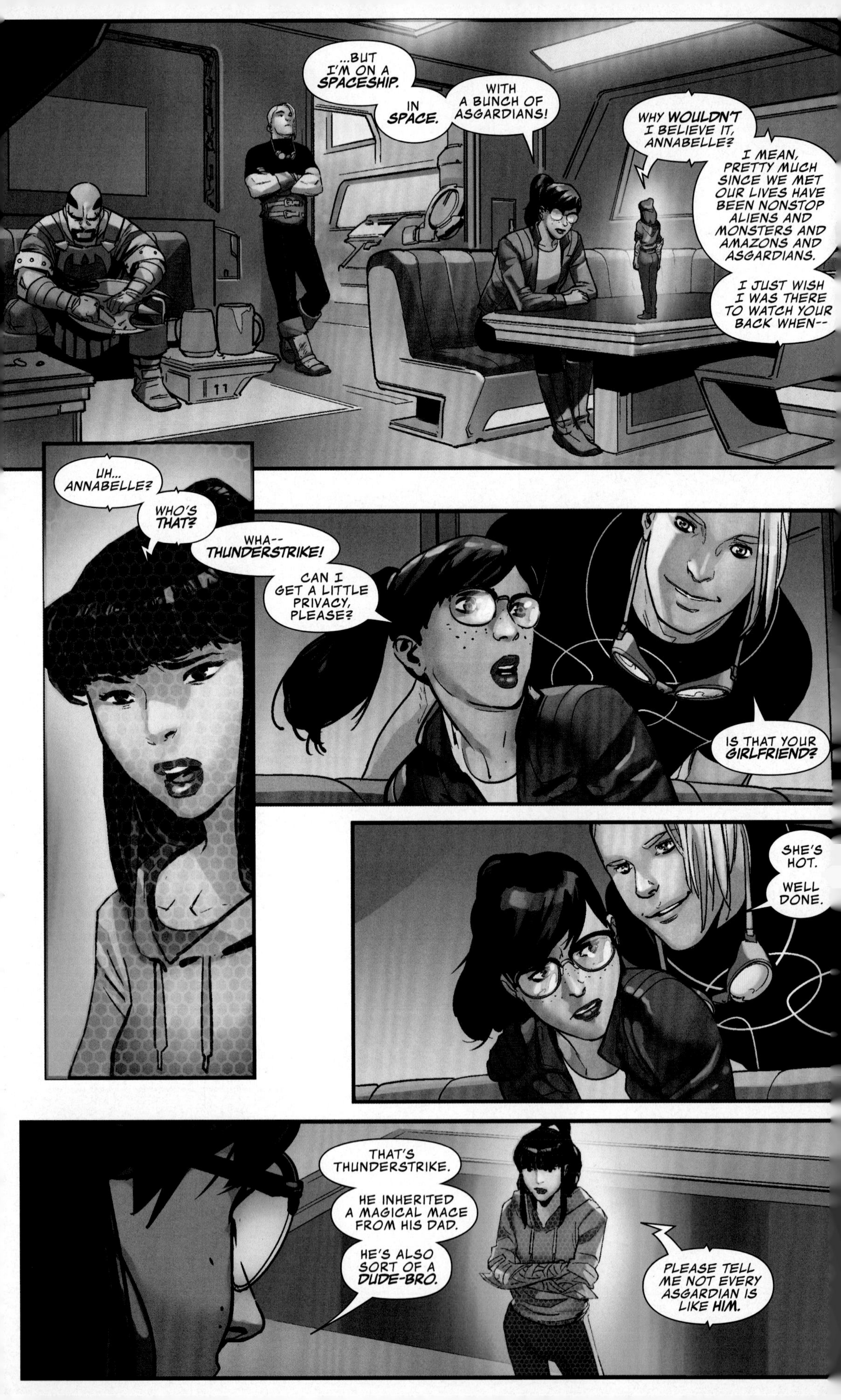

...BUT I'M ON A SPACESHIP.
IN SPACE.
WITH A BUNCH OF ASGARDIANS!
WHY WOULDN'T I BELIEVE IT, ANNABELLE?
I MEAN, PRETTY MUCH SINCE WE MET OUR LIVES HAVE BEEN NONSTOP ALIENS AND MONSTERS AND AMAZONS AND ASGARDIANS.
I JUST WISH I WAS THERE TO WATCH YOUR BACK WHEN--
UH... ANNABELLE?
WHO'S THAT?
WHA-- THUNDERSTRIKE!
CAN I GET A LITTLE PRIVACY, PLEASE?
IS THAT YOUR GIRLFRIEND?
SHE'S HOT.
WELL DONE.
THAT'S THUNDERSTRIKE.
HE INHERITED A MAGICAL MACE FROM HIS DAD.
HE'S ALSO SORT OF A DUDE-BRO.
PLEASE TELL ME NOT EVERY ASGARDIAN IS LIKE HIM.

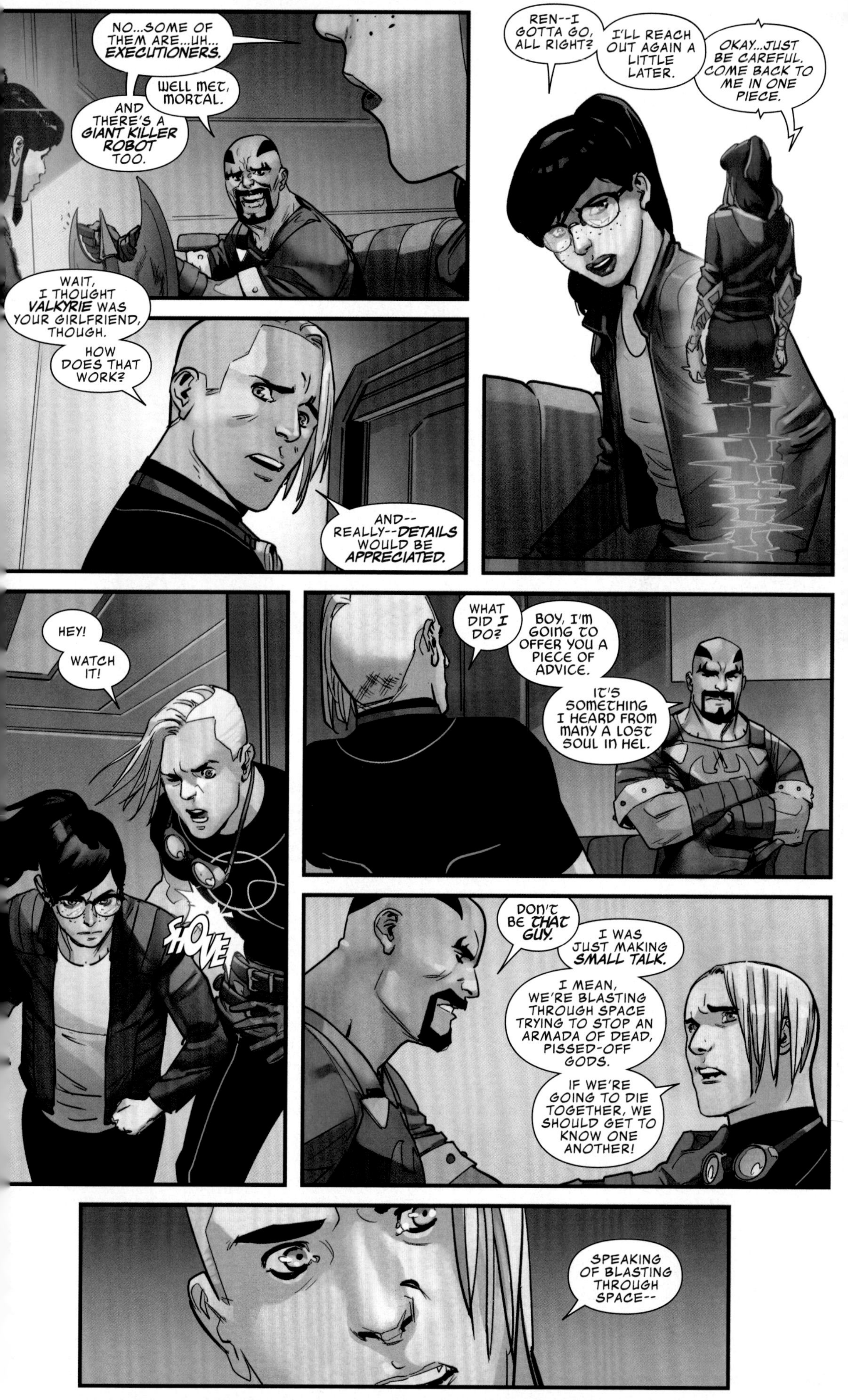

NO...SOME OF THEM ARE...UH... EXECUTIONERS.
AND THERE'S A GIANT KILLER ROBOT TOO.
WELL MET, MORTAL.
REN--I GOTTA GO, ALL RIGHT?
I'LL REACH OUT AGAIN A LITTLE LATER.
OKAY...JUST BE CAREFUL. COME BACK TO ME IN ONE PIECE.
WAIT, I THOUGHT VALKYRIE WAS YOUR GIRLFRIEND, THOUGH.
HOW DOES THAT WORK?
AND--REALLY--DETAILS WOULD BE APPRECIATED.
HEY!
WATCH IT!
SHOVE
WHAT DID I DO?
BOY, I'M GOING TO OFFER YOU A PIECE OF ADVICE.
IT'S SOMETHING I HEARD FROM MANY A LOST SOUL IN HEL.
DON'T BE THAT GUY.
I WAS JUST MAKING SMALL TALK.
I MEAN, WE'RE BLASTING THROUGH SPACE TRYING TO STOP AN ARMADA OF DEAD, PISSED-OFF GODS.
IF WE'RE GOING TO DIE TOGETHER, WE SHOULD GET TO KNOW ONE ANOTHER!
SPEAKING OF BLASTING THROUGH SPACE--

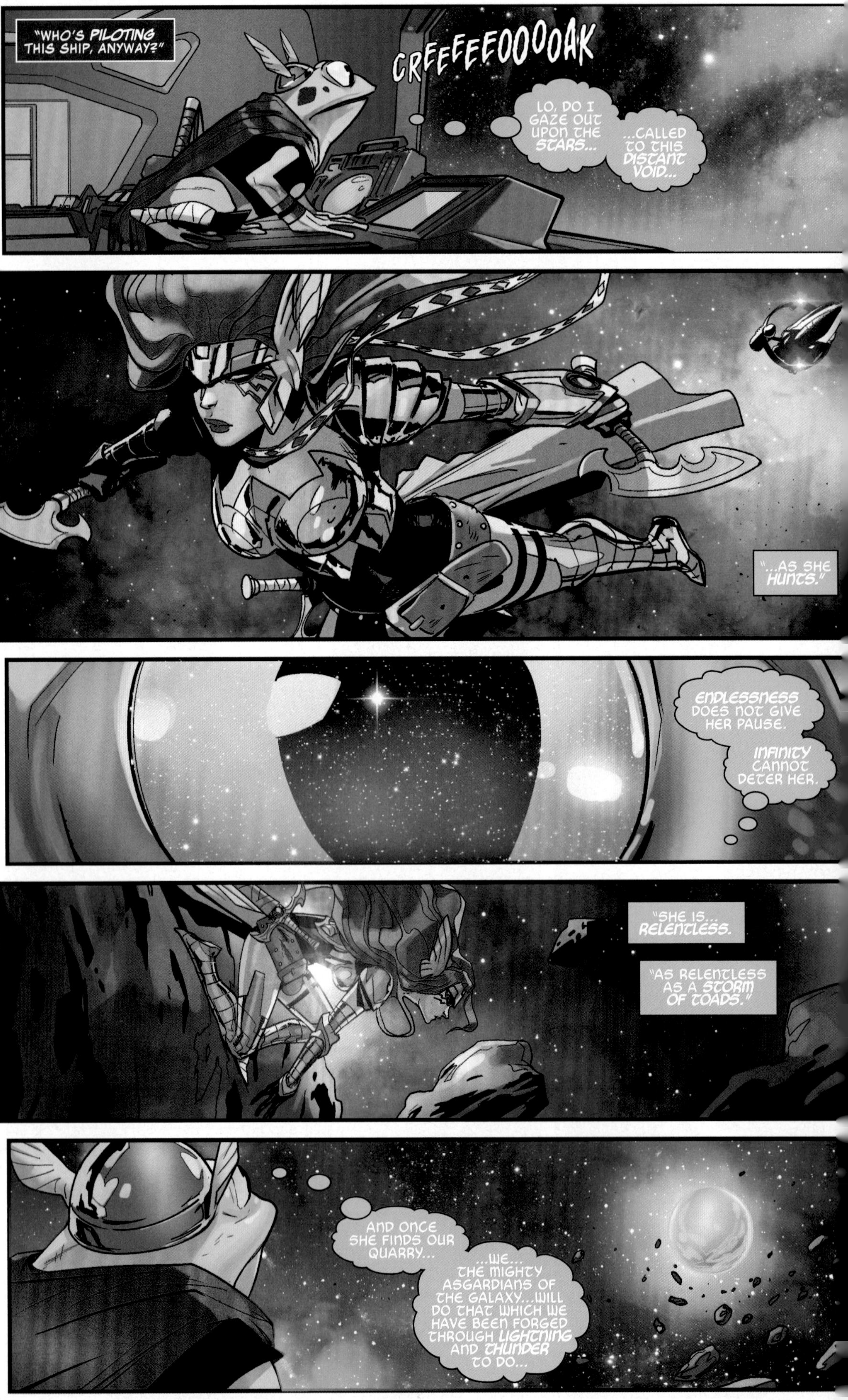

"WHO'S PILOTING THIS SHIP, ANYWAY?"
CREEEEEOOOOAK
LO, DO I GAZE OUT UPON THE STARS...
...CALLED TO THIS DISTANT VOID...
"...AS SHE HUNTS."
ENDLESSNESS DOES NOT GIVE HER PAUSE.
INFINITY CANNOT DETER HER.
"SHE IS... RELENTLESS.
"AS RELENTLESS AS A STORM OF TOADS."
AND ONCE SHE FINDS OUR QUARRY...
...WE... THE MIGHTY ASGARDIANS OF THE GALAXY...WILL DO THAT WHICH WE HAVE BEEN FORGED THROUGH LIGHTNING AND THUNDER TO DO...

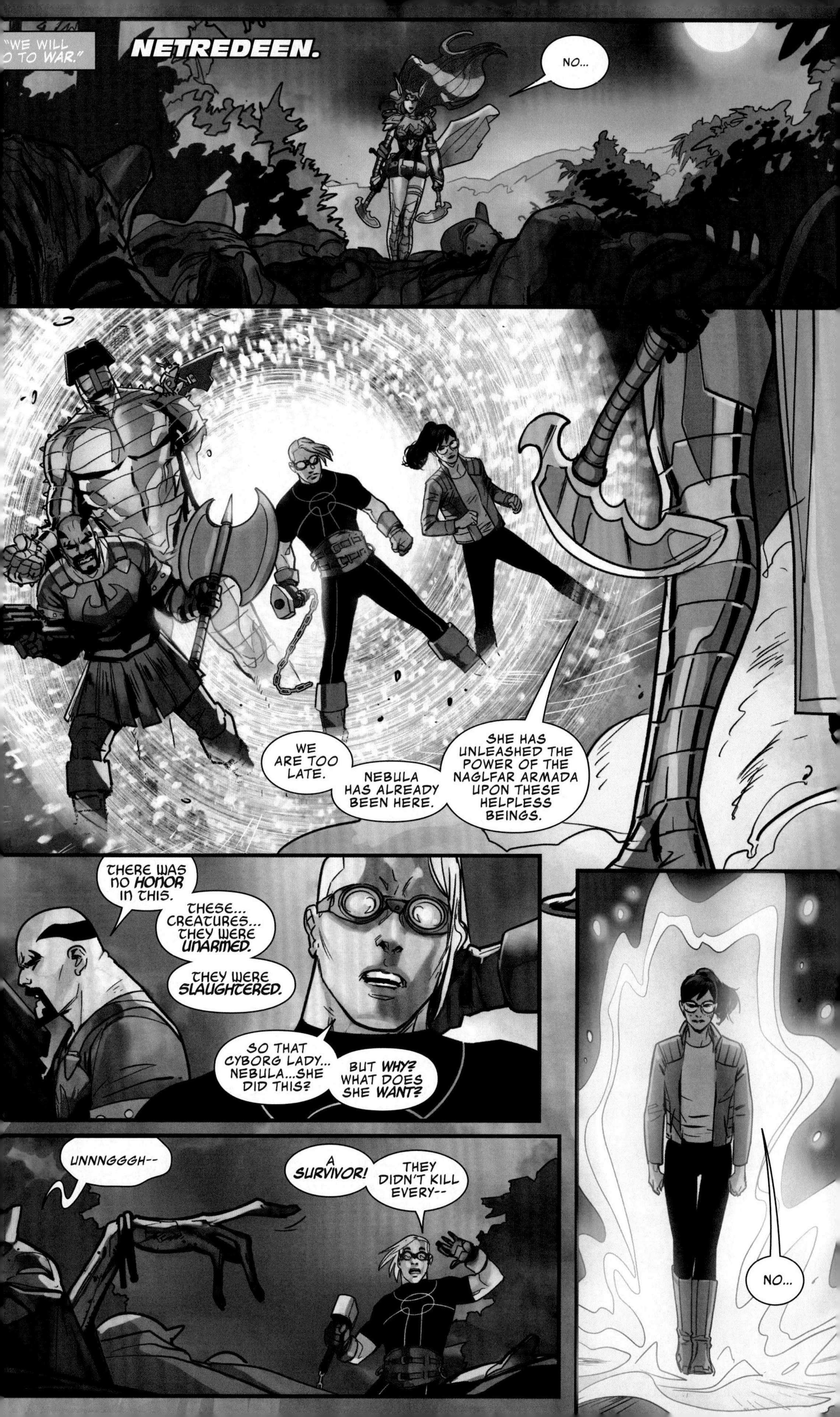
"WE WILL
O TO WAR."
NETREDEEN.
NO...
WE ARE TOO LATE.
NEBULA HAS ALREADY BEEN HERE.
SHE HAS UNLEASHED THE POWER OF THE NAGLFAR ARMADA UPON THESE HELPLESS BEINGS.
THERE WAS NO HONOR IN THIS.
THESE... CREATURES... THEY WERE UNARMED.
THEY WERE SLAUGHTERED.
SO THAT CYBORG LADY... NEBULA...SHE DID THIS?
BUT WHY? WHAT DOES SHE WANT?
UNNNGGGH--
A SURVIVOR!
THEY DIDN'T KILL EVERY--
NO...

...THERE WILL SOON BE *NO* SURVIVORS.

HOW DOES SHE KNOW?

SHE'S A *VALKYRIE,* BOY.

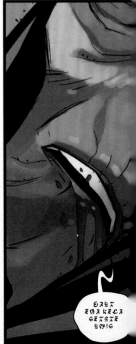

SHE CARRIES THE DEAD TO THEIR FINAL RESTING PLACE.

AND SHE CAN SEE THE *VEIL OF DEATH* WHEN IT LOOMS OVER OTHERS.

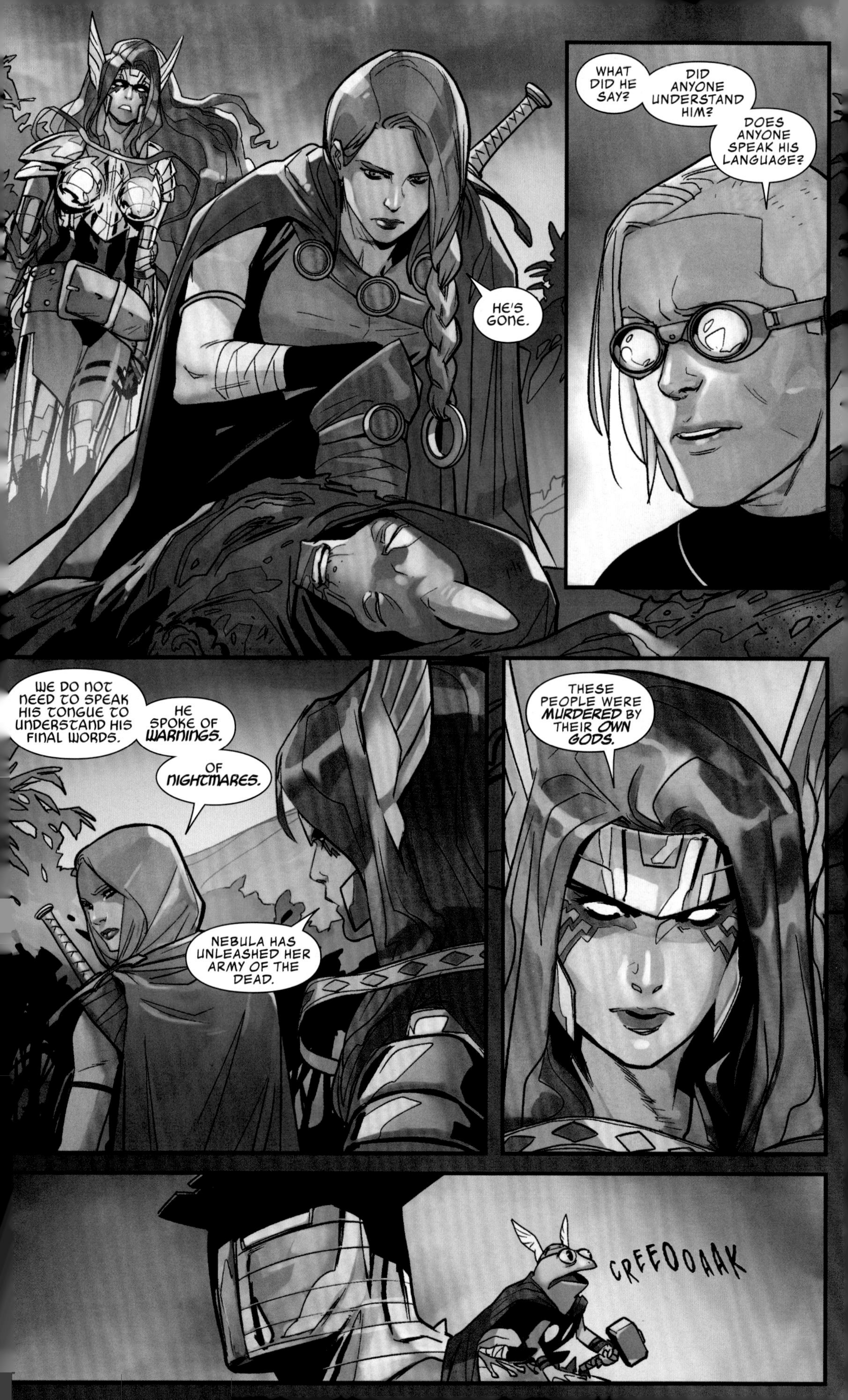
HE'S GONE.
WHAT DID HE SAY?
DID ANYONE UNDERSTAND HIM?
DOES ANYONE SPEAK HIS LANGUAGE?
WE DO NOT NEED TO SPEAK HIS TONGUE TO UNDERSTAND HIS FINAL WORDS.
HE SPOKE OF WARNINGS.
OF NIGHTMARES.
NEBULA HAS UNLEASHED HER ARMY OF THE DEAD.
THESE PEOPLE WERE MURDERED BY THEIR OWN GODS.
CREEOOAAK

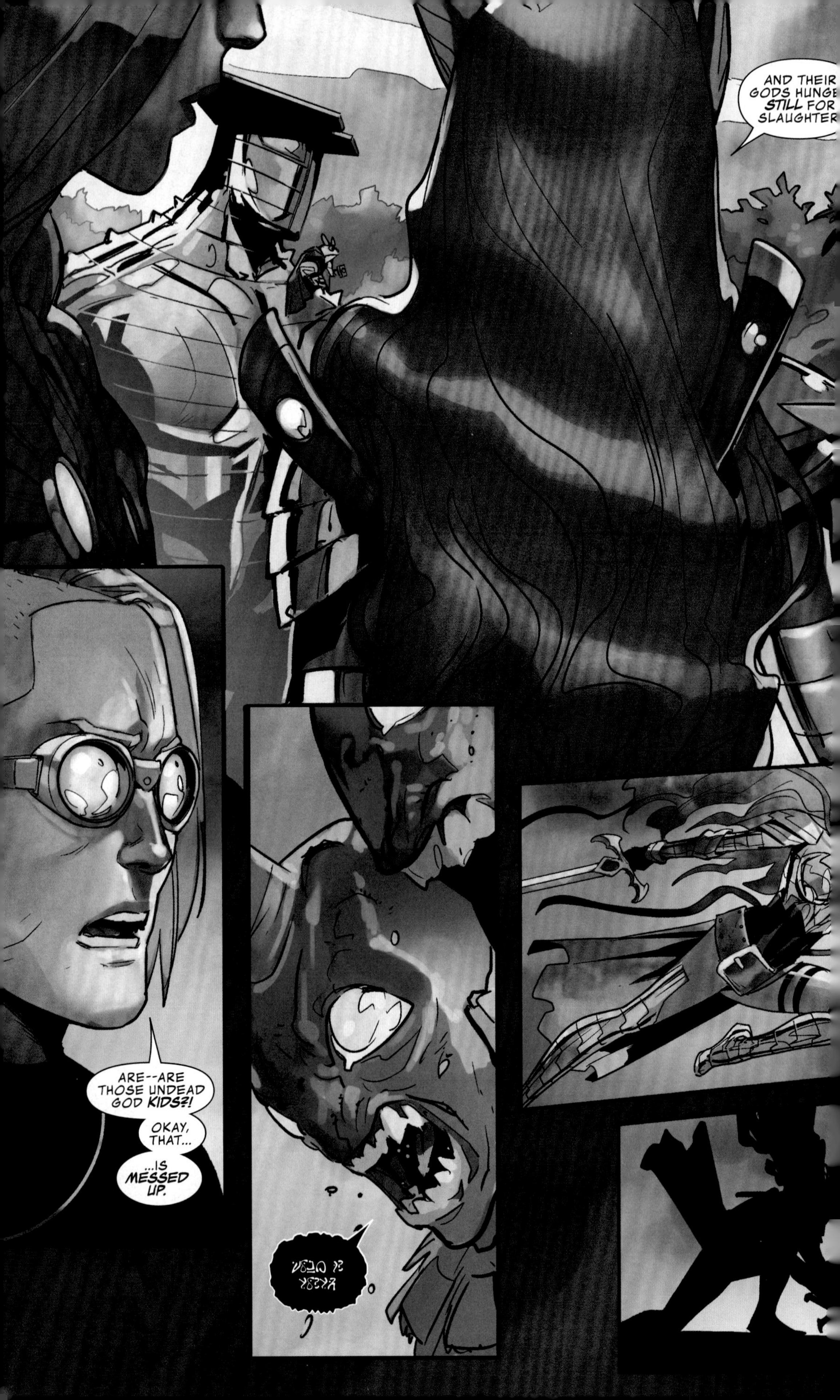

AND THEIR GODS HUNGE STILL FOR SLAUGHTER
ARE--ARE THOSE UNDEAD GOD KIDS?!
OKAY, THAT...
...IS MESSED UP.

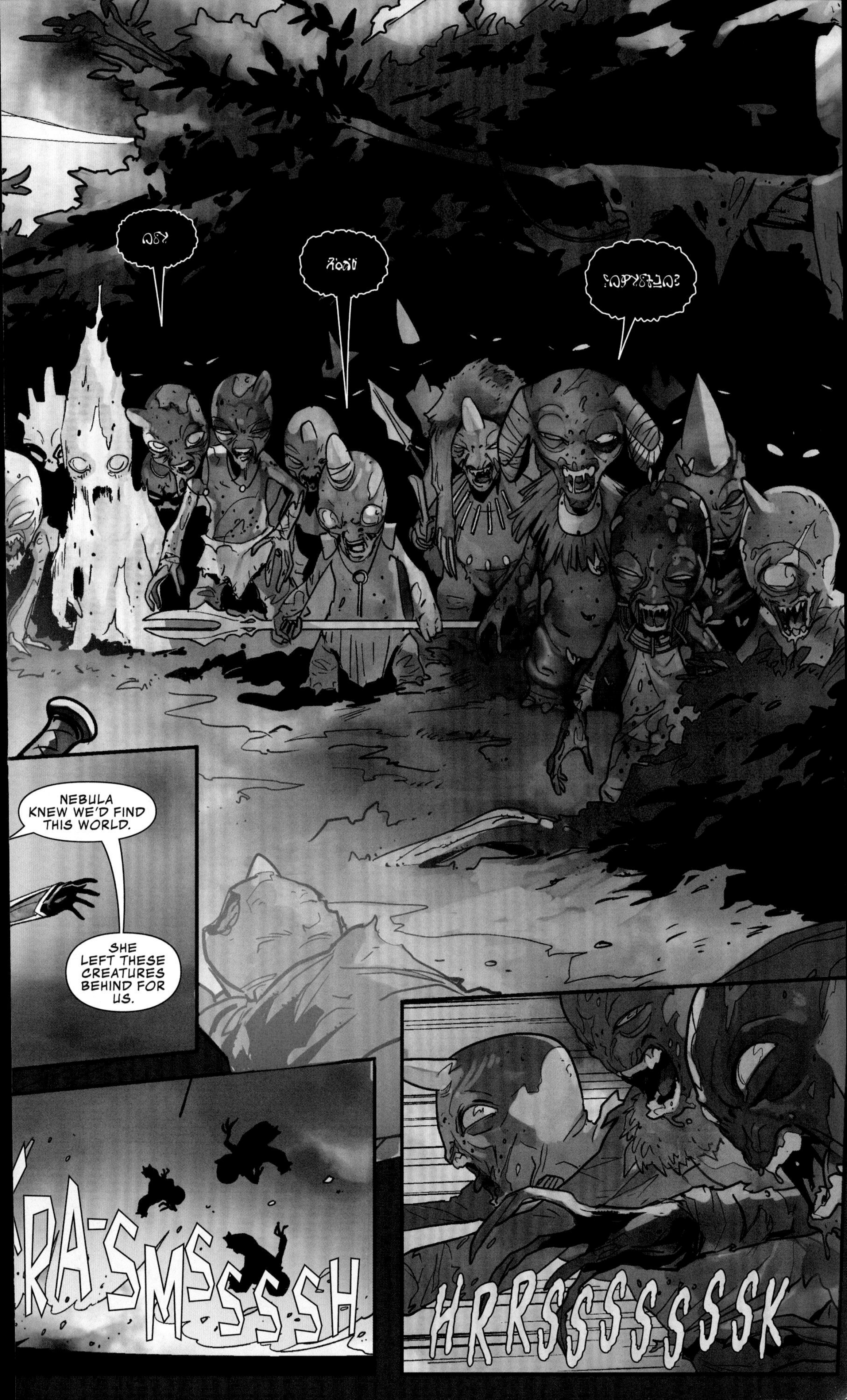
NEBULA KNEW WE'D FIND THIS WORLD.
SHE LEFT THESE CREATURES BEHIND FOR US.
RA-SMSSSSH
HRRSSSSSSSK

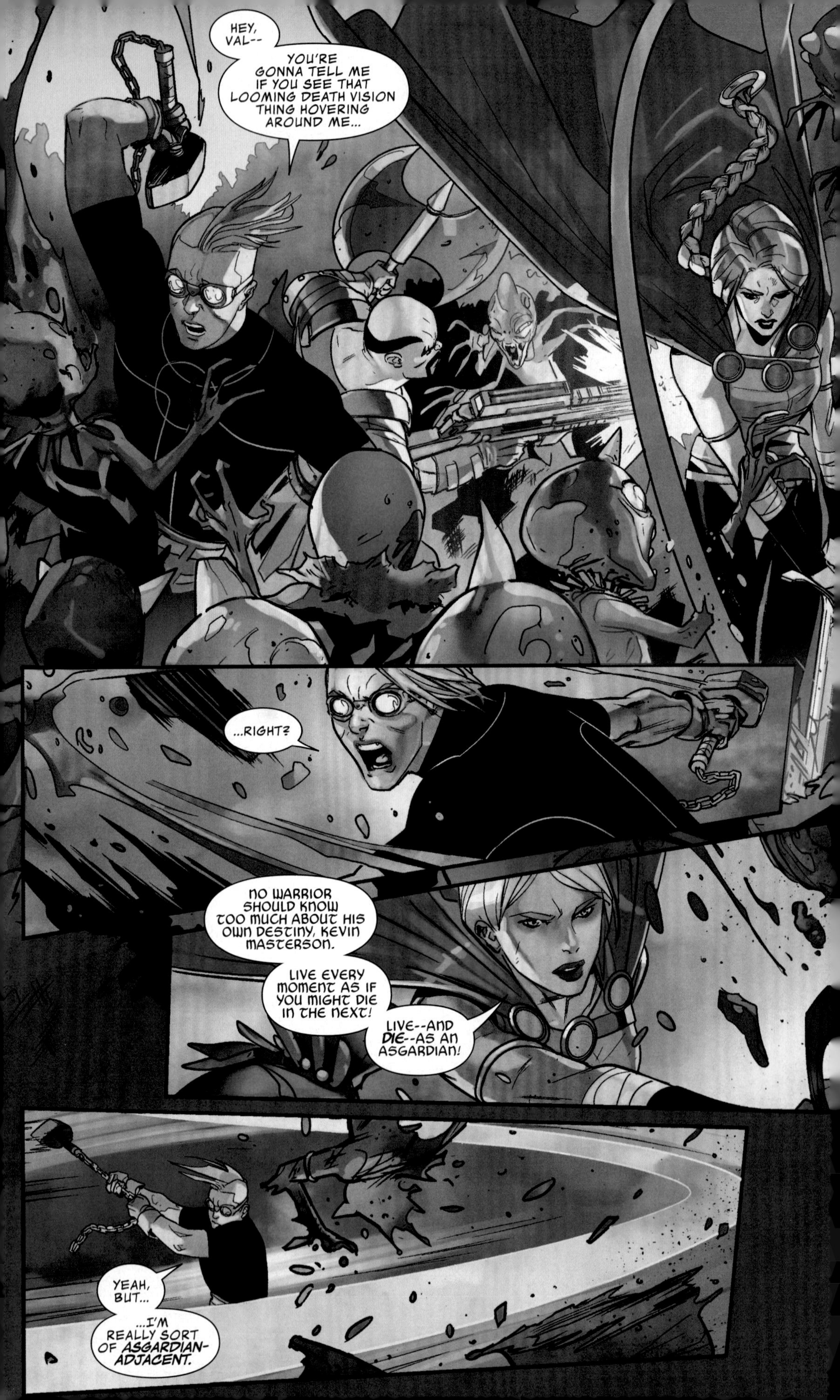
HEY, VAL--
YOU'RE GONNA TELL ME IF YOU SEE THAT LOOMING DEATH VISION THING HOVERING AROUND ME...
...RIGHT?
NO WARRIOR SHOULD KNOW TOO MUCH ABOUT HIS OWN DESTINY, KEVIN MASTERSON.
LIVE EVERY MOMENT AS IF YOU MIGHT DIE IN THE NEXT!
LIVE--AND DIE--AS AN ASGARDIAN!
YEAH, BUT...
...I'M REALLY SORT OF ASGARDIAN-ADJACENT.

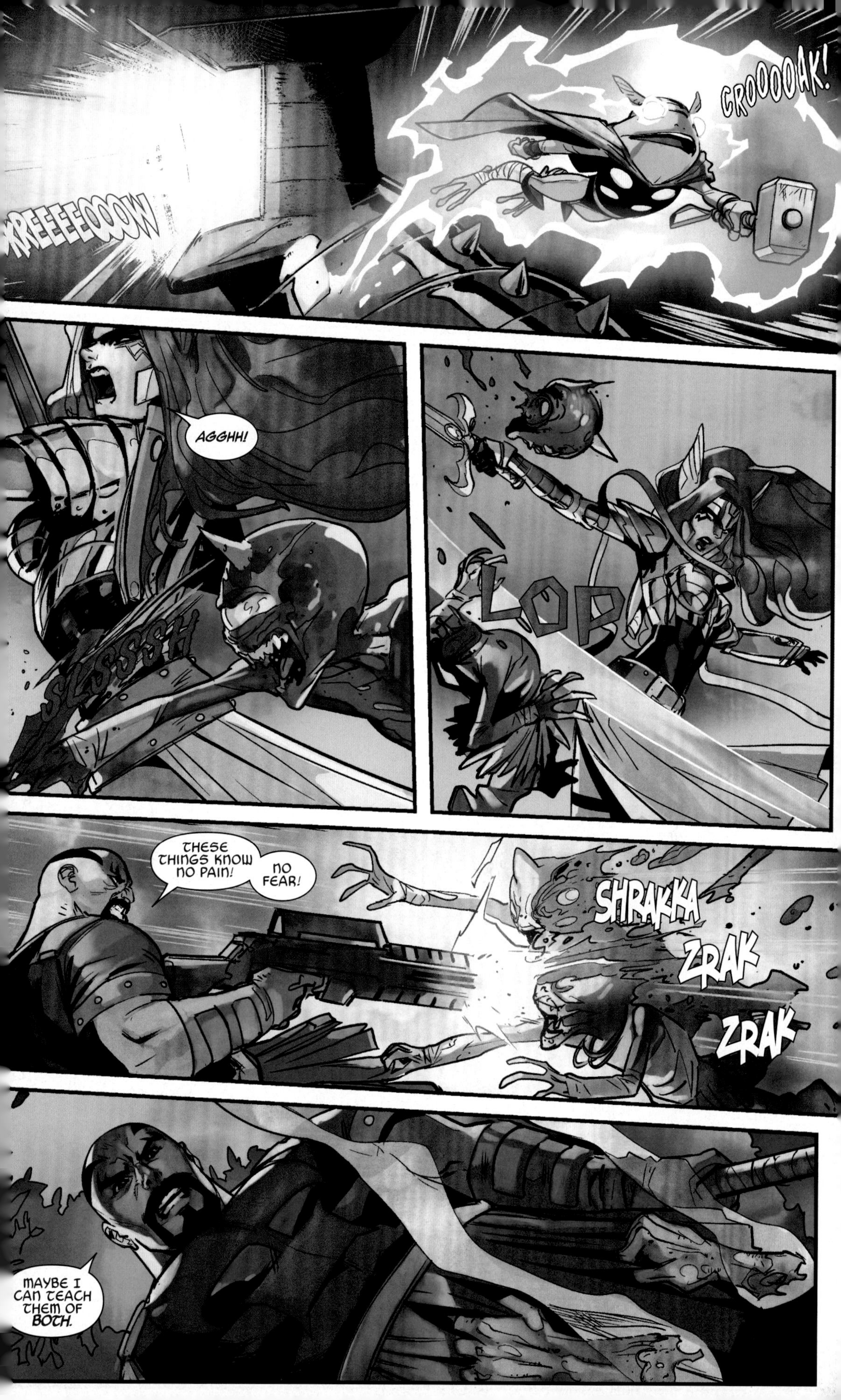
CROOOOAK!
KREEEEOOOW
AGGHH!
SLSSSSH
LOP
THESE THINGS KNOW NO PAIN!
NO FEAR!
SHRAKKA
ZRAK
ZRAK
MAYBE I CAN TEACH THEM OF BOTH.

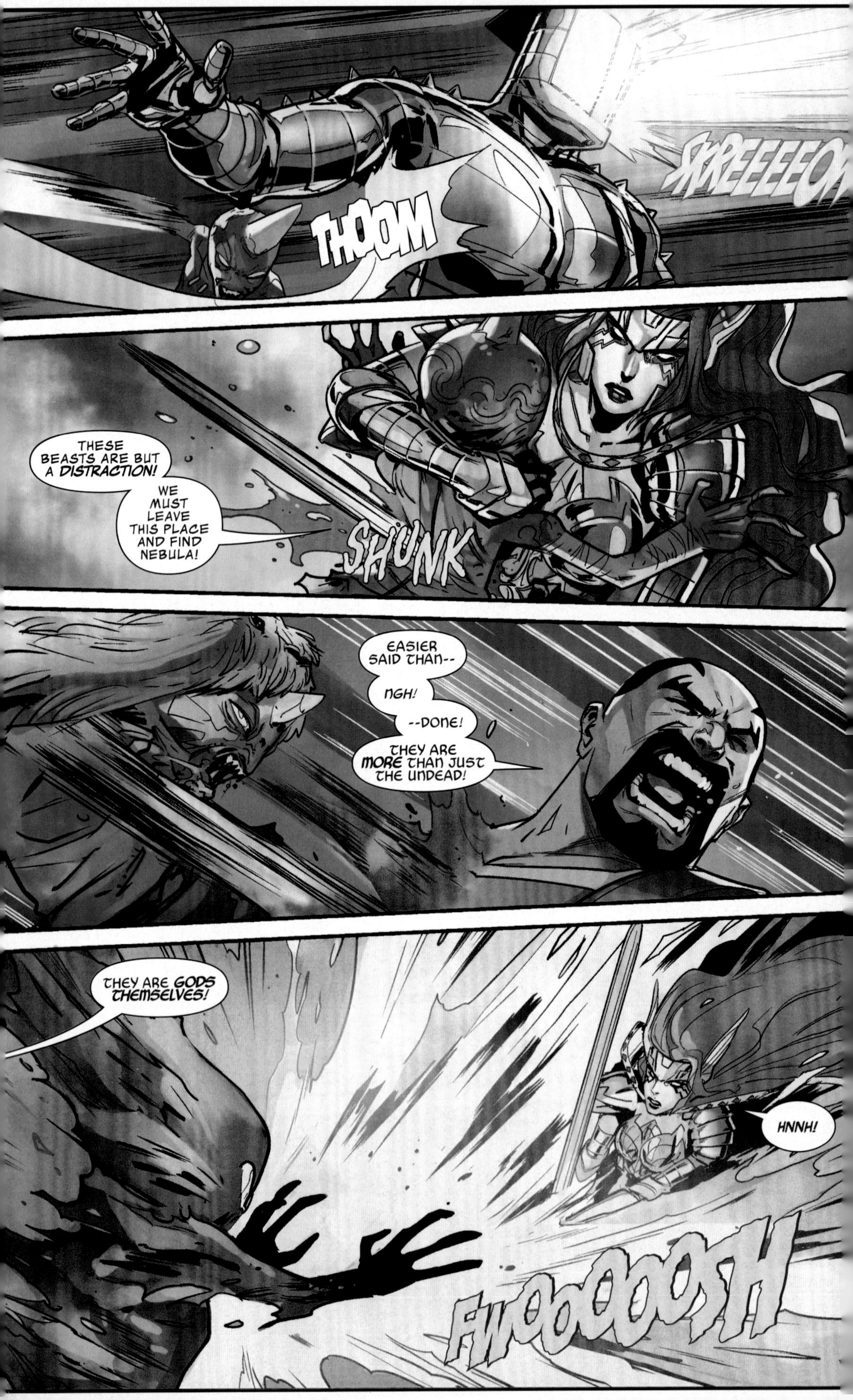
SKREEEEOW
THOOM
THESE BEASTS ARE BUT A DISTRACTION!
WE MUST LEAVE THIS PLACE AND FIND NEBULA!
SHUNK
EASIER SAID THAN--
NGH!
--DONE!
THEY ARE MORE THAN JUST THE UNDEAD!
THEY ARE GODS THEMSELVES!
HNNH!
FWOOOOOSH

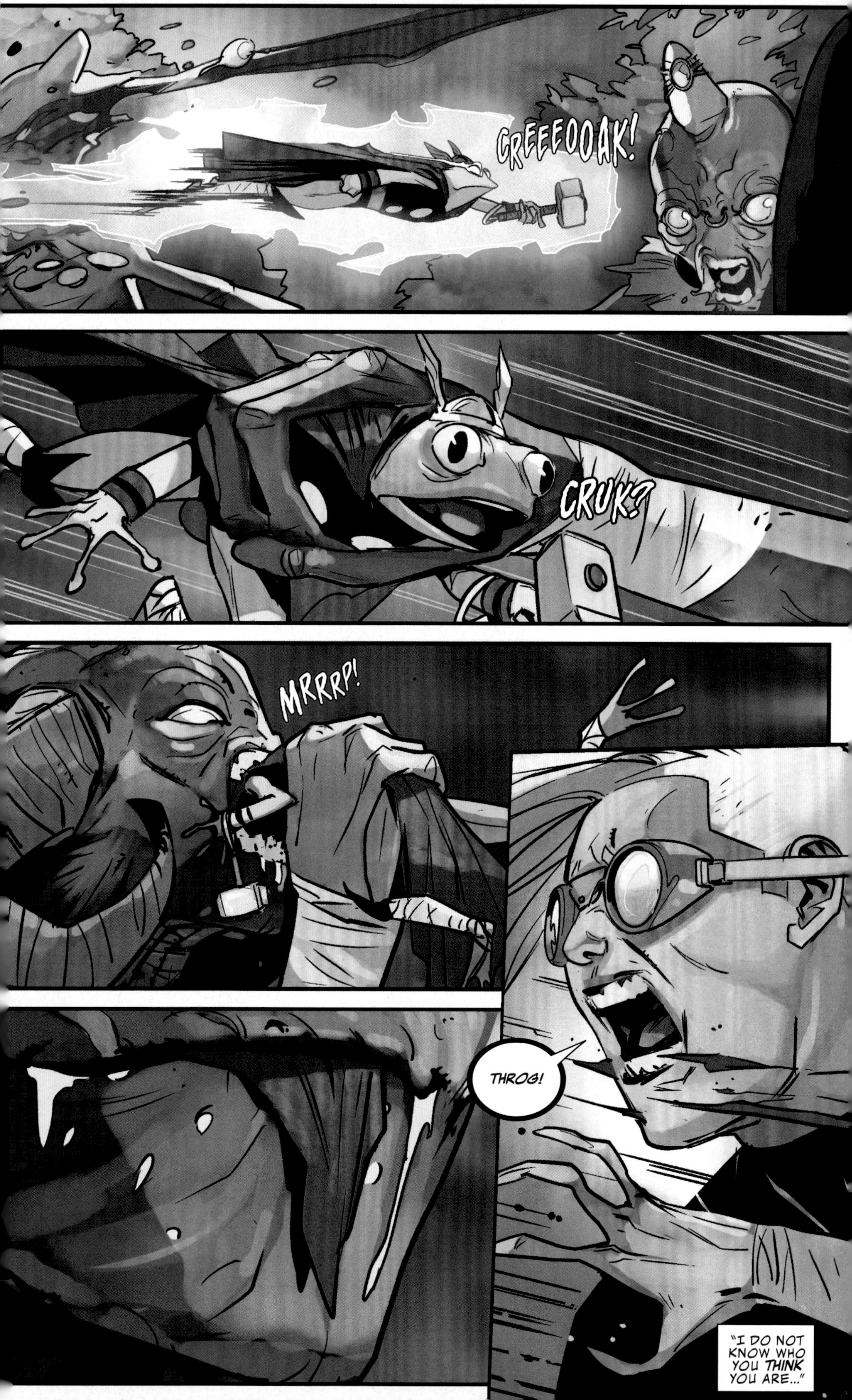
CREEEOOAK!
CRUK?
MRRRP!
THROG!
"I DO NOT KNOW WHO YOU THINK YOU ARE..."

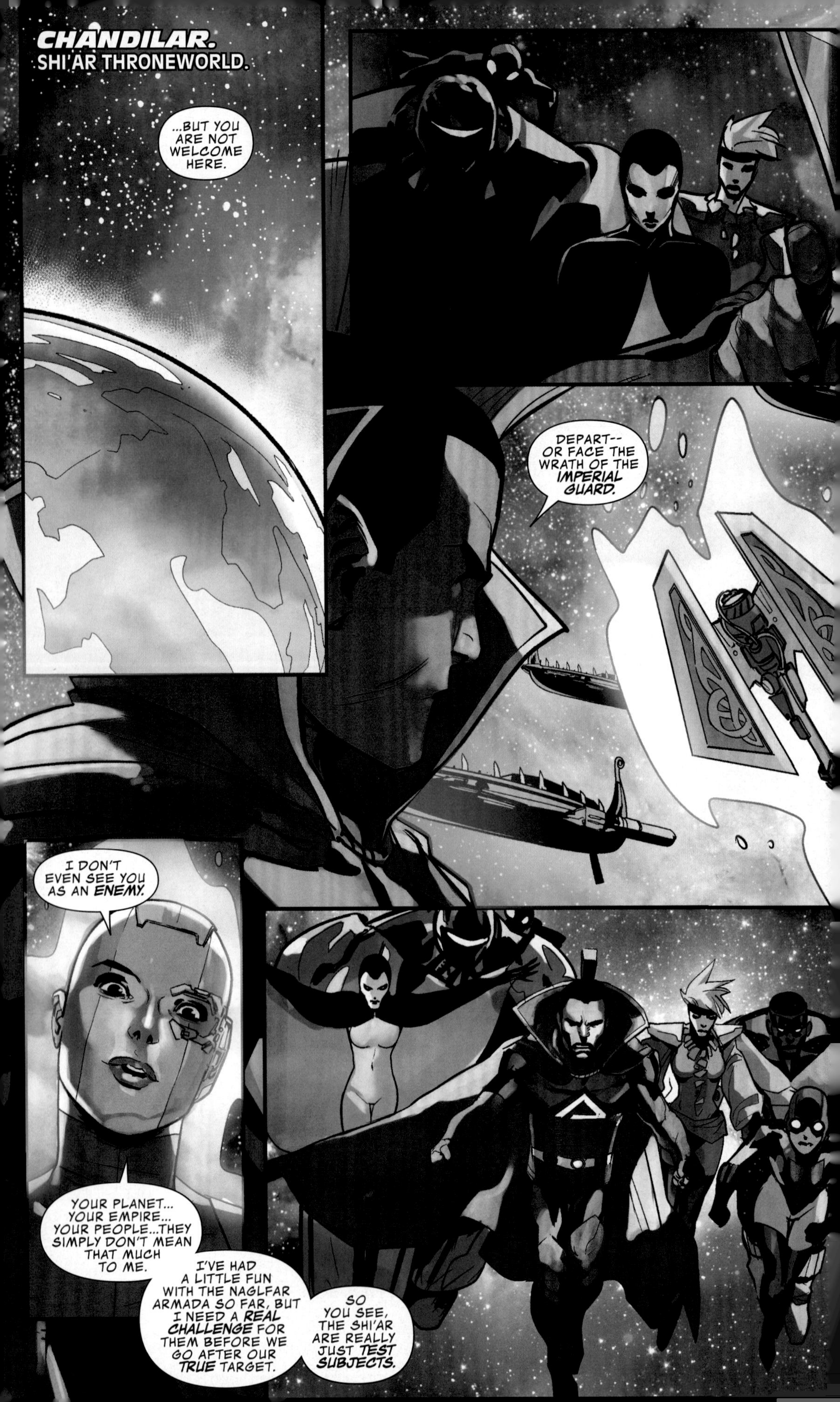
CHANDILAR.
SHI'AR THRONEWORLD.
...BUT YOU ARE NOT WELCOME HERE.
DEPART-- OR FACE THE WRATH OF THE IMPERIAL GUARD.
I DON'T EVEN SEE YOU AS AN ENEMY.
YOUR PLANET... YOUR EMPIRE... YOUR PEOPLE...THEY SIMPLY DON'T MEAN THAT MUCH TO ME.
I'VE HAD A LITTLE FUN WITH THE NAGLFAR ARMADA SO FAR, BUT I NEED A REAL CHALLENGE FOR THEM BEFORE WE GO AFTER OUR TRUE TARGET.
SO YOU SEE, THE SHI'AR ARE REALLY JUST TEST SUBJECTS.

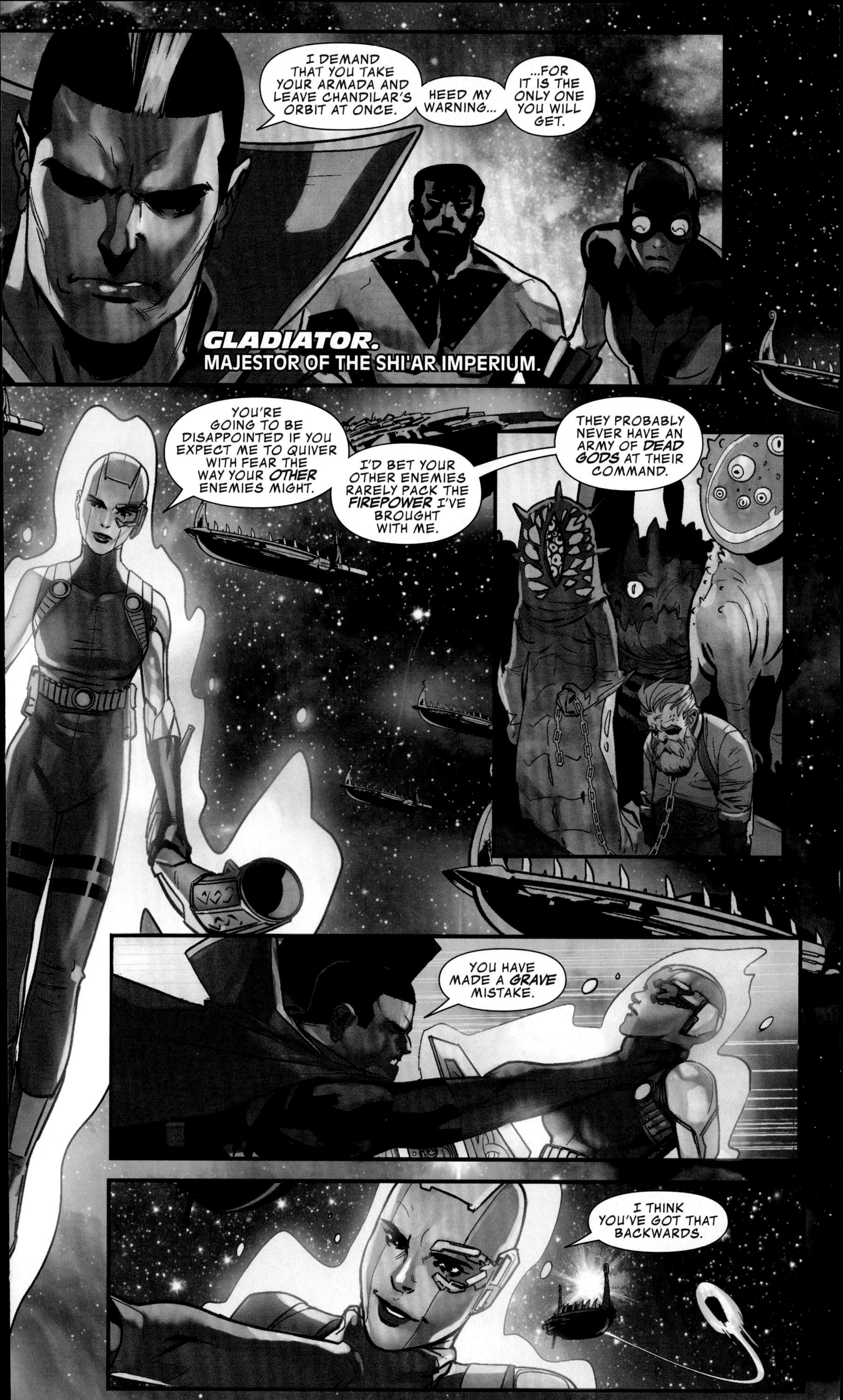

I DEMAND THAT YOU TAKE YOUR ARMADA AND LEAVE CHANDILAR'S ORBIT AT ONCE.
HEED MY WARNING...
...FOR IT IS THE ONLY ONE YOU WILL GET.
GLADIATOR. MAJESTOR OF THE SHI'AR IMPERIUM.
YOU'RE GOING TO BE DISAPPOINTED IF YOU EXPECT ME TO QUIVER WITH FEAR THE WAY YOUR OTHER ENEMIES MIGHT.
I'D BET YOUR OTHER ENEMIES RARELY PACK THE FIREPOWER I'VE BROUGHT WITH ME.
THEY PROBABLY NEVER HAVE AN ARMY OF DEAD GODS AT THEIR COMMAND.
YOU HAVE MADE A GRAVE MISTAKE.
I THINK YOU'VE GOT THAT BACKWARDS.

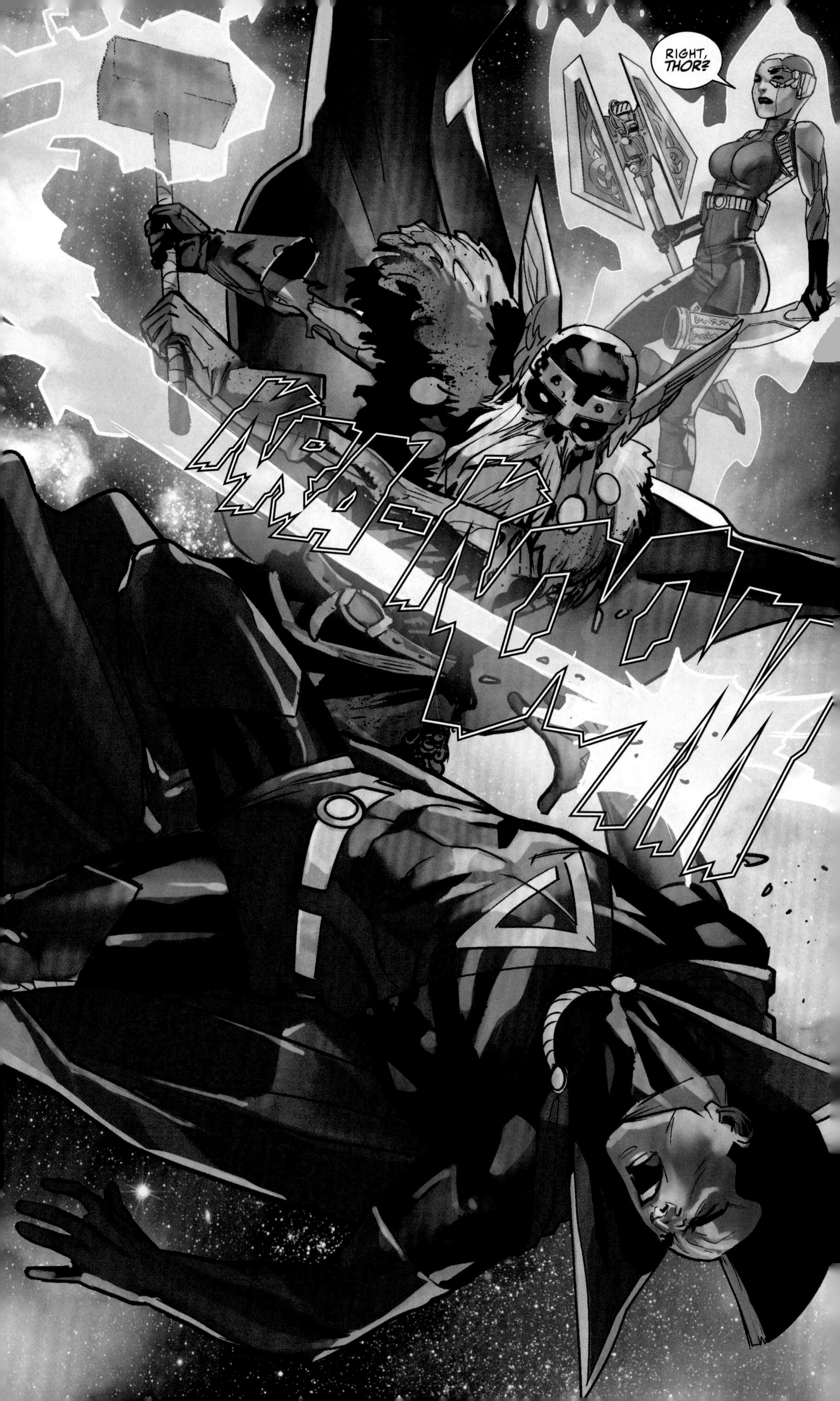
RIGHT, THOR?

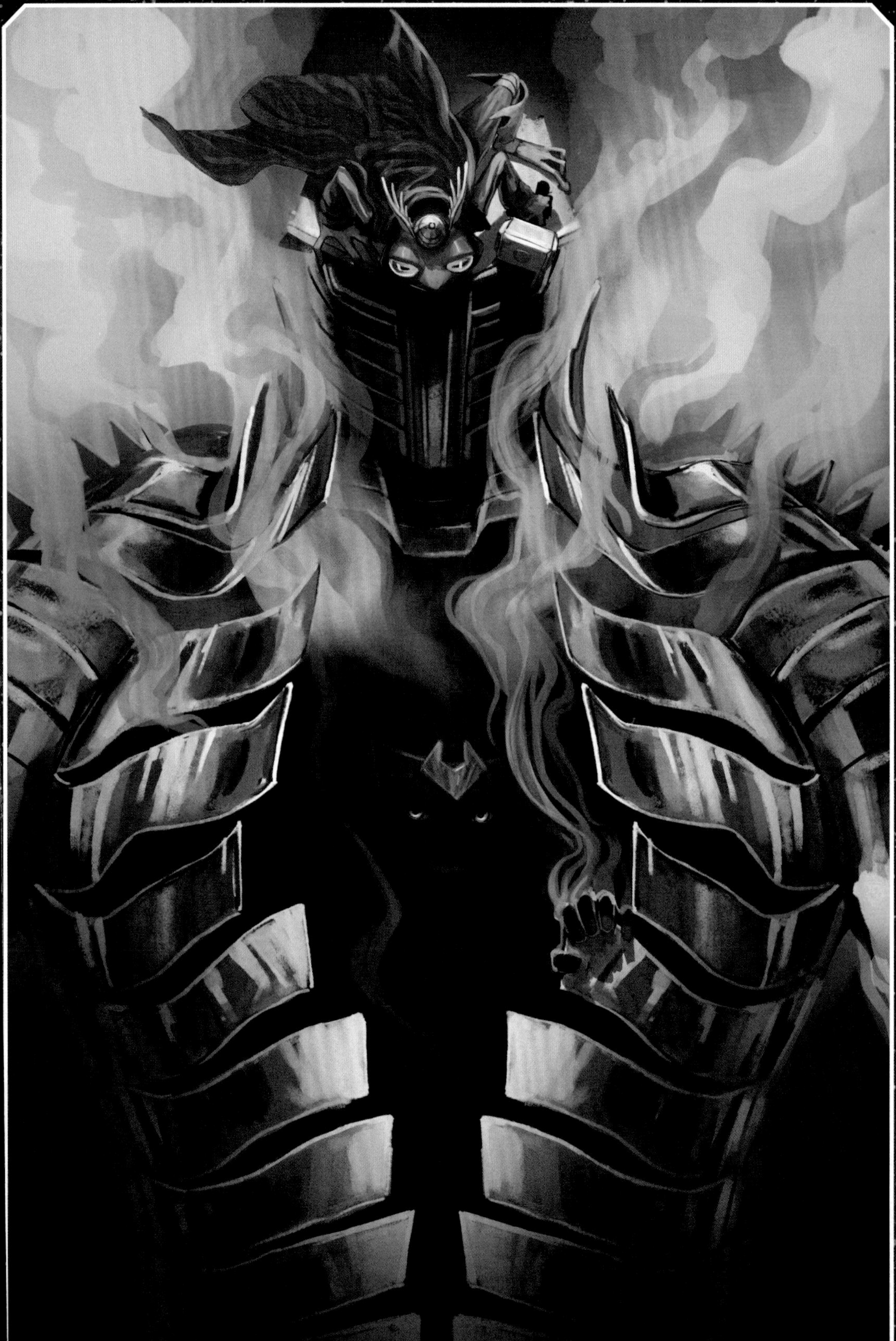

STEPHANIE HANS
#2 VARIANT

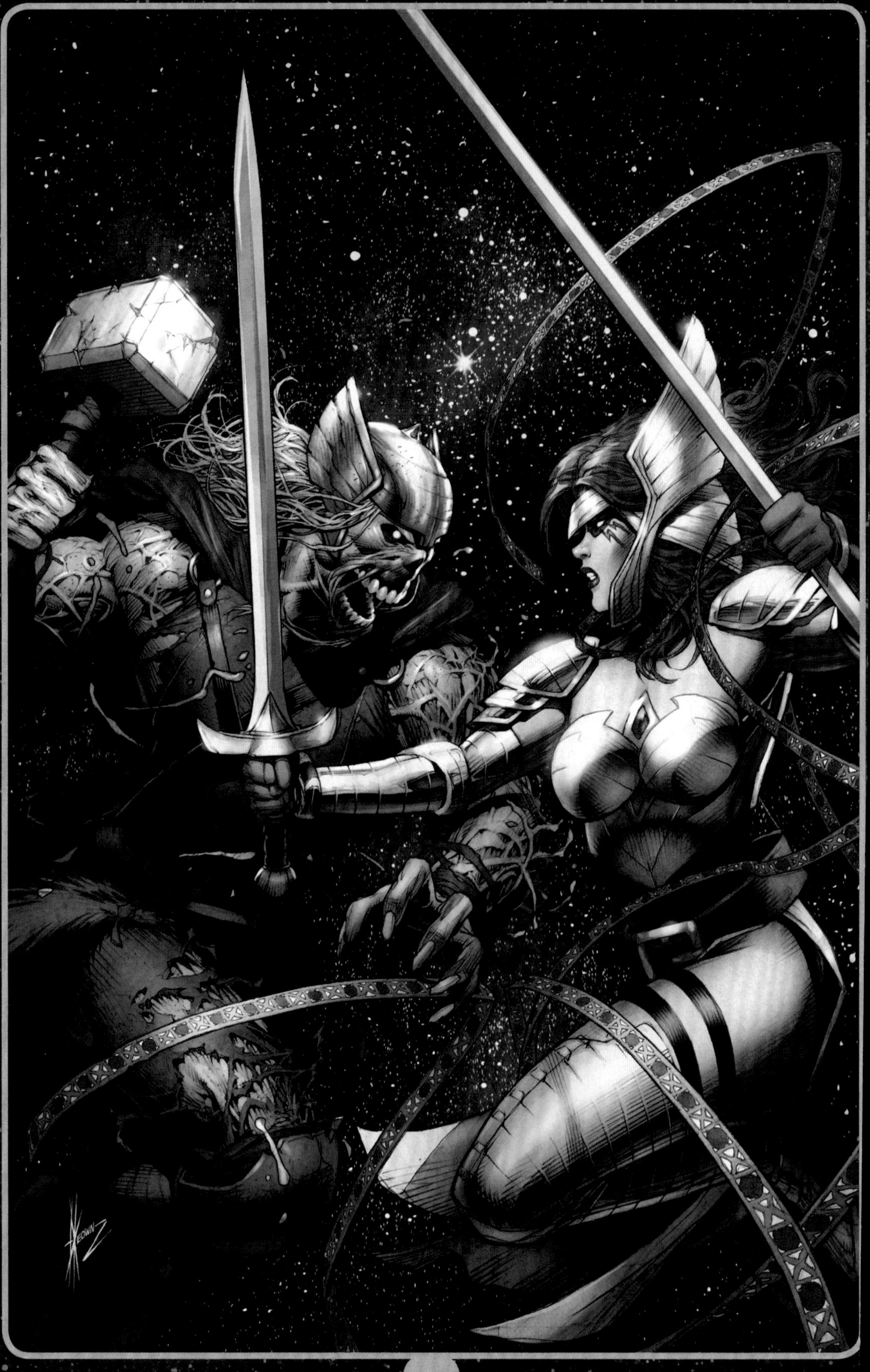

3

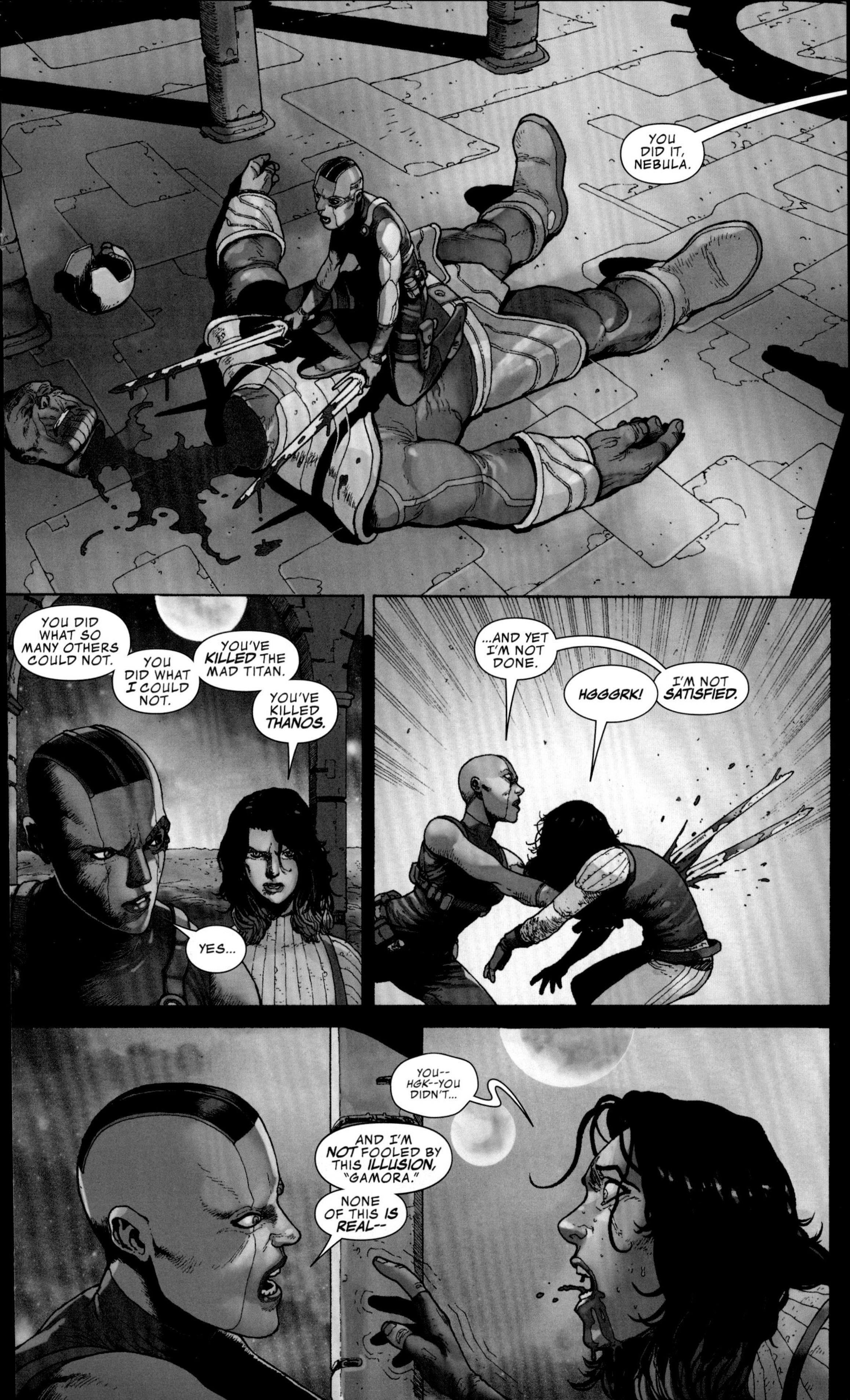
YOU DID IT, NEBULA.
YOU DID WHAT SO MANY OTHERS COULD NOT.
YOU DID WHAT I COULD NOT.
YOU'VE KILLED THE MAD TITAN.
YOU'VE KILLED THANOS.
YES...
...AND YET I'M NOT DONE.
I'M NOT SATISFIED.
HGGGRK!
YOU-- HGK--YOU DIDN'T...
AND I'M NOT FOOLED BY THIS ILLUSION, "GAMORA."
NONE OF THIS IS REAL--

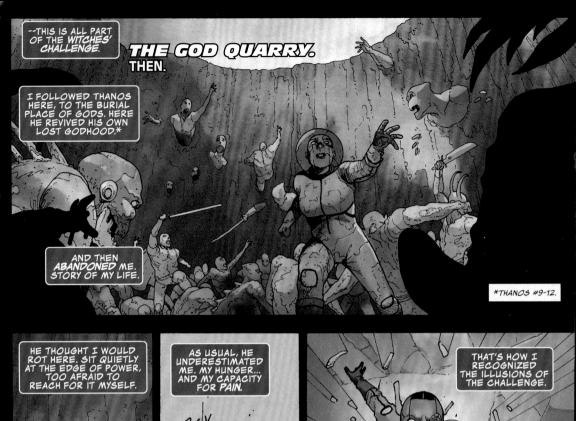

--THIS IS ALL PART OF THE *WITCHES'* CHALLENGE.

THE GOD QUARRY.
THEN.

I FOLLOWED THANOS HERE, TO THE BURIAL PLACE OF GODS. HERE HE REVIVED HIS OWN LOST GODHOOD.*

AND THEN *ABANDONED* ME. STORY OF MY LIFE.

*THANOS #9-12.

HE THOUGHT I WOULD ROT HERE. SIT QUIETLY AT THE EDGE OF POWER, TOO AFRAID TO REACH FOR IT MYSELF.

CRCK
CRCK
CRCK
CRCK

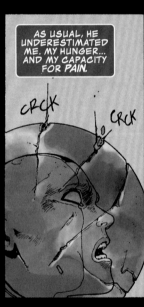

AS USUAL, HE UNDERESTIMATED ME. MY HUNGER... AND MY CAPACITY FOR *PAIN.*

CRCK
CRCK

THAT'S HOW I RECOGNIZED THE ILLUSIONS OF THE CHALLENGE.

I WASN'T *SUFFERING* ENOUGH.

ALL THE GODS THAT HAD COME HERE TO DIE...

...TRAPPED BY LIES...

PITIFUL.

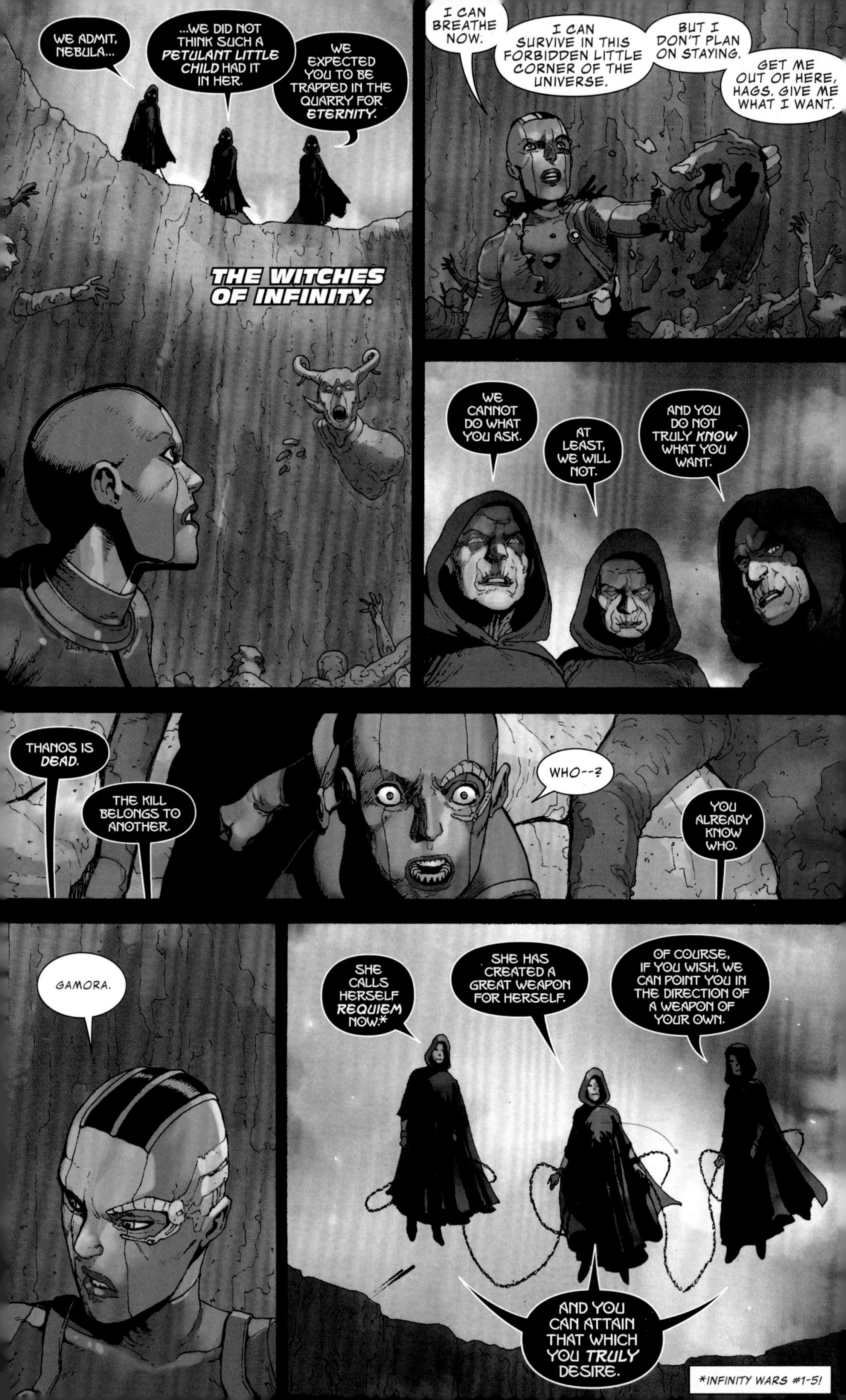
WE ADMIT, NEBULA...
...WE DID NOT THINK SUCH A PETULANT LITTLE CHILD HAD IT IN HER.
WE EXPECTED YOU TO BE TRAPPED IN THE QUARRY FOR ETERNITY.
THE WITCHES OF INFINITY.
I CAN BREATHE NOW.
I CAN SURVIVE IN THIS FORBIDDEN LITTLE CORNER OF THE UNIVERSE.
BUT I DON'T PLAN ON STAYING.
GET ME OUT OF HERE, HAGS. GIVE ME WHAT I WANT.
WE CANNOT DO WHAT YOU ASK.
AT LEAST, WE WILL NOT.
AND YOU DO NOT TRULY KNOW WHAT YOU WANT.
THANOS IS DEAD.
THE KILL BELONGS TO ANOTHER.
WHO--?
YOU ALREADY KNOW WHO.
GAMORA.
SHE CALLS HERSELF REQUIEM NOW.*
SHE HAS CREATED A GREAT WEAPON FOR HERSELF.
OF COURSE, IF YOU WISH, WE CAN POINT YOU IN THE DIRECTION OF A WEAPON OF YOUR OWN.
AND YOU CAN ATTAIN THAT WHICH YOU TRULY DESIRE.
*INFINITY WARS #1-5!

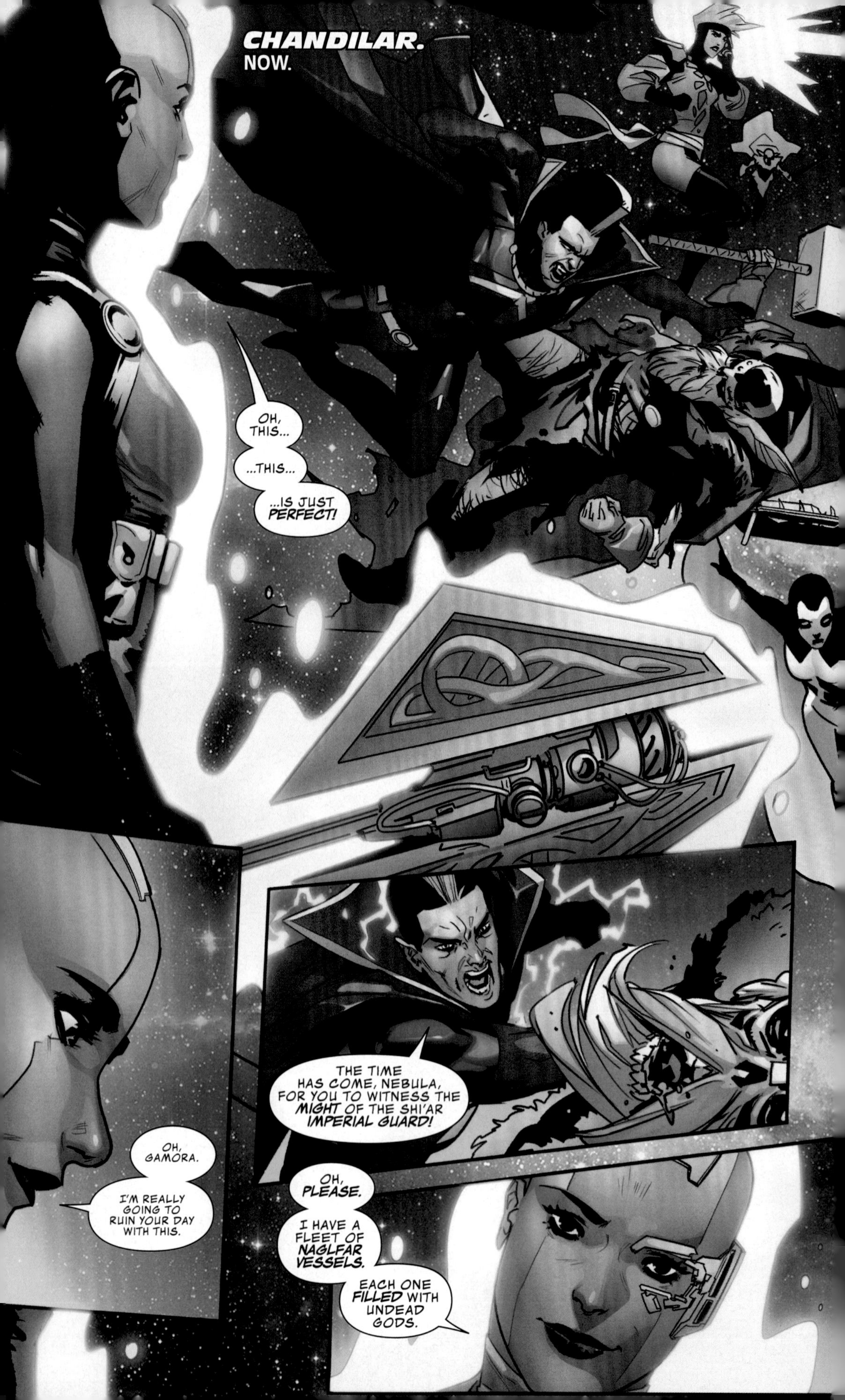
CHANDILAR.
NOW.
OH, THIS...
...THIS...
...IS JUST PERFECT!
THE TIME HAS COME, NEBULA, FOR YOU TO WITNESS THE MIGHT OF THE SHI'AR IMPERIAL GUARD!
OH, GAMORA.
I'M REALLY GOING TO RUIN YOUR DAY WITH THIS.
OH, PLEASE.
I HAVE A FLEET OF NAGLFAR VESSELS.
EACH ONE FILLED WITH UNDEAD GODS.

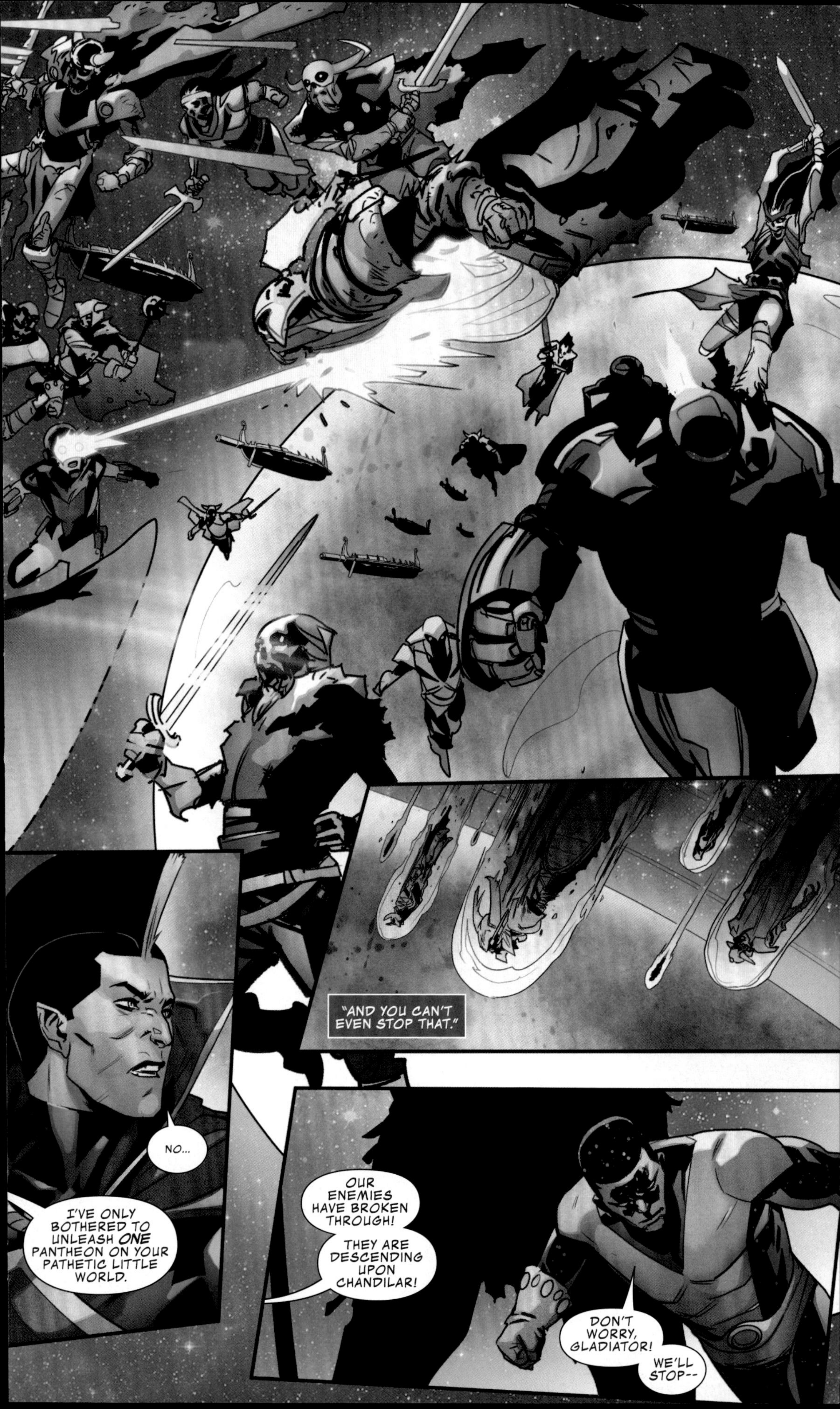
"AND YOU CAN'T EVEN STOP THAT."
NO...
I'VE ONLY BOTHERED TO UNLEASH ONE PANTHEON ON YOUR PATHETIC LITTLE WORLD.
OUR ENEMIES HAVE BROKEN THROUGH!
THEY ARE DESCENDING UPON CHANDILAR!
DON'T WORRY, GLADIATOR!
WE'LL STOP--

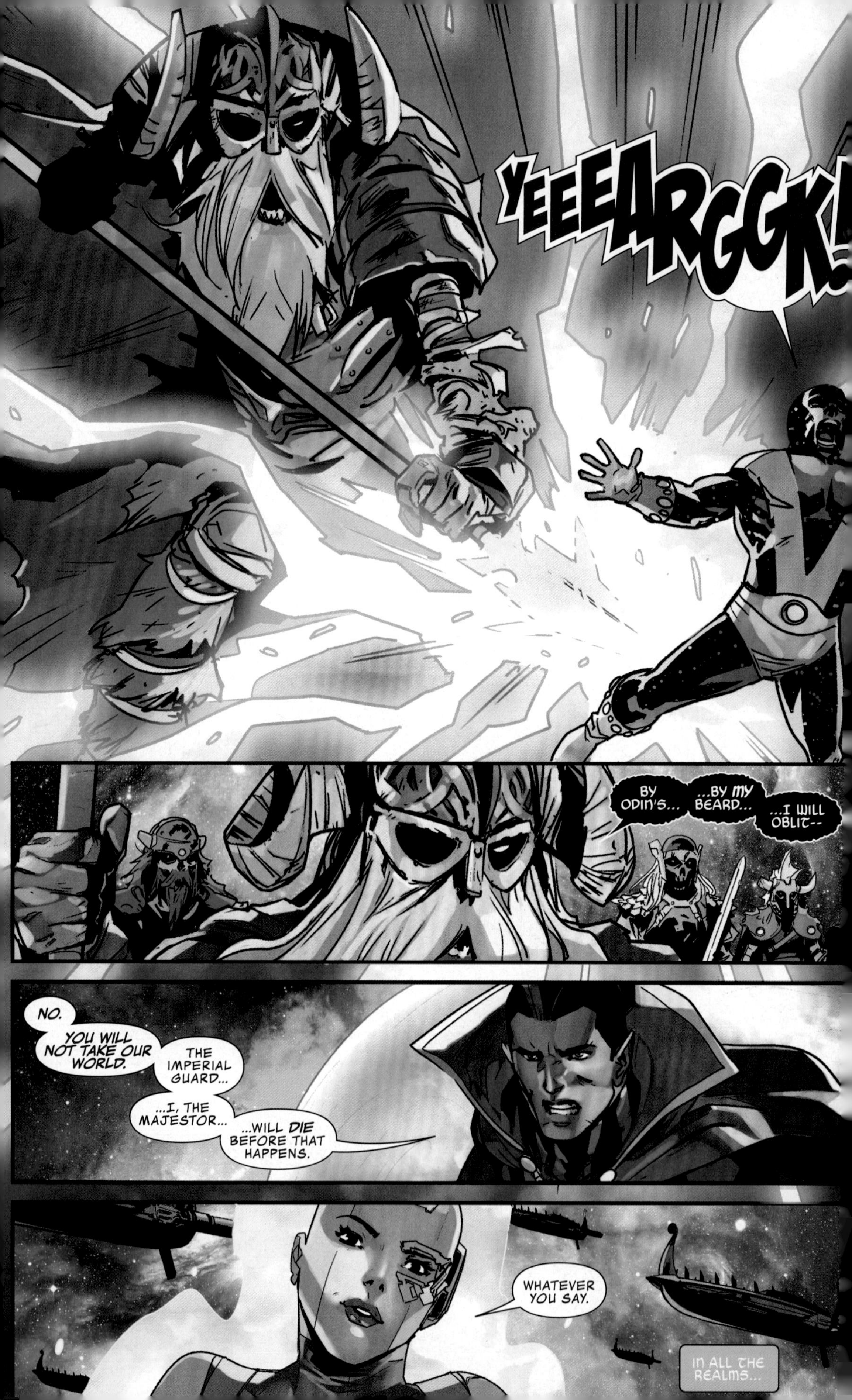
YEEEARGGK!
BY ODIN'S...
...BY MY BEARD...
...I WILL OBLIT--
NO.
YOU WILL NOT TAKE OUR WORLD.
THE IMPERIAL GUARD...
...I, THE MAJESTOR...
...WILL DIE BEFORE THAT HAPPENS.
WHATEVER YOU SAY.
IN ALL THE REALMS...

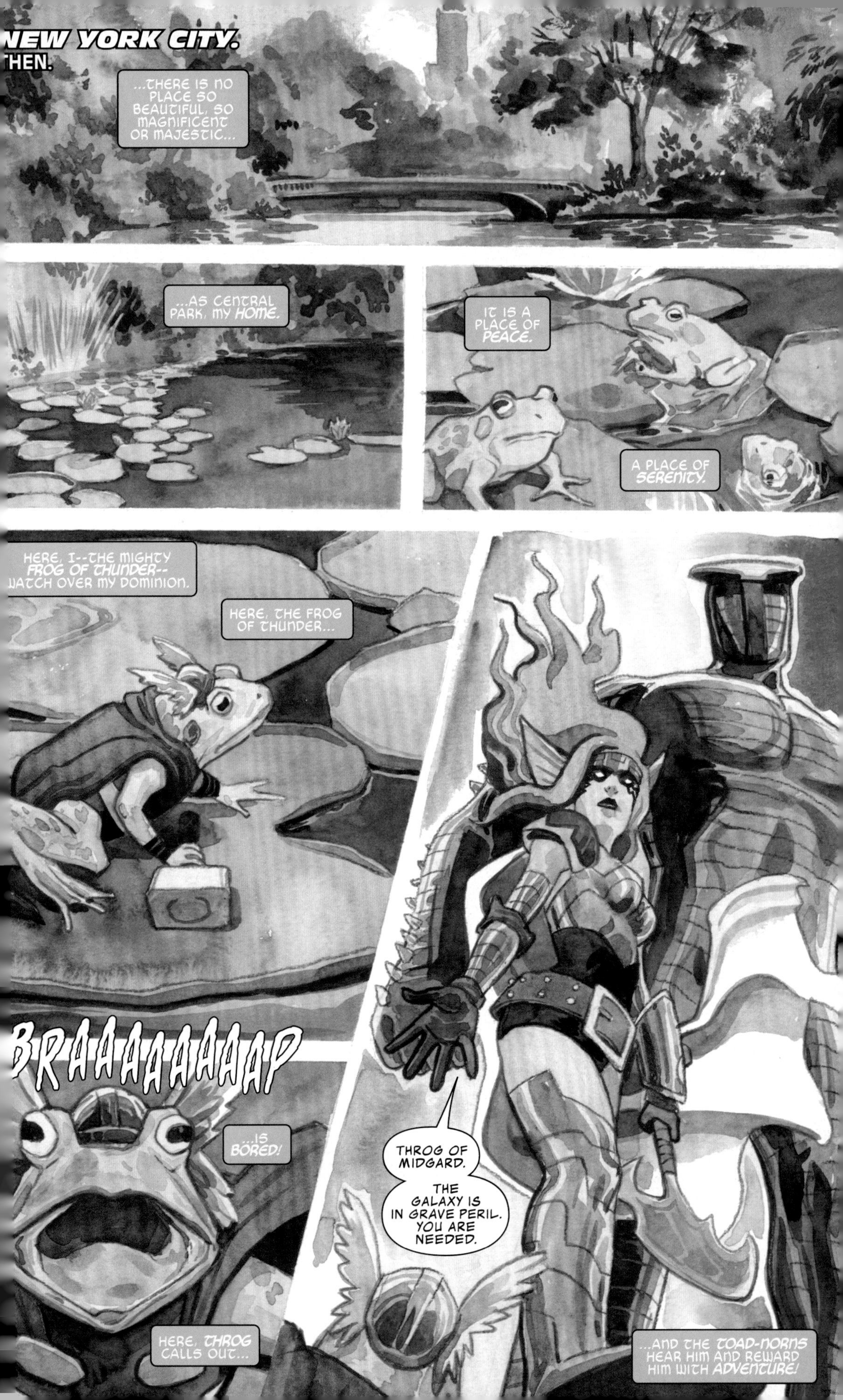
NEW YORK CITY.
THEN.
...THERE IS NO PLACE SO BEAUTIFUL, SO MAGNIFICENT OR MAJESTIC...
...AS CENTRAL PARK, MY HOME.
IT IS A PLACE OF PEACE.
A PLACE OF SERENITY.
HERE, I--THE MIGHTY FROG OF THUNDER-- WATCH OVER MY DOMINION.
HERE, THE FROG OF THUNDER...
BRAAAAAAAAP
...IS BORED!
HERE, THROG CALLS OUT...
THROG OF MIDGARD.
THE GALAXY IS IN GRAVE PERIL. YOU ARE NEEDED.
...AND THE TOAD-NORNS HEAR HIM AND REWARD HIM WITH ADVENTURE!

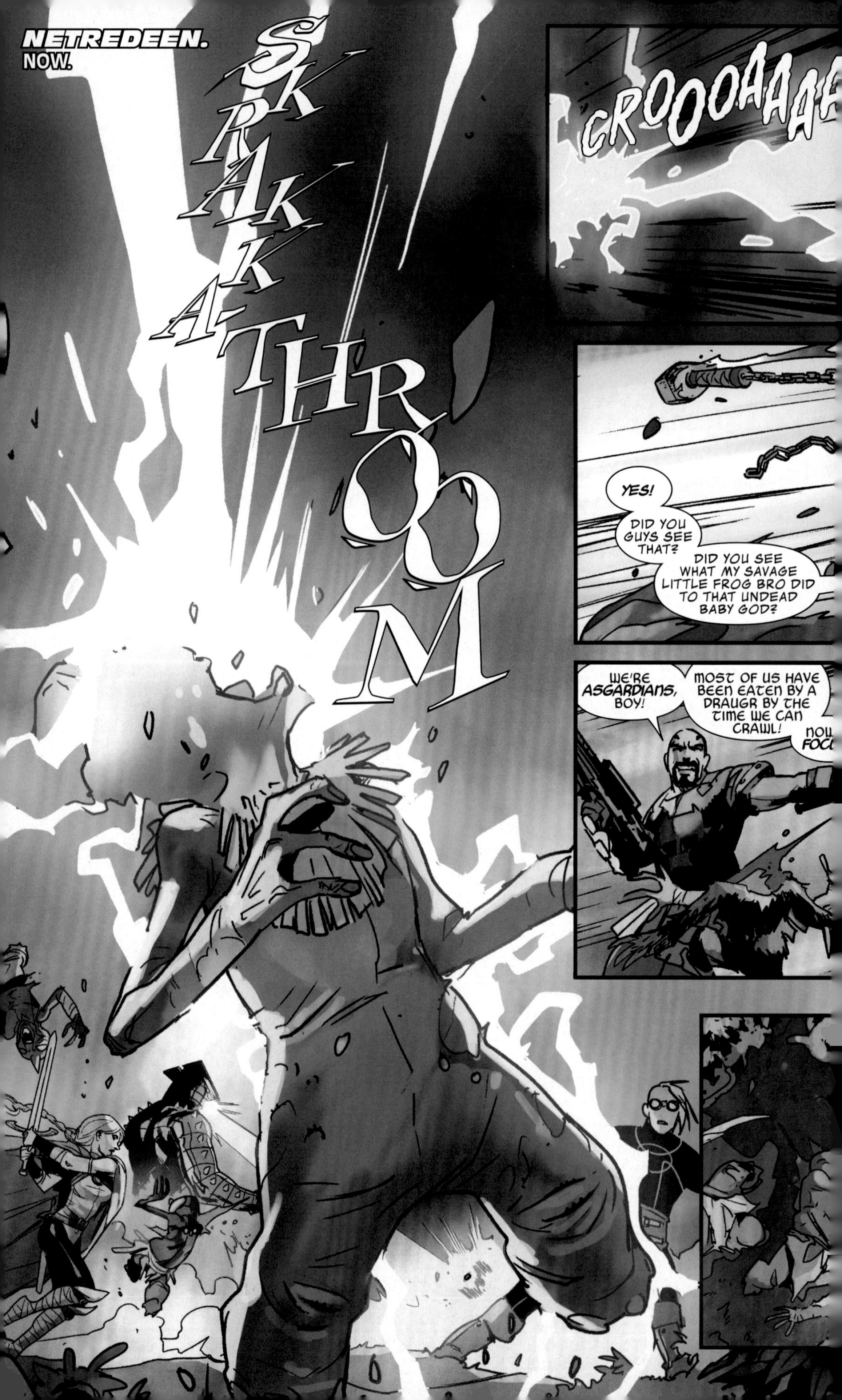

NETREDEEN.
NOW.
SKRAKKATHROOM
CROOOAAAAH
YES!
DID YOU GUYS SEE THAT?
DID YOU SEE WHAT MY SAVAGE LITTLE FROG BRO DID TO THAT UNDEAD BABY GOD?
WE'RE ASGARDIANS, BOY!
MOST OF US HAVE BEEN EATEN BY A DRAUGR BY THE TIME WE CAN CRAWL!

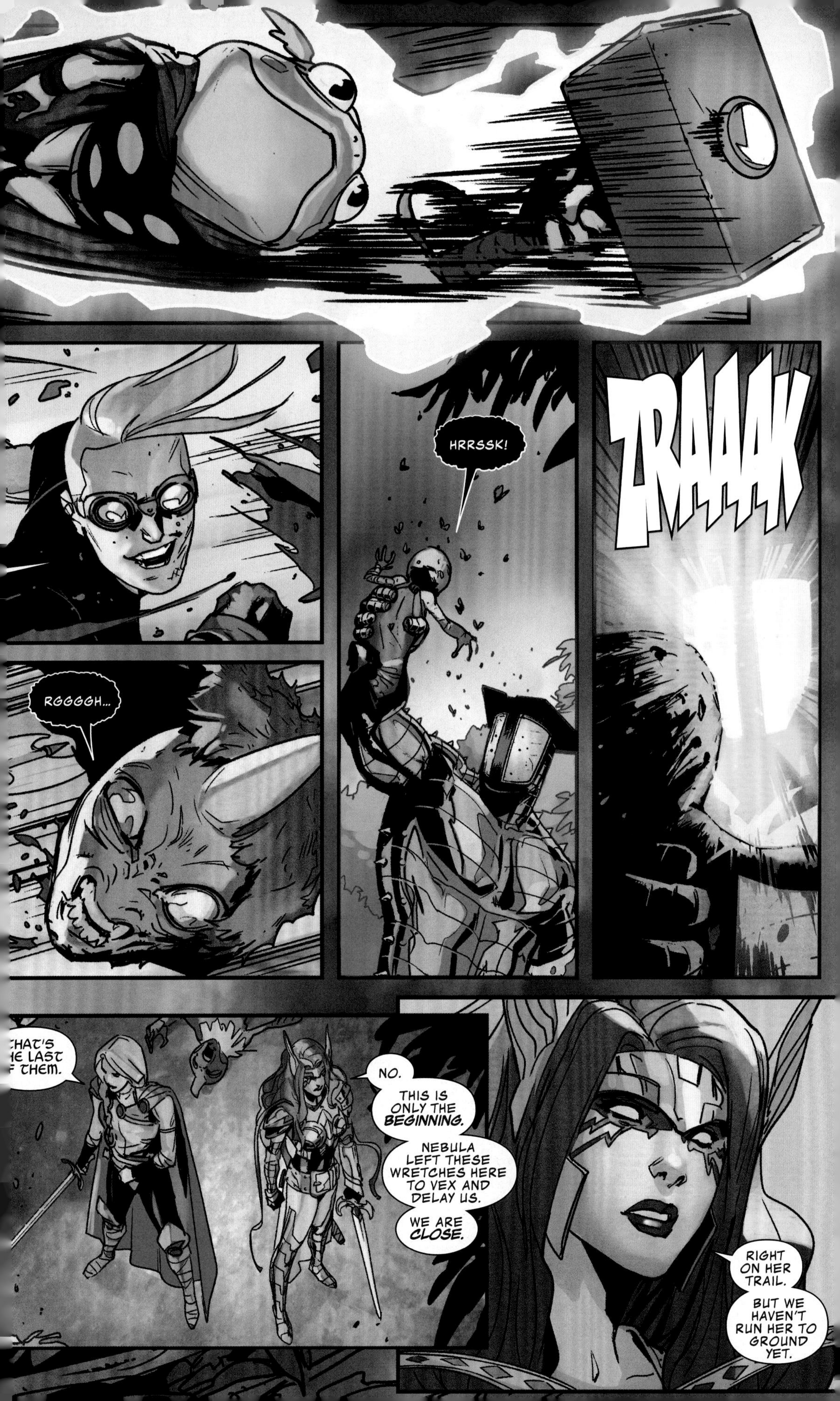

RGGGGH...
HRRSSK!
ZRAAAK
THAT'S THE LAST OF THEM.
NO.
THIS IS ONLY THE BEGINNING.
NEBULA LEFT THESE WRETCHES HERE TO VEX AND DELAY US.
WE ARE CLOSE.
RIGHT ON HER TRAIL.
BUT WE HAVEN'T RUN HER TO GROUND YET.

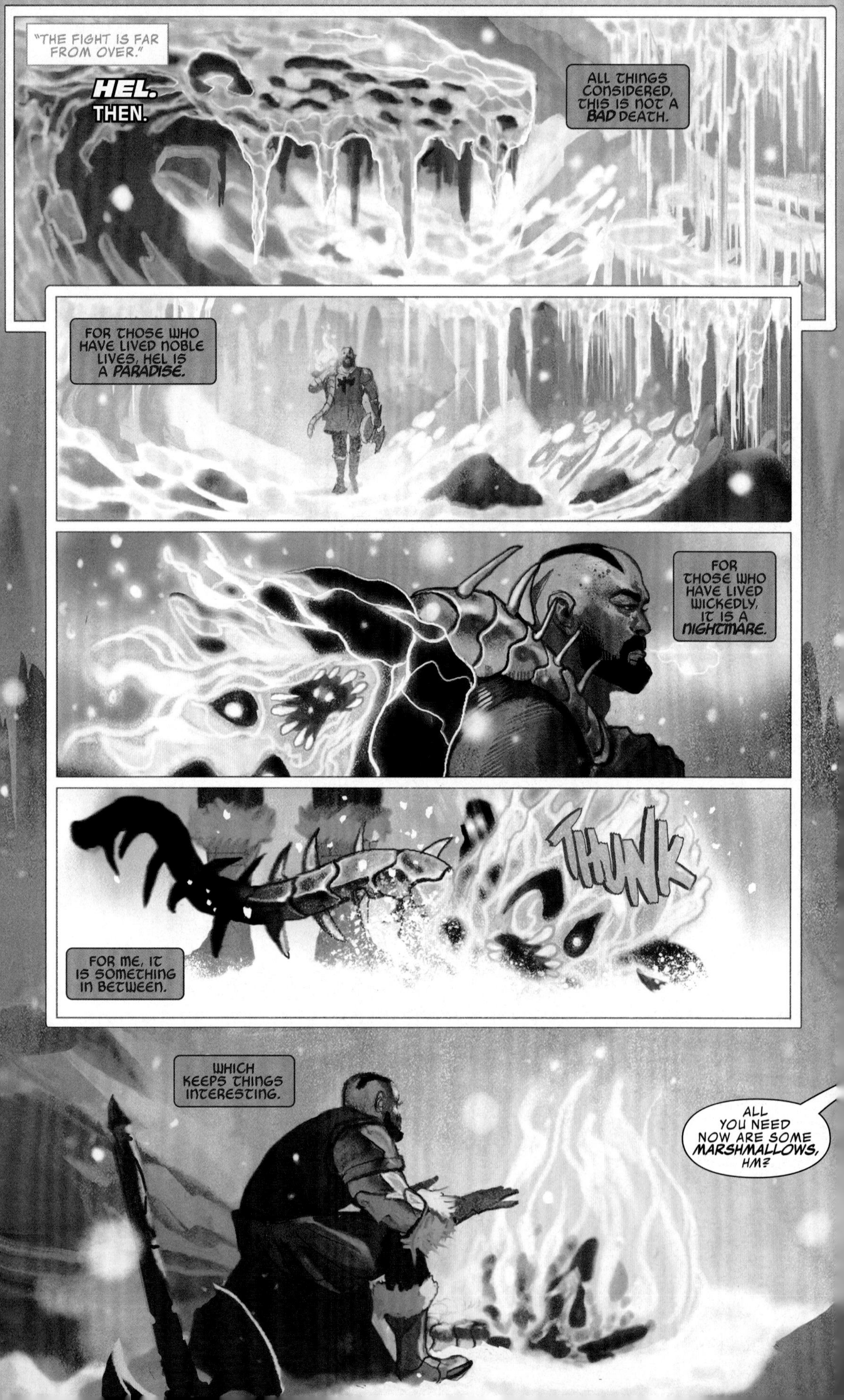
"THE FIGHT IS FAR FROM OVER."
HEL. THEN.
ALL THINGS CONSIDERED, THIS IS NOT A BAD DEATH.
FOR THOSE WHO HAVE LIVED NOBLE LIVES, HEL IS A PARADISE.
FOR THOSE WHO HAVE LIVED WICKEDLY, IT IS A NIGHTMARE.
THUNK
FOR ME, IT IS SOMETHING IN BETWEEN.
WHICH KEEPS THINGS INTERESTING.
ALL YOU NEED NOW ARE SOME MARSHMALLOWS, HM?

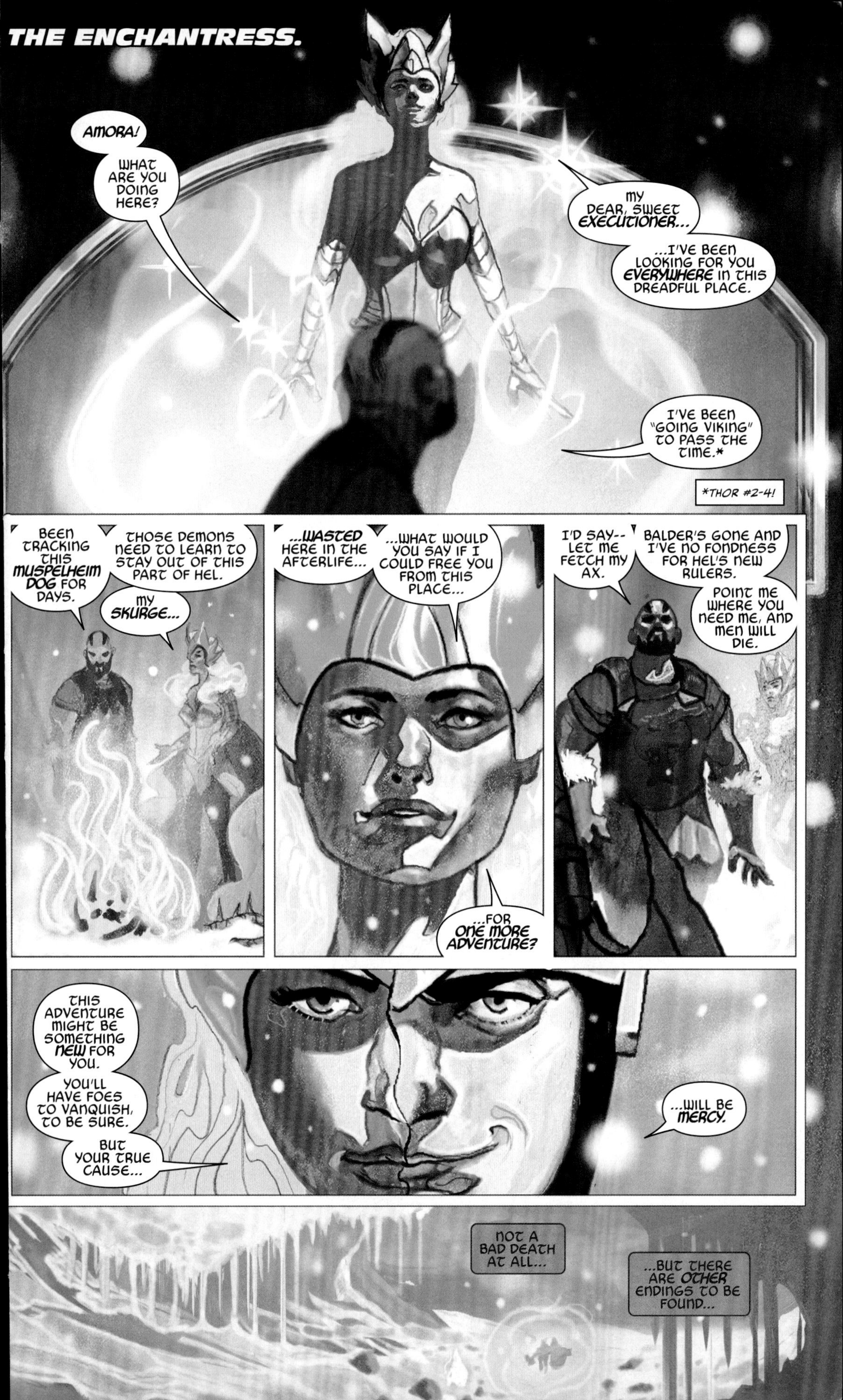
THE ENCHANTRESS.
AMORA!
WHAT ARE YOU DOING HERE?
MY DEAR, SWEET EXECUTIONER...
...I'VE BEEN LOOKING FOR YOU EVERYWHERE IN THIS DREADFUL PLACE.
I'VE BEEN "GOING VIKING" TO PASS THE TIME.*
*THOR #2-4!
BEEN TRACKING THIS MUSPELHEIM DOG FOR DAYS.
THOSE DEMONS NEED TO LEARN TO STAY OUT OF THIS PART OF HEL.
MY SKURGE...
...WASTED HERE IN THE AFTERLIFE...
...WHAT WOULD YOU SAY IF I COULD FREE YOU FROM THIS PLACE...
...FOR ONE MORE ADVENTURE?
I'D SAY-- LET ME FETCH MY AX.
BALDER'S GONE AND I'VE NO FONDNESS FOR HEL'S NEW RULERS.
POINT ME WHERE YOU NEED ME, AND MEN WILL DIE.
THIS ADVENTURE MIGHT BE SOMETHING NEW FOR YOU.
YOU'LL HAVE FOES TO VANQUISH, TO BE SURE.
BUT YOUR TRUE CAUSE...
...WILL BE MERCY.
NOT A BAD DEATH AT ALL...
...BUT THERE ARE OTHER ENDINGS TO BE FOUND...

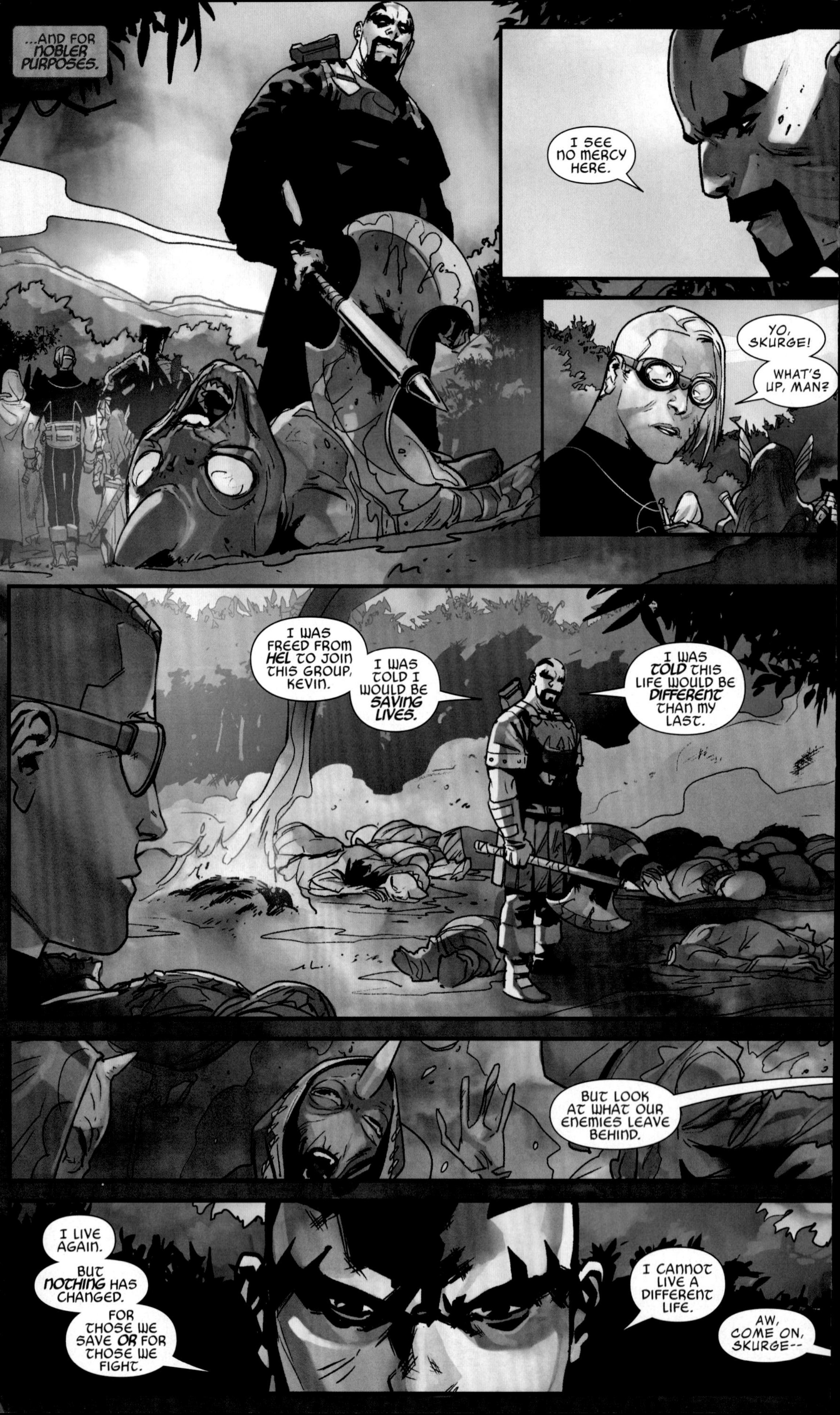
...AND FOR NOBLER PURPOSES.
I SEE NO MERCY HERE.
YO, SKURGE!
WHAT'S UP, MAN?
I WAS FREED FROM HEL TO JOIN THIS GROUP, KEVIN.
I WAS TOLD I WOULD BE SAVING LIVES.
I WAS TOLD THIS LIFE WOULD BE DIFFERENT THAN MY LAST.
BUT LOOK AT WHAT OUR ENEMIES LEAVE BEHIND.
I LIVE AGAIN.
BUT NOTHING HAS CHANGED.
FOR THOSE WE SAVE OR FOR THOSE WE FIGHT.
I CANNOT LIVE A DIFFERENT LIFE.
AW, COME ON, SKURGE--

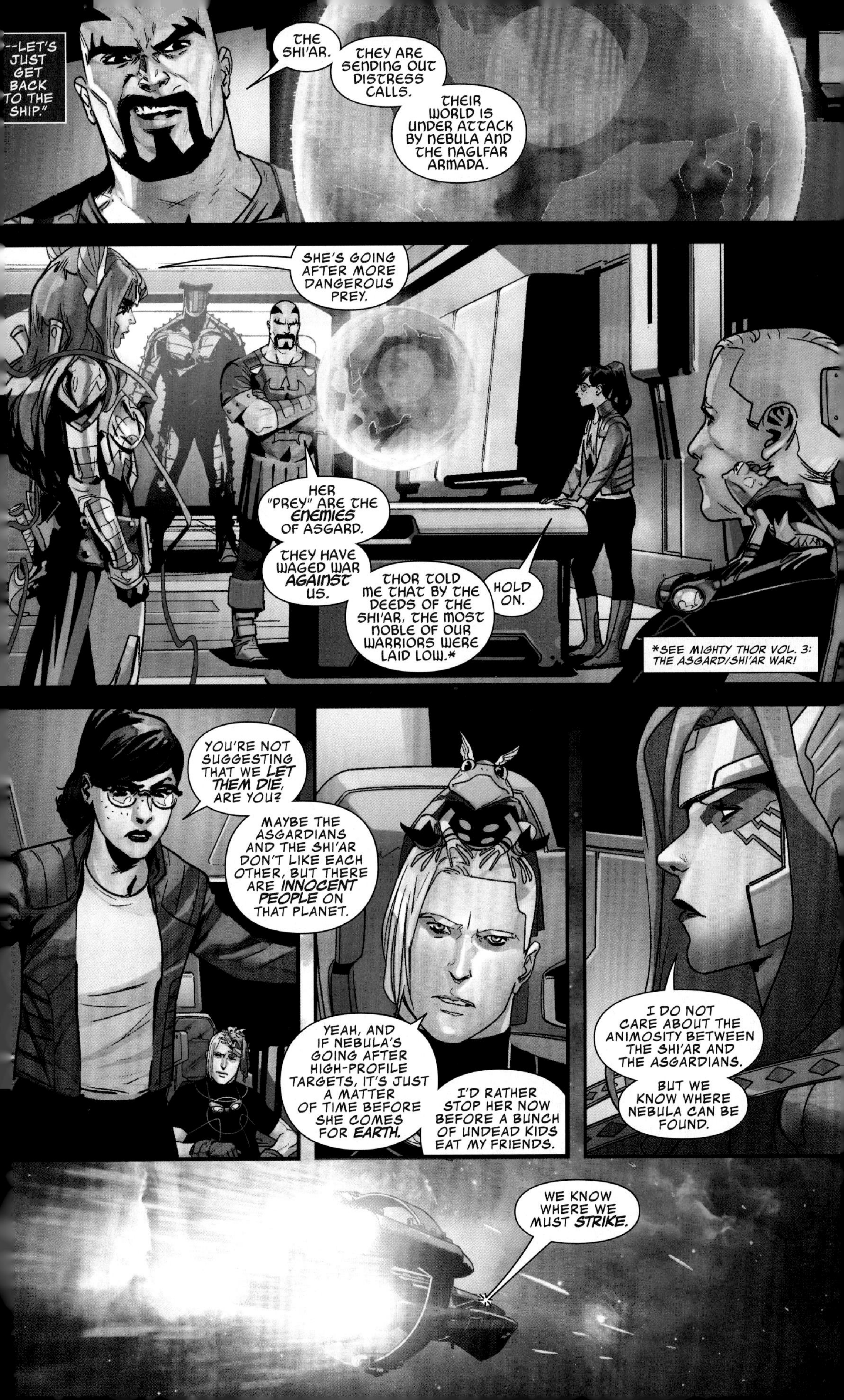

"--LET'S JUST GET BACK TO THE SHIP."
THE SHI'AR.
THEY ARE SENDING OUT DISTRESS CALLS.
THEIR WORLD IS UNDER ATTACK BY NEBULA AND THE NAGLFAR ARMADA.
SHE'S GOING AFTER MORE DANGEROUS PREY.
HER "PREY" ARE THE ENEMIES OF ASGARD.
THEY HAVE WAGED WAR AGAINST US.
THOR TOLD ME THAT BY THE DEEDS OF THE SHI'AR, THE MOST NOBLE OF OUR WARRIORS WERE LAID LOW.*
HOLD ON.
*SEE MIGHTY THOR VOL. 3: THE ASGARD/SHI'AR WAR!
YOU'RE NOT SUGGESTING THAT WE LET THEM DIE, ARE YOU?
MAYBE THE ASGARDIANS AND THE SHI'AR DON'T LIKE EACH OTHER, BUT THERE ARE INNOCENT PEOPLE ON THAT PLANET.
YEAH, AND IF NEBULA'S GOING AFTER HIGH-PROFILE TARGETS, IT'S JUST A MATTER OF TIME BEFORE SHE COMES FOR EARTH.
I'D RATHER STOP HER NOW BEFORE A BUNCH OF UNDEAD KIDS EAT MY FRIENDS.
I DO NOT CARE ABOUT THE ANIMOSITY BETWEEN THE SHI'AR AND THE ASGARDIANS.
BUT WE KNOW WHERE NEBULA CAN BE FOUND.
WE KNOW WHERE WE MUST STRIKE.

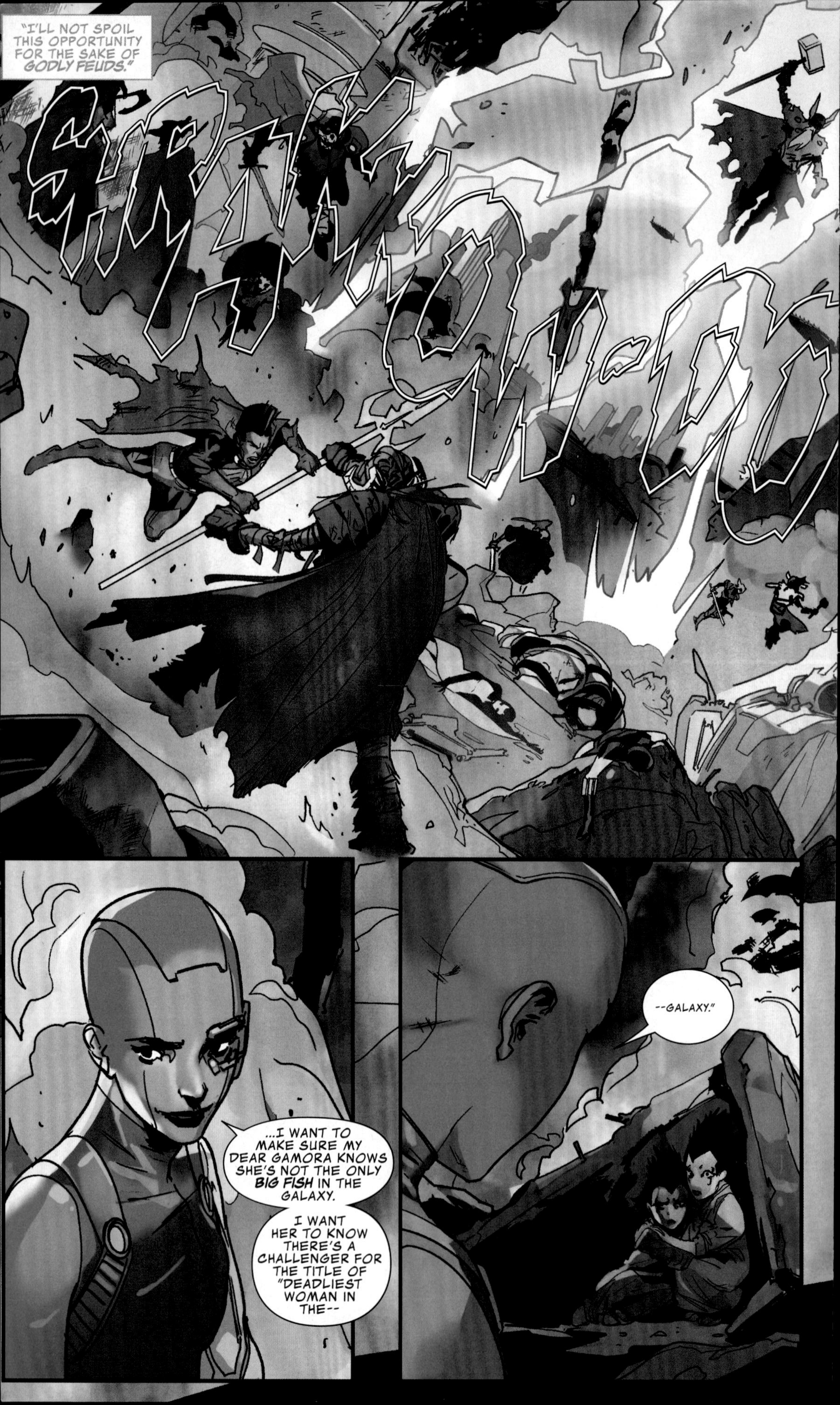

"I'LL NOT SPOIL THIS OPPORTUNITY FOR THE SAKE OF GODLY FEUDS."
...I WANT TO MAKE SURE MY DEAR GAMORA KNOWS SHE'S NOT THE ONLY BIG FISH IN THE GALAXY.
I WANT HER TO KNOW THERE'S A CHALLENGER FOR THE TITLE OF "DEADLIEST WOMAN IN THE--
--GALAXY."

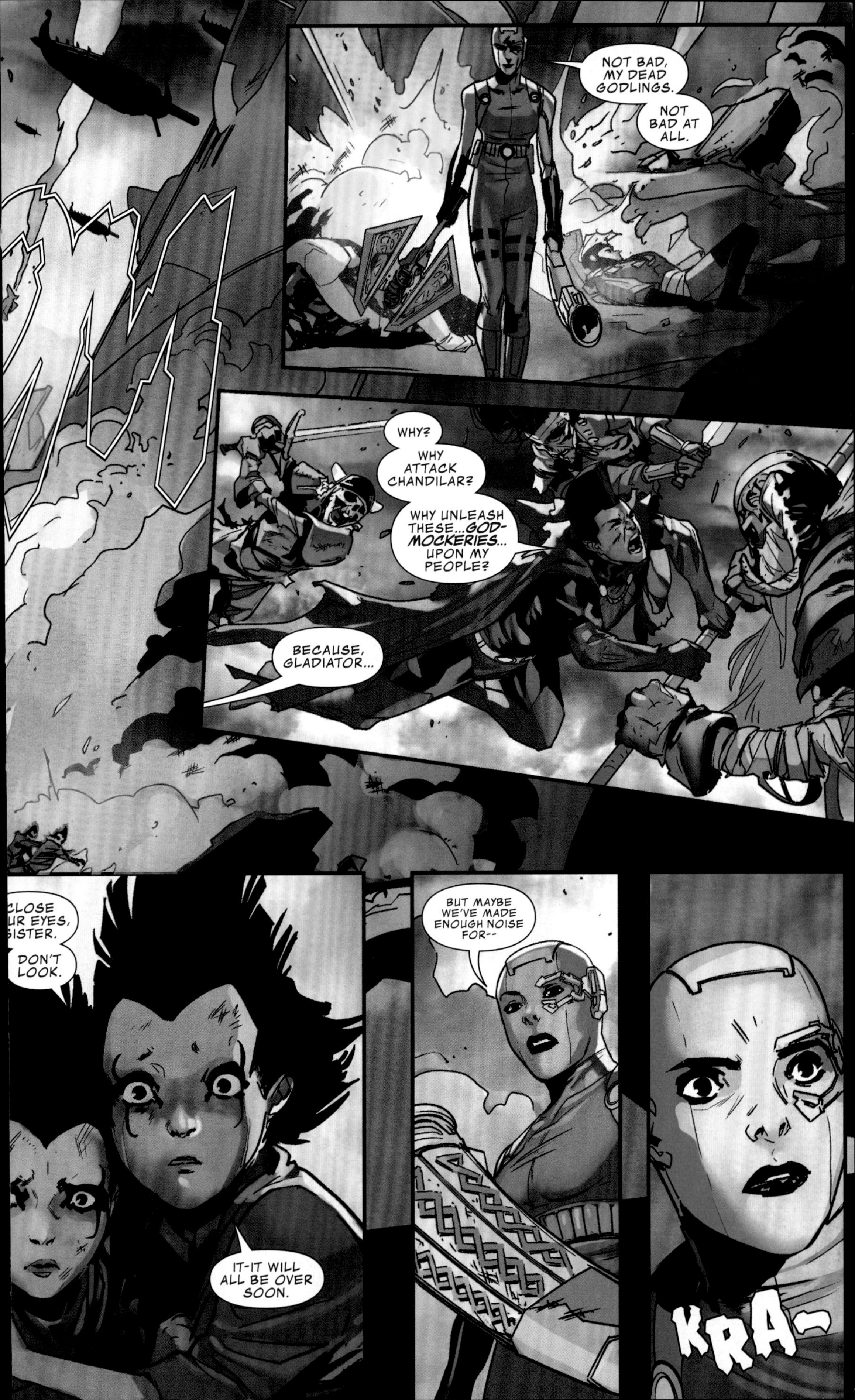
NOT BAD, MY DEAD GODLINGS.
NOT BAD AT ALL.
WHY?
WHY ATTACK CHANDILAR?
WHY UNLEASH THESE...GOD-MOCKERIES... UPON MY PEOPLE?
BECAUSE, GLADIATOR...
CLOSE UR EYES, SISTER.
DON'T LOOK.
IT-IT WILL ALL BE OVER SOON.
BUT MAYBE WE'VE MADE ENOUGH NOISE FOR--
KRA-

NEBULA IS OUR TARGET!

FIND HER AND WE FIND THE WEAPON!

TAKE THE WEAPON AND WE END THIS BATTLE!

WHERE'S THE FUN IN *THAT?*

RUN NOW, CHILDREN, WHILE YOU HAVE THE CHANCE.

GO FAR FROM HERE.

PRAY TO *YOUR* GODS THAT *MY* GODS DO NOT FOLLOW YOU.

WE'VE ALL GOT BETTER PLACES TO BE.

AND I'VE SEEN ALL I NEED TO.

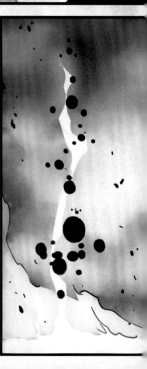

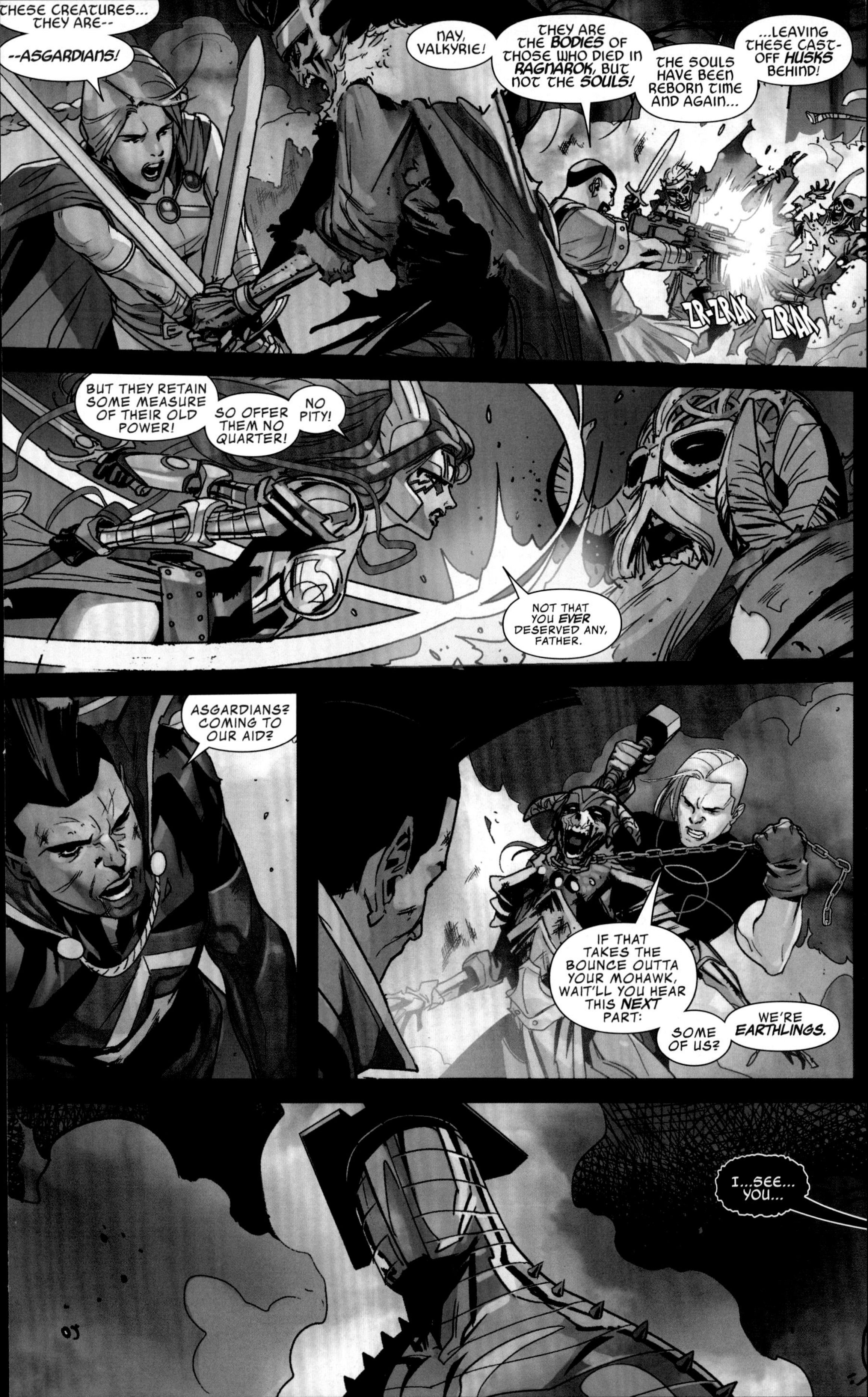
THESE CREATURES... THEY ARE--
--ASGARDIANS!
NAY, VALKYRIE!
THEY ARE THE BODIES OF THOSE WHO DIED IN RAGNAROK, BUT NOT THE SOULS!
THE SOULS HAVE BEEN REBORN TIME AND AGAIN...
...LEAVING THESE CAST-OFF HUSKS BEHIND!
ZR-ZRAK
ZRAK
BUT THEY RETAIN SOME MEASURE OF THEIR OLD POWER!
SO OFFER THEM NO QUARTER!
NO PITY!
NOT THAT YOU EVER DESERVED ANY, FATHER.
ASGARDIANS? COMING TO OUR AID?
IF THAT TAKES THE BOUNCE OUTTA YOUR MOHAWK, WAIT'LL YOU HEAR THIS NEXT PART:
SOME OF US?
WE'RE EARTHLINGS.
I...SEE... YOU...

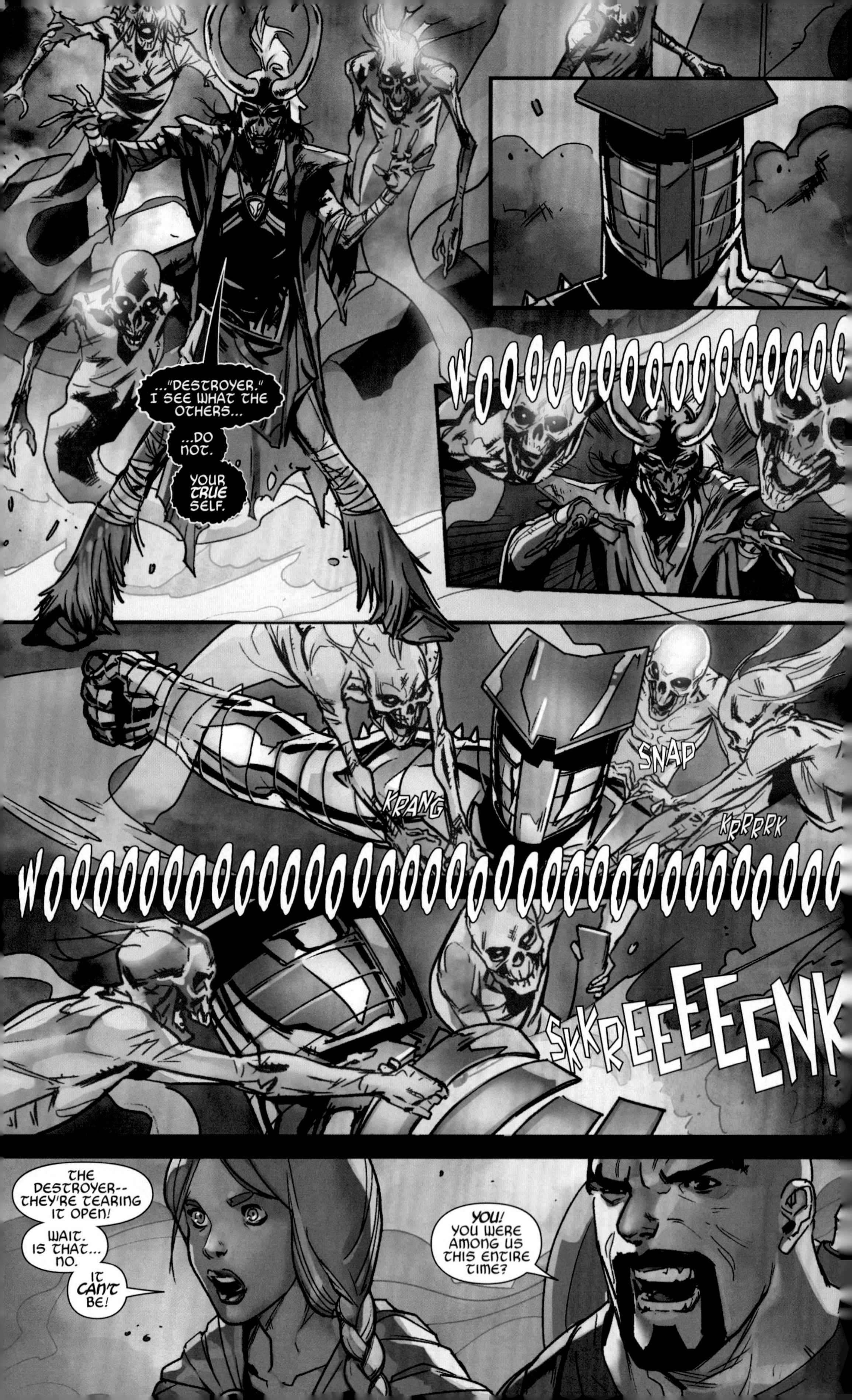
..."DESTROYER." I SEE WHAT THE OTHERS...
...DO NOT.
YOUR TRUE SELF.
WOOOOOOOOOOOOOOO
SNAP
KRANG
KRRRRK
WOOOOOOOOOOOOOOOOOOOOOOOOOOOOOOOOO
SKKREEEEEENK
THE DESTROYER-- THEY'RE TEARING IT OPEN!
WAIT. IS THAT... NO.
IT CAN'T BE!
YOU! YOU WERE AMONG US THIS ENTIRE TIME?

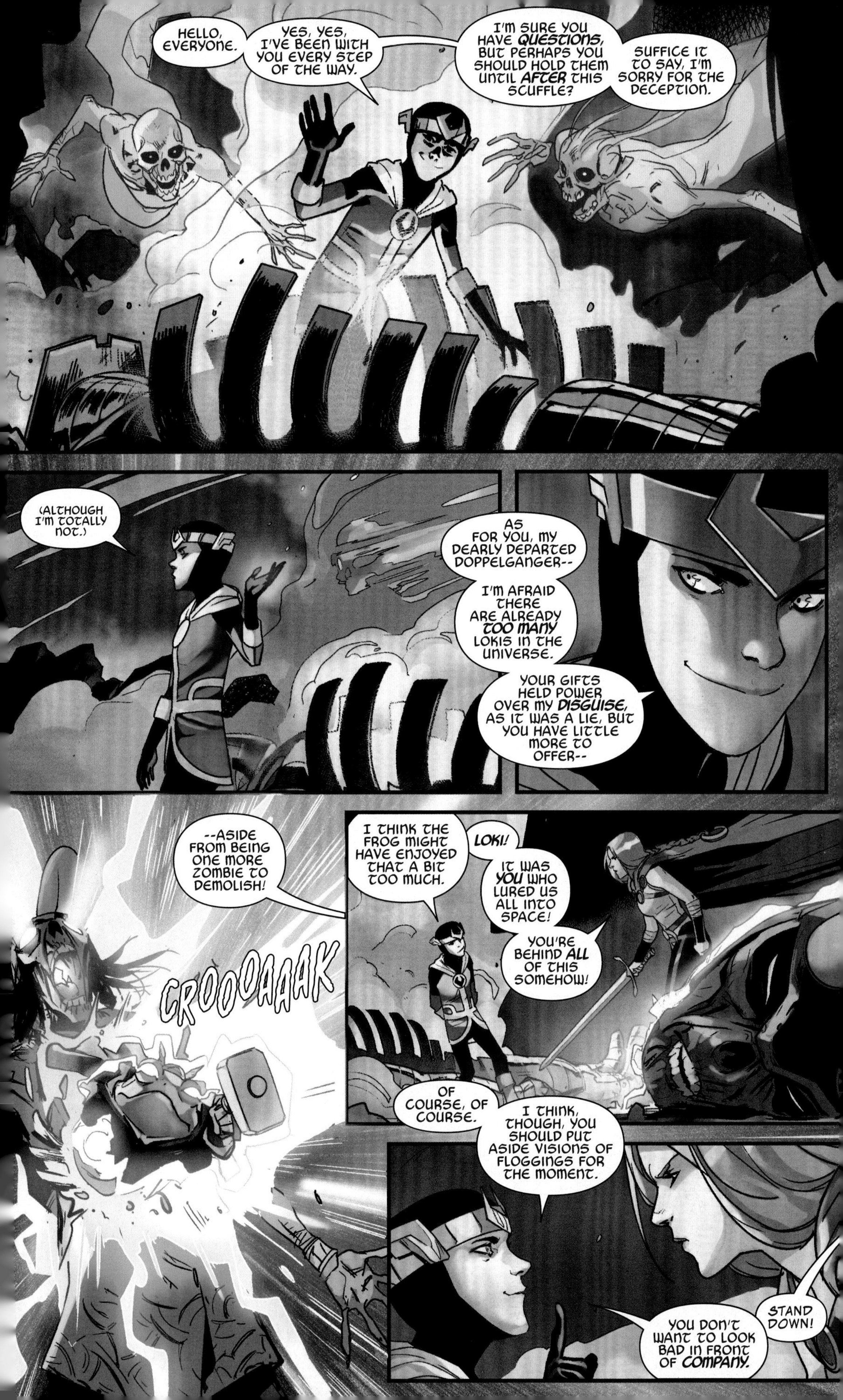
HELLO, EVERYONE.
YES, YES, I'VE BEEN WITH YOU EVERY STEP OF THE WAY.
I'M SURE YOU HAVE QUESTIONS, BUT PERHAPS YOU SHOULD HOLD THEM UNTIL AFTER THIS SCUFFLE?
SUFFICE IT TO SAY, I'M SORRY FOR THE DECEPTION.
(ALTHOUGH I'M TOTALLY NOT.)
AS FOR YOU, MY DEARLY DEPARTED DOPPELGANGER--
I'M AFRAID THERE ARE ALREADY TOO MANY LOKIS IN THE UNIVERSE.
YOUR GIFTS HELD POWER OVER MY DISGUISE, AS IT WAS A LIE, BUT YOU HAVE LITTLE MORE TO OFFER--
--ASIDE FROM BEING ONE MORE ZOMBIE TO DEMOLISH!
CROOOAAAK
I THINK THE FROG MIGHT HAVE ENJOYED THAT A BIT TOO MUCH.
LOKI!
IT WAS YOU WHO LURED US ALL INTO SPACE!
YOU'RE BEHIND ALL OF THIS SOMEHOW!
OF COURSE, OF COURSE.
I THINK, THOUGH, YOU SHOULD PUT ASIDE VISIONS OF FLOGGINGS FOR THE MOMENT.
YOU DON'T WANT TO LOOK BAD IN FRONT OF COMPANY.
STAND DOWN!

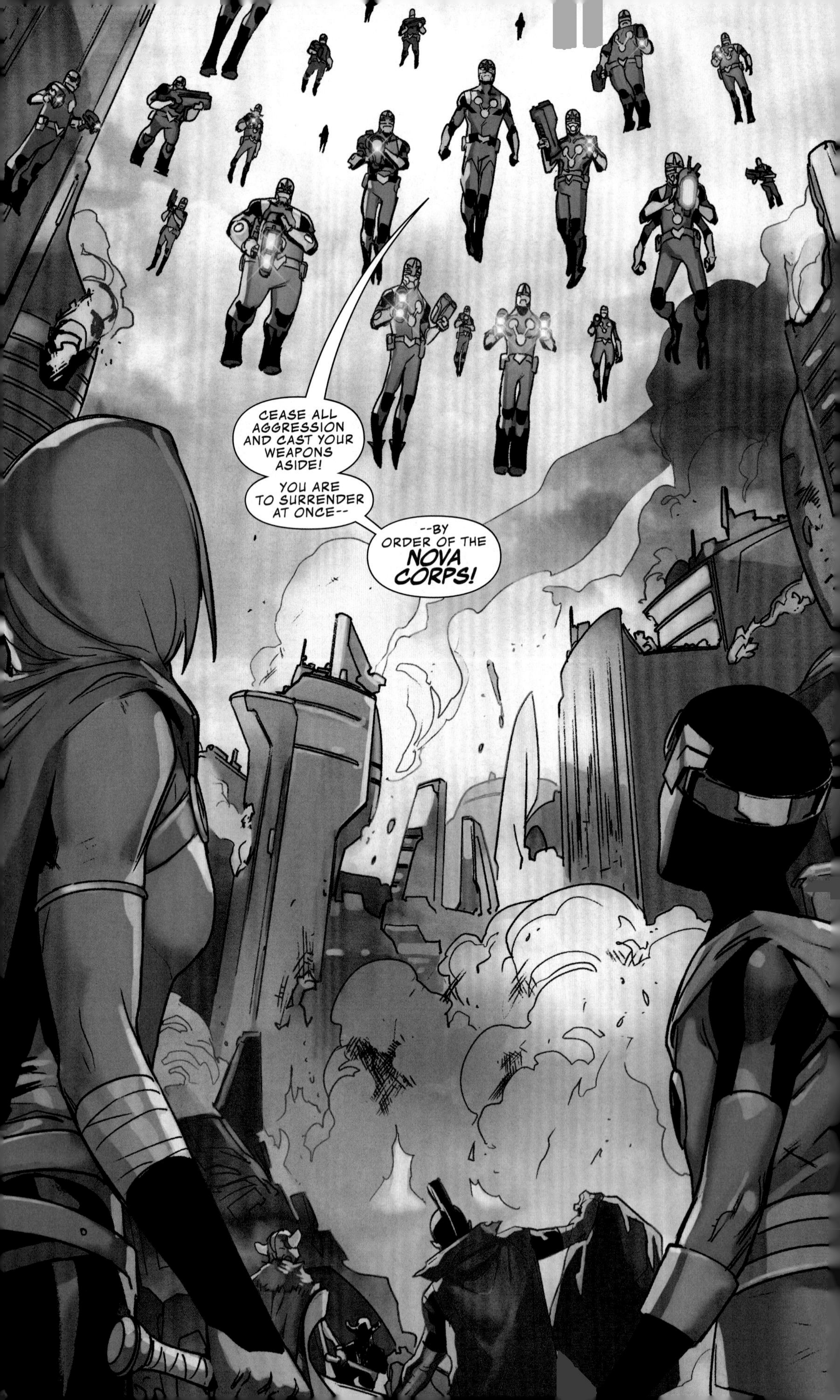
CEASE ALL AGGRESSION AND CAST YOUR WEAPONS ASIDE!
YOU ARE TO SURRENDER AT ONCE--
--BY ORDER OF THE NOVA CORPS!

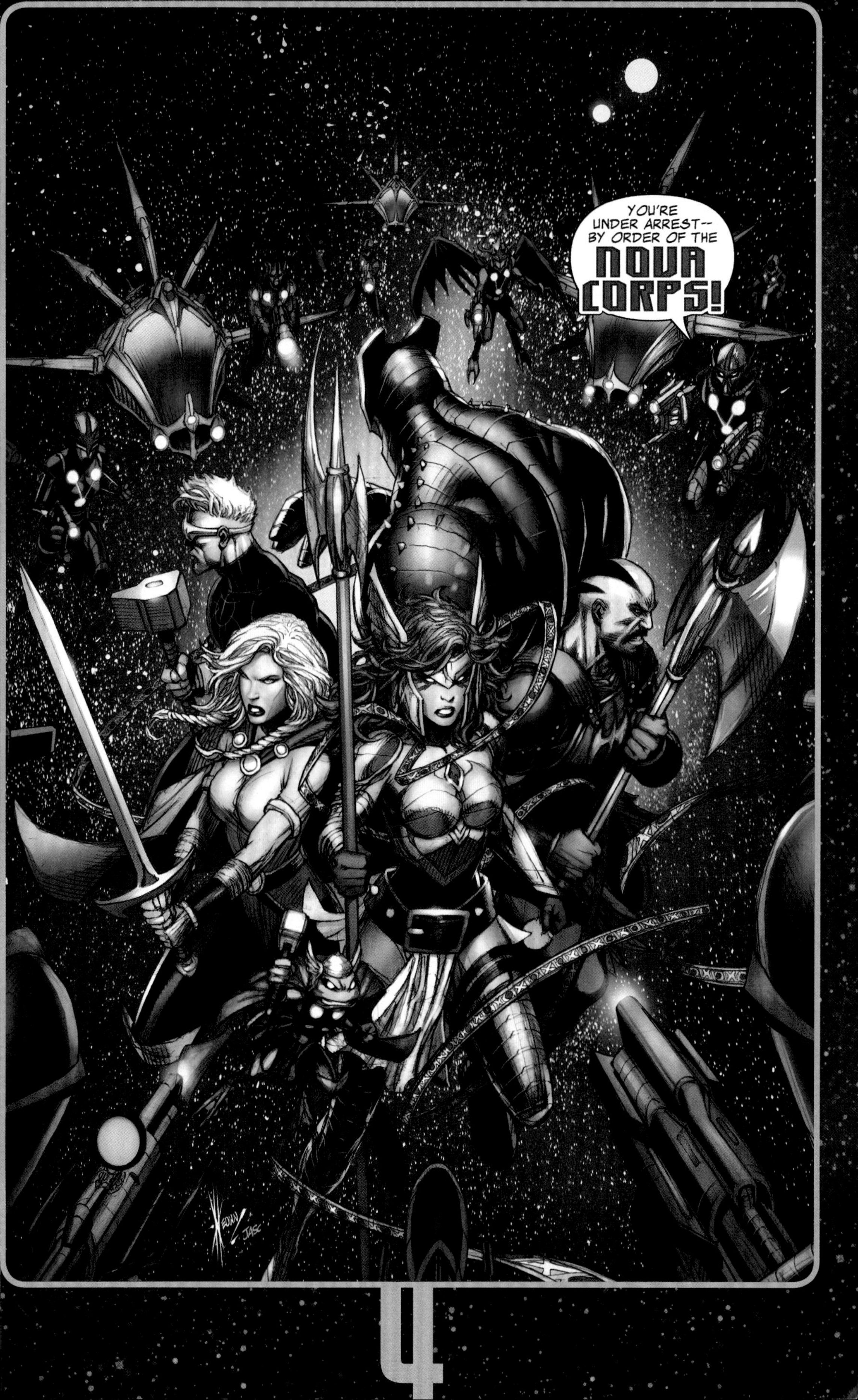
YOU'RE UNDER ARREST-- BY ORDER OF THE NOVA CORPS!

4

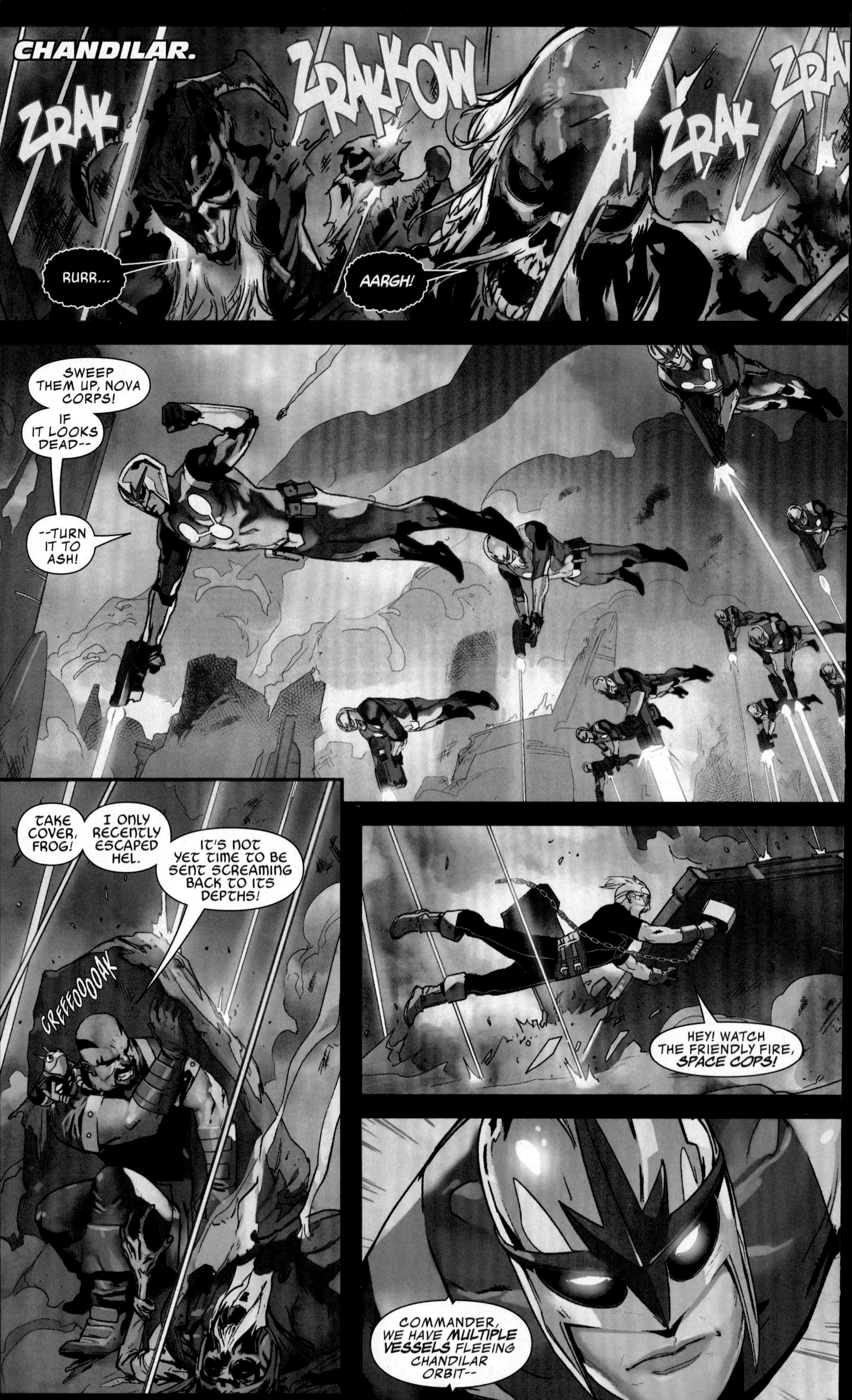
CHANDILAR.
ZRAK
ZRAKKOW
ZRAK
ZRA
RURR...
AARGH!
SWEEP THEM UP, NOVA CORPS!
IF IT LOOKS DEAD--
--TURN IT TO ASH!
TAKE COVER, FROG!
I ONLY RECENTLY ESCAPED HEL.
IT'S NOT YET TIME TO BE SENT SCREAMING BACK TO ITS DEPTHS!
CREEEOOOAK
HEY! WATCH THE FRIENDLY FIRE, SPACE COPS!
COMMANDER, WE HAVE MULTIPLE VESSELS FLEEING CHANDILAR ORBIT--

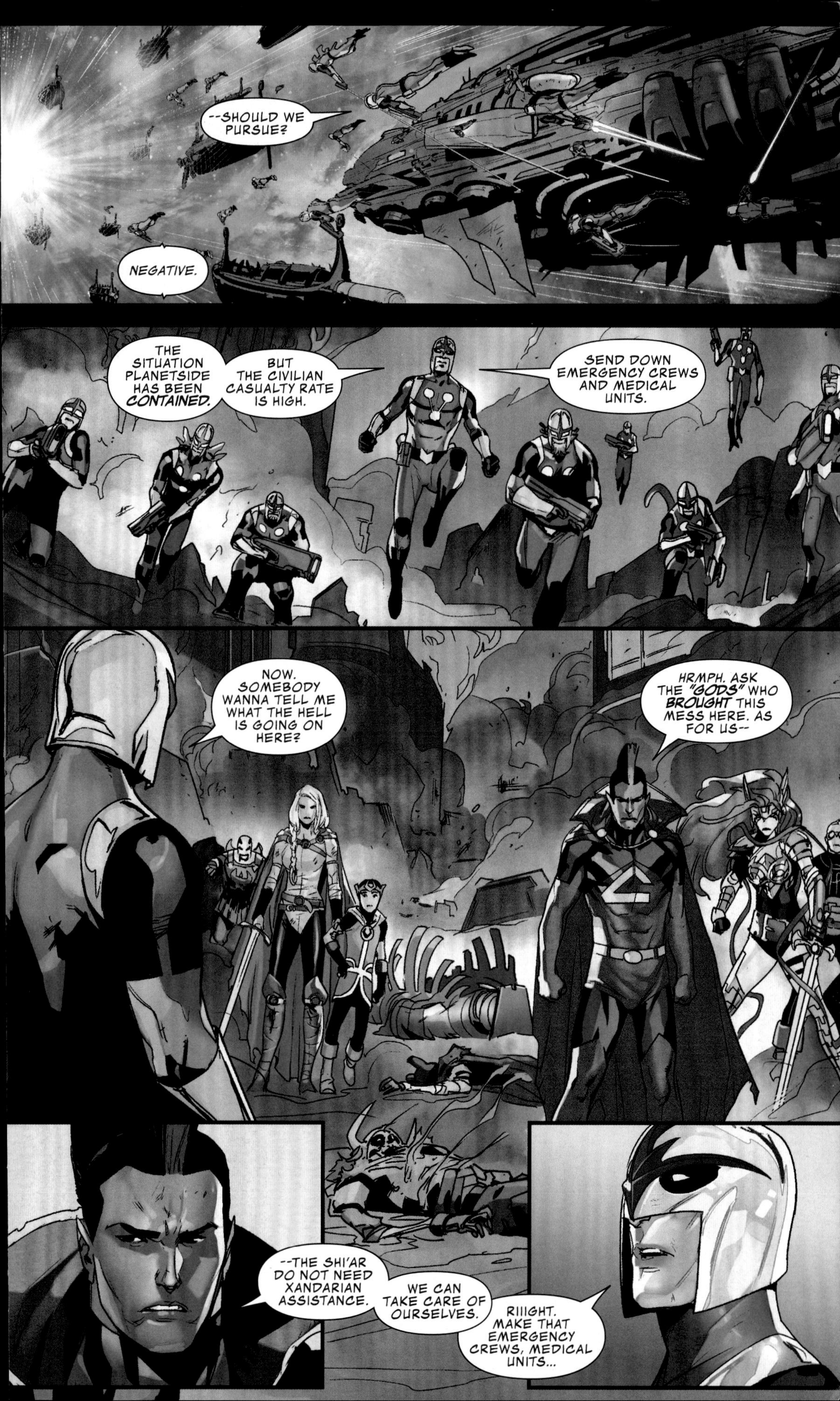
--SHOULD WE PURSUE?
NEGATIVE.
THE SITUATION PLANETSIDE HAS BEEN CONTAINED.
BUT THE CIVILIAN CASUALTY RATE IS HIGH.
SEND DOWN EMERGENCY CREWS AND MEDICAL UNITS.
NOW. SOMEBODY WANNA TELL ME WHAT THE HELL IS GOING ON HERE?
HRMPH. ASK THE "GODS" WHO BROUGHT THIS MESS HERE. AS FOR US--
--THE SHI'AR DO NOT NEED XANDARIAN ASSISTANCE.
WE CAN TAKE CARE OF OURSELVES.
RIIIGHT. MAKE THAT EMERGENCY CREWS, MEDICAL UNITS...

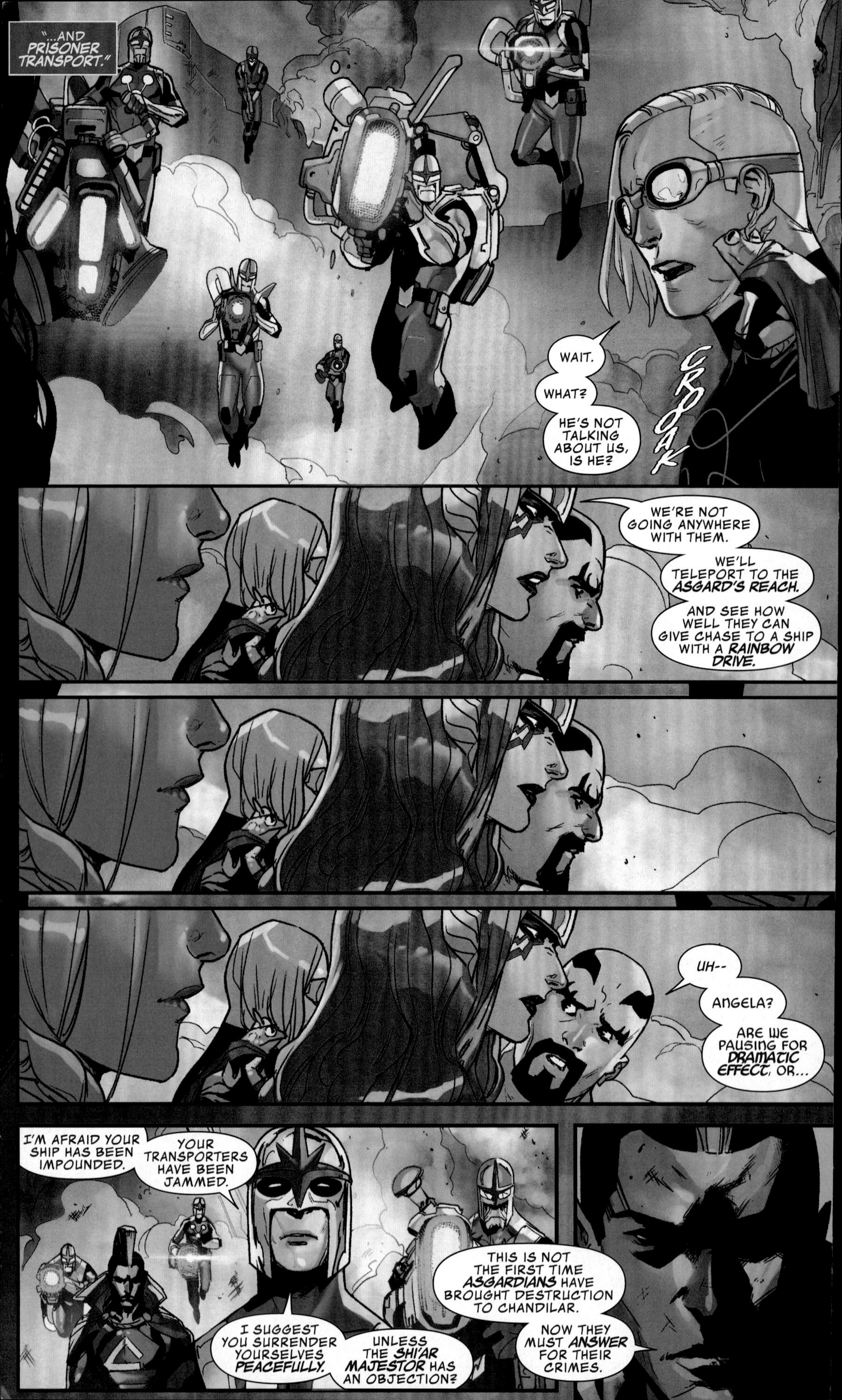
"...AND PRISONER TRANSPORT."
WAIT.
WHAT?
HE'S NOT TALKING ABOUT US, IS HE?
CROAK
WE'RE NOT GOING ANYWHERE WITH THEM.
WE'LL TELEPORT TO THE ASGARD'S REACH.
AND SEE HOW WELL THEY CAN GIVE CHASE TO A SHIP WITH A RAINBOW DRIVE.
UH--
ANGELA?
ARE WE PAUSING FOR DRAMATIC EFFECT, OR...
I'M AFRAID YOUR SHIP HAS BEEN IMPOUNDED.
YOUR TRANSPORTERS HAVE BEEN JAMMED.
I SUGGEST YOU SURRENDER YOURSELVES PEACEFULLY.
UNLESS THE SHI'AR MAJESTOR HAS AN OBJECTION?
THIS IS NOT THE FIRST TIME ASGARDIANS HAVE BROUGHT DESTRUCTION TO CHANDILAR.
NOW THEY MUST ANSWER FOR THEIR CRIMES.

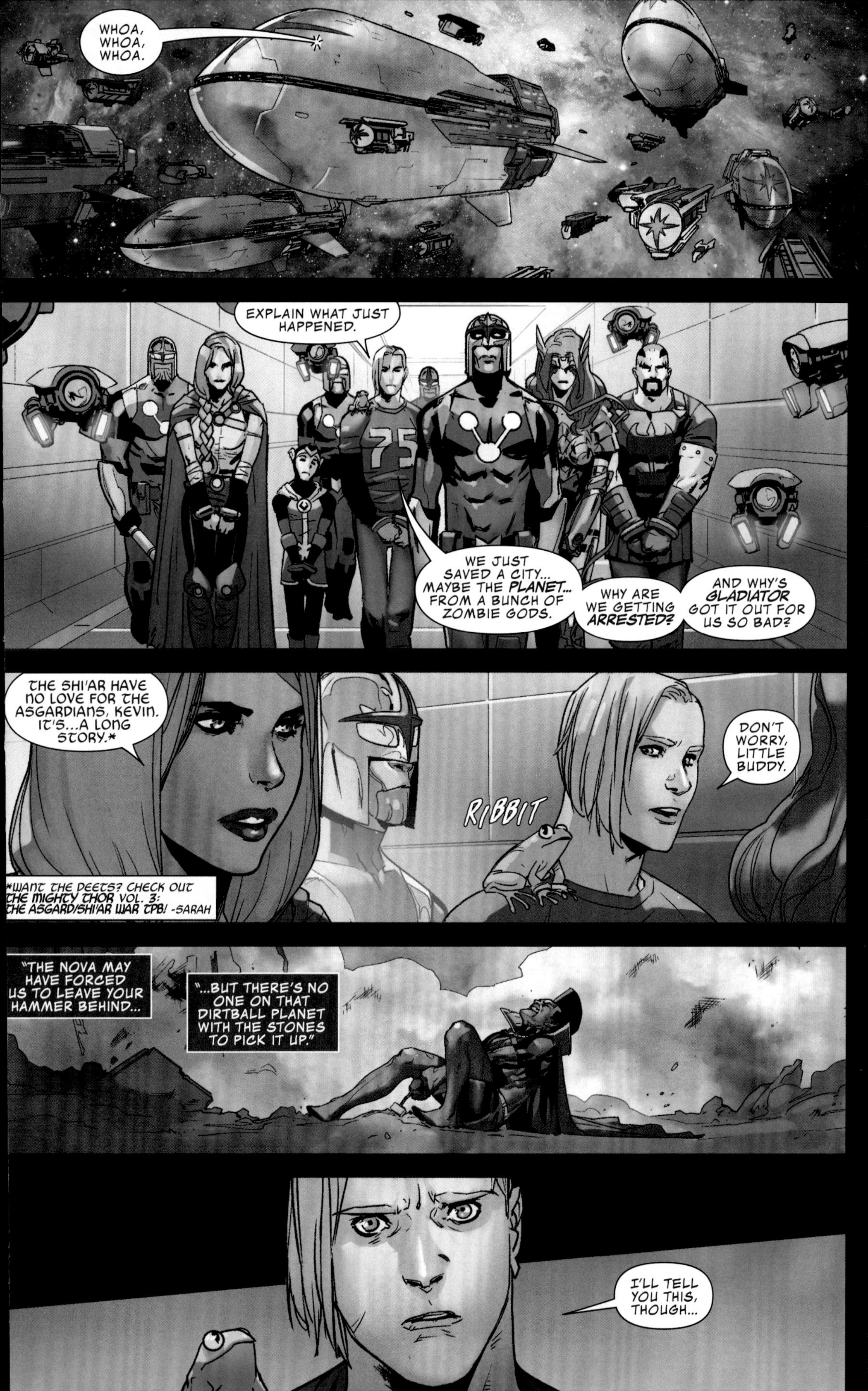
WHOA, WHOA, WHOA.
EXPLAIN WHAT JUST HAPPENED.
WE JUST SAVED A CITY... MAYBE THE PLANET... FROM A BUNCH OF ZOMBIE GODS.
WHY ARE WE GETTING ARRESTED?
AND WHY'S GLADIATOR GOT IT OUT FOR US SO BAD?
THE SHI'AR HAVE NO LOVE FOR THE ASGARDIANS, KEVIN. IT'S...A LONG STORY.*
DON'T WORRY, LITTLE BUDDY.
RIBBIT
*WANT THE DEETS? CHECK OUT THE MIGHTY THOR VOL. 3: THE ASGARD/SHI'AR WAR TPB! -SARAH
"THE NOVA MAY HAVE FORCED US TO LEAVE YOUR HAMMER BEHIND...
"...BUT THERE'S NO ONE ON THAT DIRTBALL PLANET WITH THE STONES TO PICK IT UP."
I'LL TELL YOU THIS, THOUGH...

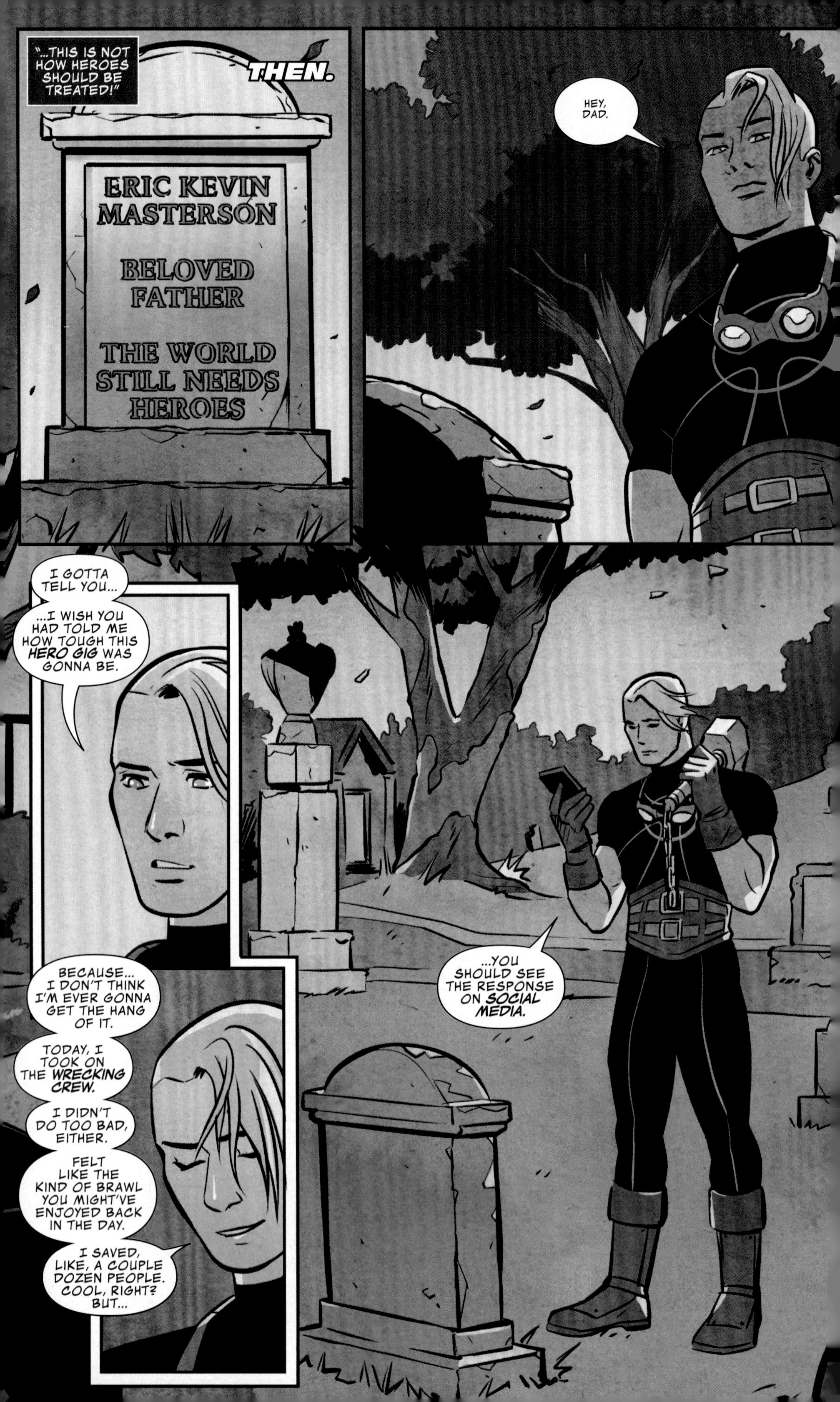

"...THIS IS NOT HOW HEROES SHOULD BE TREATED!"
THEN.
ERIC KEVIN MASTERSON
BELOVED FATHER
THE WORLD STILL NEEDS HEROES
HEY, DAD.
I GOTTA TELL YOU...
...I WISH YOU HAD TOLD ME HOW TOUGH THIS HERO GIG WAS GONNA BE.
BECAUSE... I DON'T THINK I'M EVER GONNA GET THE HANG OF IT.
TODAY, I TOOK ON THE WRECKING CREW.
I DIDN'T DO TOO BAD, EITHER.
FELT LIKE THE KIND OF BRAWL YOU MIGHT'VE ENJOYED BACK IN THE DAY.
I SAVED, LIKE, A COUPLE DOZEN PEOPLE. COOL, RIGHT? BUT...
...YOU SHOULD SEE THE RESPONSE ON SOCIAL MEDIA.

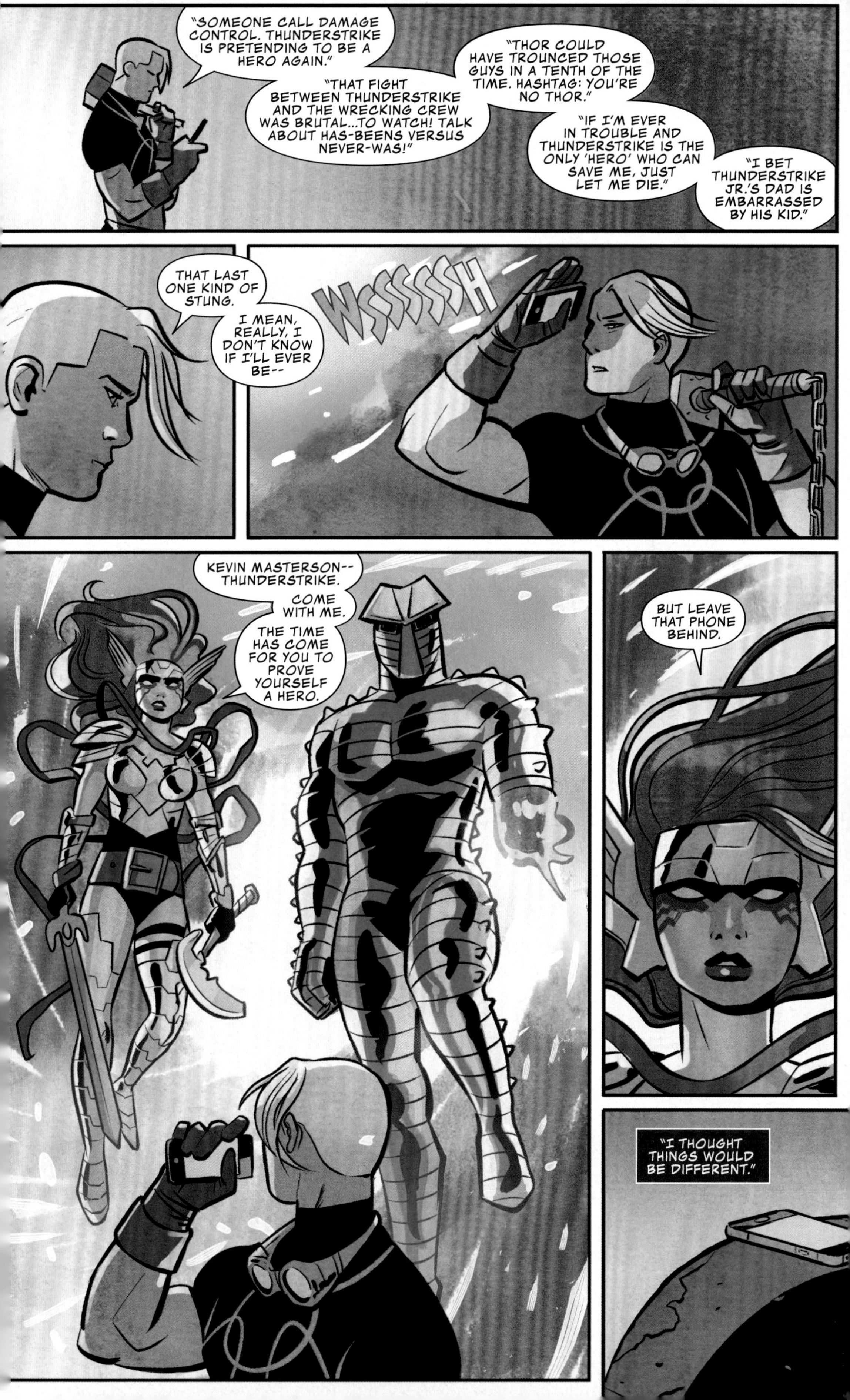
"SOMEONE CALL DAMAGE CONTROL. THUNDERSTRIKE IS PRETENDING TO BE A HERO AGAIN."
"THAT FIGHT BETWEEN THUNDERSTRIKE AND THE WRECKING CREW WAS BRUTAL...TO WATCH! TALK ABOUT HAS-BEENS VERSUS NEVER-WAS!"
"THOR COULD HAVE TROUNCED THOSE GUYS IN A TENTH OF THE TIME. HASHTAG: YOU'RE NO THOR."
"IF I'M EVER IN TROUBLE AND THUNDERSTRIKE IS THE ONLY 'HERO' WHO CAN SAVE ME, JUST LET ME DIE."
"I BET THUNDERSTRIKE JR.'S DAD IS EMBARRASSED BY HIS KID."
THAT LAST ONE KIND OF STUNG.
I MEAN, REALLY, I DON'T KNOW IF I'LL EVER BE--
WSSSSSH
KEVIN MASTERSON-- THUNDERSTRIKE.
COME WITH ME.
THE TIME HAS COME FOR YOU TO PROVE YOURSELF A HERO.
BUT LEAVE THAT PHONE BEHIND.
"I THOUGHT THINGS WOULD BE DIFFERENT."

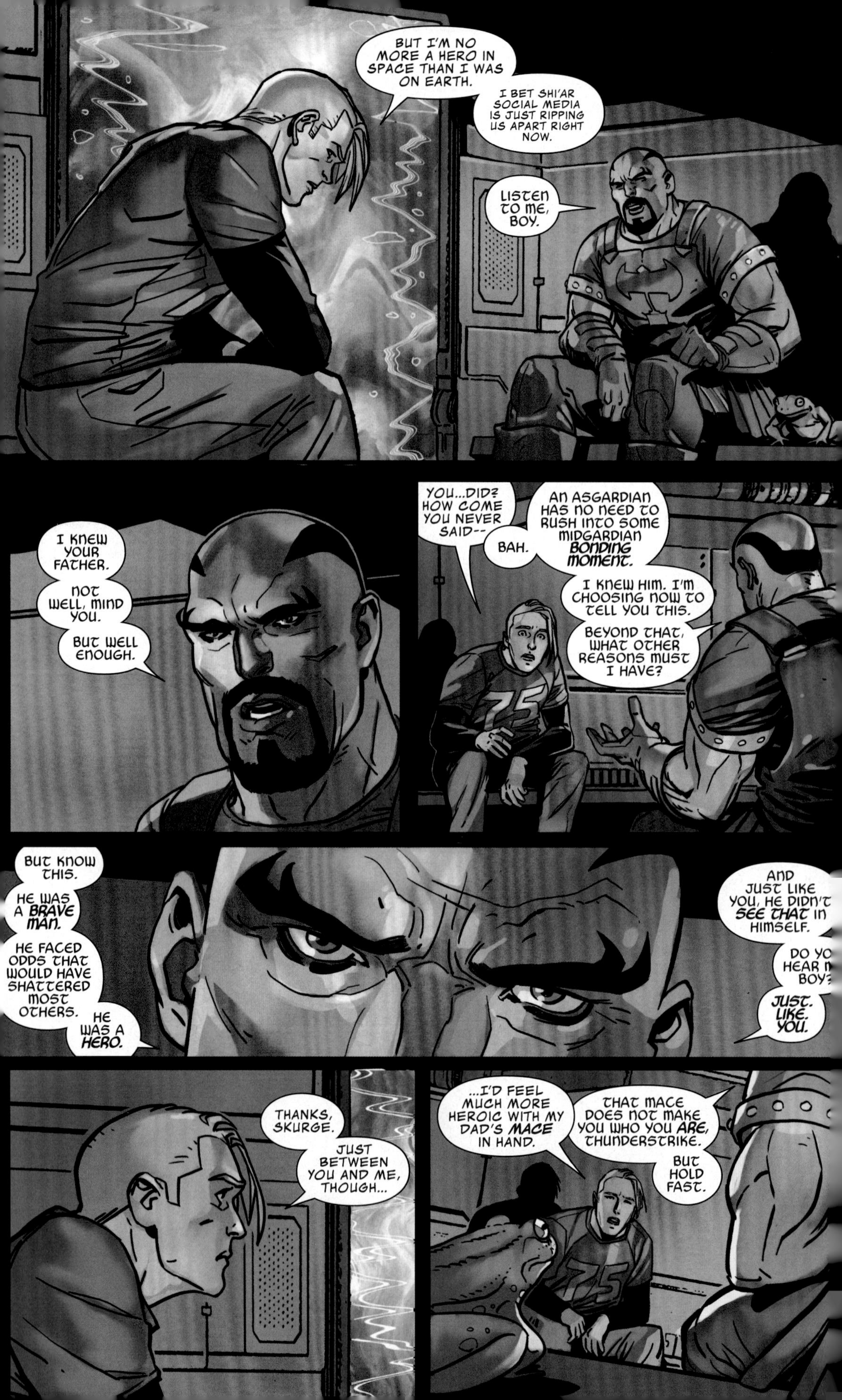

BUT I'M NO MORE A HERO IN SPACE THAN I WAS ON EARTH.
I BET SHI'AR SOCIAL MEDIA IS JUST RIPPING US APART RIGHT NOW.
LISTEN TO ME, BOY.
I KNEW YOUR FATHER.
NOT WELL, MIND YOU.
BUT WELL ENOUGH.
YOU...DID? HOW COME YOU NEVER SAID--
BAH.
AN ASGARDIAN HAS NO NEED TO RUSH INTO SOME MIDGARDIAN BONDING MOMENT.
I KNEW HIM. I'M CHOOSING NOW TO TELL YOU THIS.
BEYOND THAT, WHAT OTHER REASONS MUST I HAVE?
BUT KNOW THIS.
HE WAS A BRAVE MAN.
HE FACED ODDS THAT WOULD HAVE SHATTERED MOST OTHERS.
HE WAS A HERO.
AND JUST LIKE YOU, HE DIDN'T SEE THAT IN HIMSELF.
DO YO HEAR BOY?
JUST. LIKE. YOU.
THANKS, SKURGE.
JUST BETWEEN YOU AND ME, THOUGH...
...I'D FEEL MUCH MORE HEROIC WITH MY DAD'S MACE IN HAND.
THAT MACE DOES NOT MAKE YOU WHO YOU ARE, THUNDERSTRIKE.
BUT HOLD FAST.

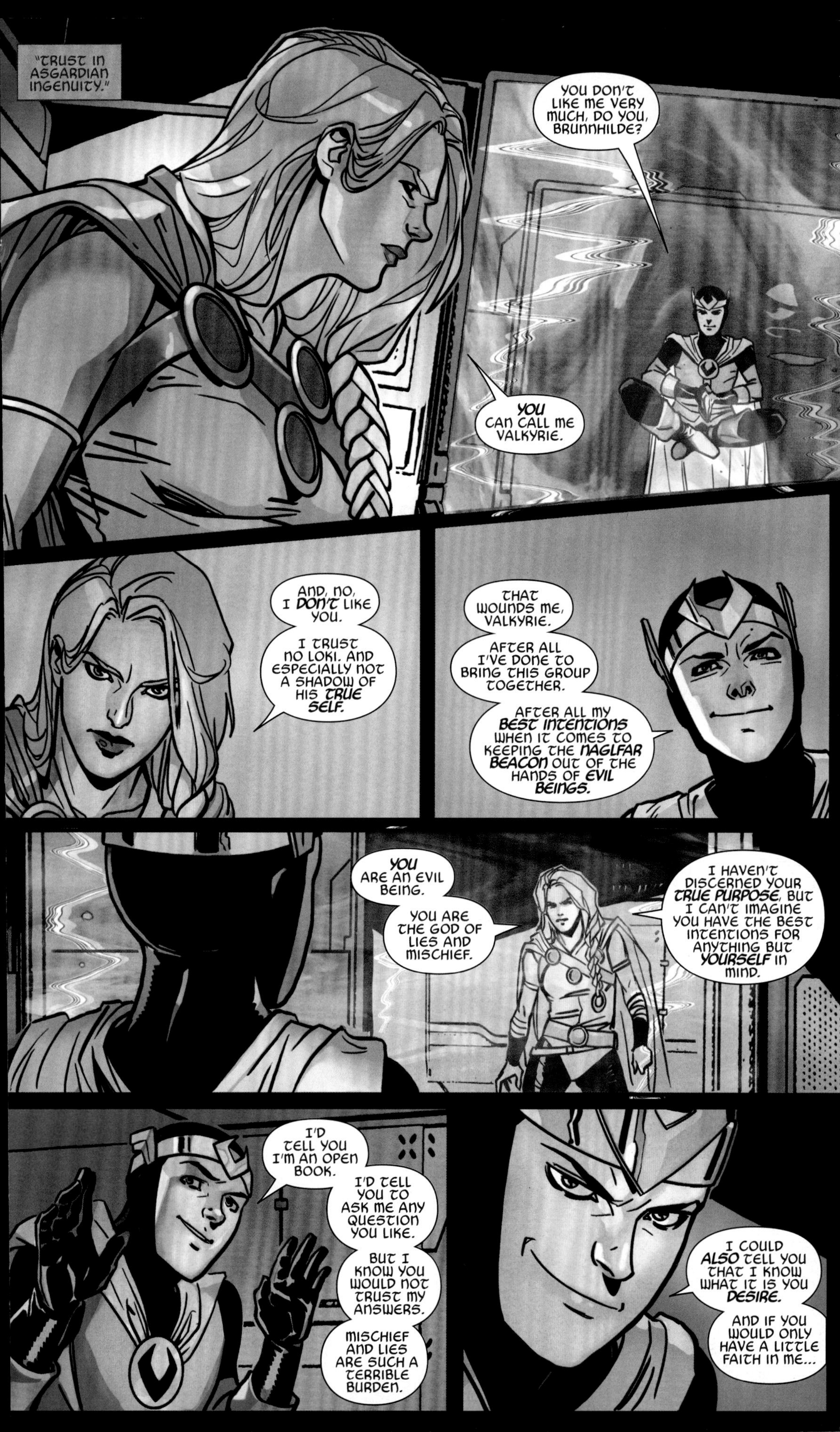

"TRUST IN ASGARDIAN INGENUITY."
YOU DON'T LIKE ME VERY MUCH, DO YOU, BRUNNHILDE?
YOU CAN CALL ME VALKYRIE.
AND, NO, I DON'T LIKE YOU.
I TRUST NO LOKI. AND ESPECIALLY NOT A SHADOW OF HIS TRUE SELF.
THAT WOUNDS ME, VALKYRIE.
AFTER ALL I'VE DONE TO BRING THIS GROUP TOGETHER.
AFTER ALL MY BEST INTENTIONS WHEN IT COMES TO KEEPING THE NAGLFAR BEACON OUT OF THE HANDS OF EVIL BEINGS.
YOU ARE AN EVIL BEING.
YOU ARE THE GOD OF LIES AND MISCHIEF.
I HAVEN'T DISCERNED YOUR TRUE PURPOSE, BUT I CAN'T IMAGINE YOU HAVE THE BEST INTENTIONS FOR ANYTHING BUT YOURSELF IN MIND.
I'D TELL YOU I'M AN OPEN BOOK.
I'D TELL YOU TO ASK ME ANY QUESTION YOU LIKE.
BUT I KNOW YOU WOULD NOT TRUST MY ANSWERS.
MISCHIEF AND LIES ARE SUCH A TERRIBLE BURDEN.
I COULD ALSO TELL YOU THAT I KNOW WHAT IT IS YOU DESIRE.
AND IF YOU WOULD ONLY HAVE A LITTLE FAITH IN ME...

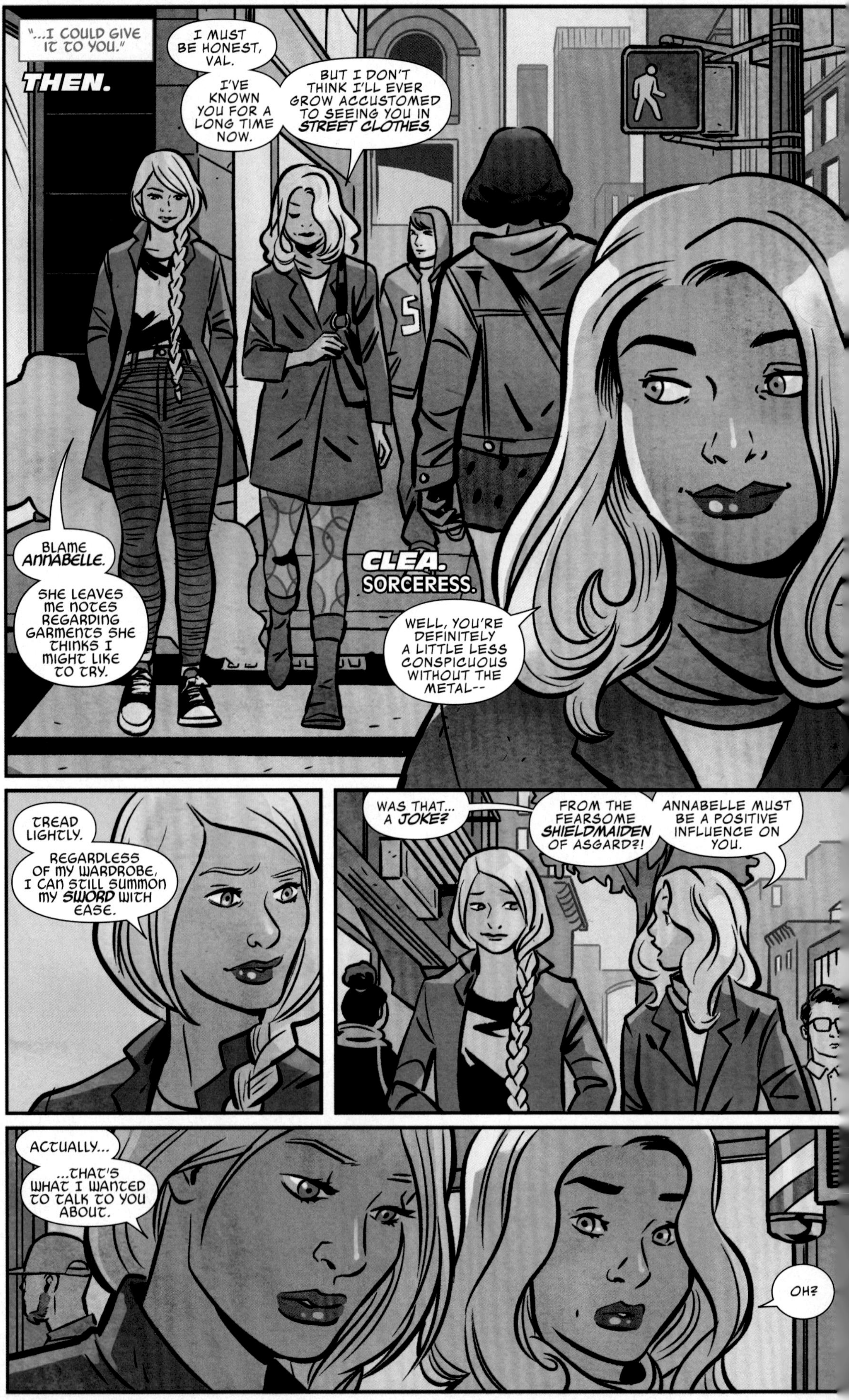
"...I COULD GIVE IT TO YOU."
THEN.
I MUST BE HONEST, VAL.
I'VE KNOWN YOU FOR A LONG TIME NOW.
BUT I DON'T THINK I'LL EVER GROW ACCUSTOMED TO SEEING YOU IN STREET CLOTHES.
BLAME ANNABELLE.
SHE LEAVES ME NOTES REGARDING GARMENTS SHE THINKS I MIGHT LIKE TO TRY.
CLEA. SORCERESS.
WELL, YOU'RE DEFINITELY A LITTLE LESS CONSPICUOUS WITHOUT THE METAL--
TREAD LIGHTLY.
REGARDLESS OF MY WARDROBE, I CAN STILL SUMMON MY SWORD WITH EASE.
WAS THAT... A JOKE?
FROM THE FEARSOME SHIELDMAIDEN OF ASGARD?!
ANNABELLE MUST BE A POSITIVE INFLUENCE ON YOU.
ACTUALLY...
...THAT'S WHAT I WANTED TO TALK TO YOU ABOUT.
OH?

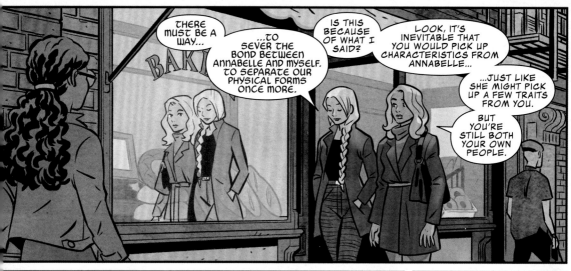

THERE MUST BE A WAY... ...TO SEVER THE BOND BETWEEN ANNABELLE AND MYSELF. TO SEPARATE OUR PHYSICAL FORMS ONCE MORE.

IS THIS BECAUSE OF WHAT I SAID?

LOOK, IT'S INEVITABLE THAT YOU WOULD PICK UP CHARACTERISTICS FROM ANNABELLE...

...JUST LIKE SHE MIGHT PICK UP A FEW TRAITS FROM YOU.

BUT YOU'RE STILL BOTH YOUR OWN PEOPLE.

IT'S NOT THAT.

I AM A WARRIOR.

I AM DESTINED FOR BATTLE.

ANNABELLE, ON THE OTHER HAND, IS MORTAL.

SHE'S GOING TO ACCOMPANY ME INTO BATTLE ONE TOO MANY TIMES AND...

VAL...I TOLD YOU WHEN YOU ASKED ME TO SAVE ANNABELLE'S LIFE, YOU ARE HER BOND TO THE MORTAL PLANE.* YOU'RE HER ANCHOR.

I'M NOT SURE THERE'S A WAY TO PULL THE TWO OF YOU APART.

I CAN'T MAKE ANY PROMISES.

I'LL LOOK INTO IT.

BUT SOMETHING LIKE THIS...

*SEE FEARLESS DEFENDERS #6-7! -SARAH

...IT'S LIKELY TO COME ONLY AT A TERRIBLE PRICE.

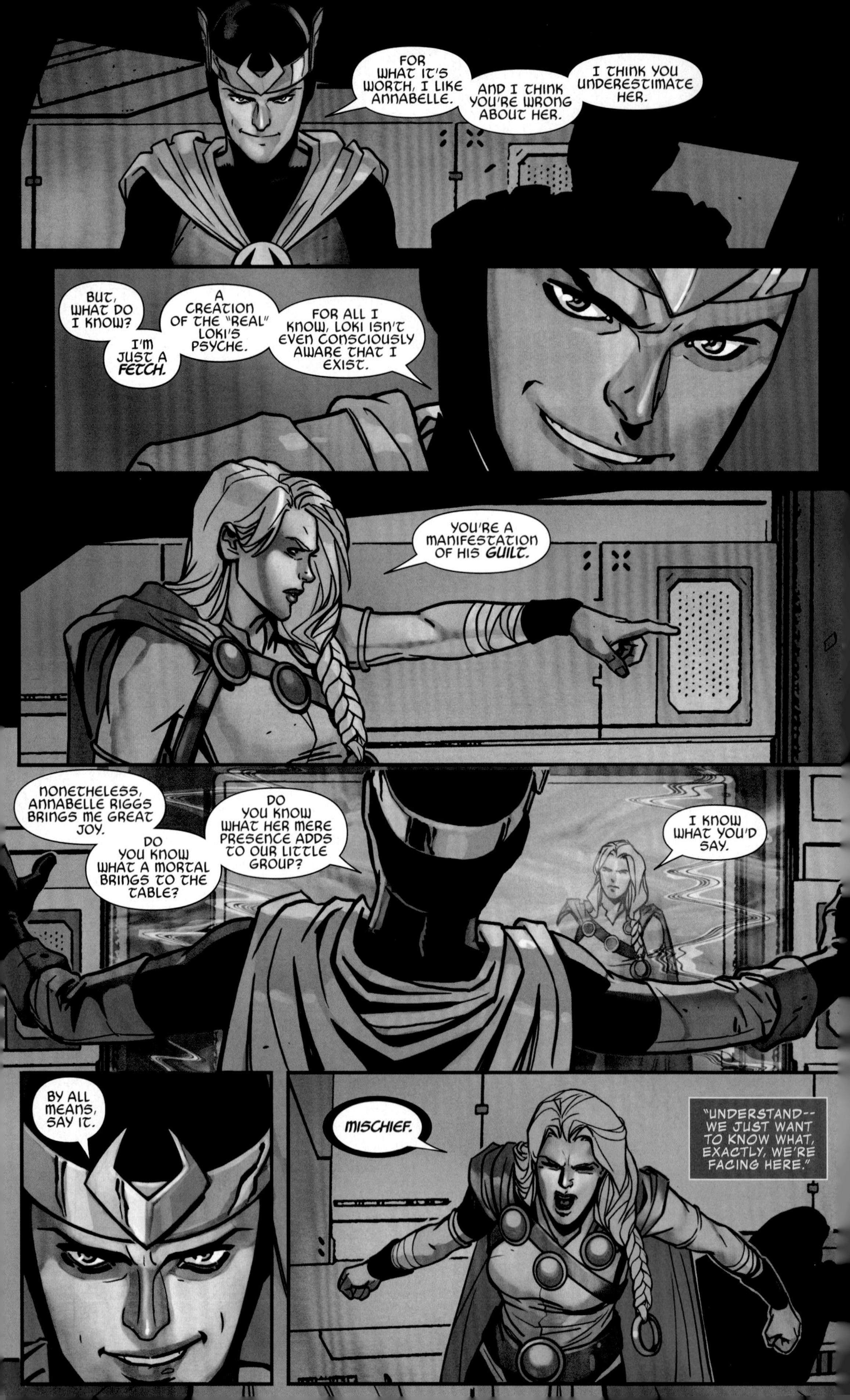
FOR WHAT IT'S WORTH, I LIKE ANNABELLE.
AND I THINK YOU'RE WRONG ABOUT HER.
I THINK YOU UNDERESTIMATE HER.
BUT, WHAT DO I KNOW?
I'M JUST A *FETCH.*
A CREATION OF THE "REAL" LOKI'S PSYCHE.
FOR ALL I KNOW, LOKI ISN'T EVEN CONSCIOUSLY AWARE THAT I EXIST.
YOU'RE A MANIFESTATION OF HIS *GUILT.*
NONETHELESS, ANNABELLE RIGGS BRINGS ME GREAT JOY.
DO YOU KNOW WHAT A MORTAL BRINGS TO THE TABLE?
DO YOU KNOW WHAT HER MERE PRESENCE ADDS TO OUR LITTLE GROUP?
I KNOW WHAT YOU'D SAY.
BY ALL MEANS, SAY IT.
MISCHIEF.
"UNDERSTAND-- WE JUST WANT TO KNOW WHAT, EXACTLY, WE'RE FACING HERE."

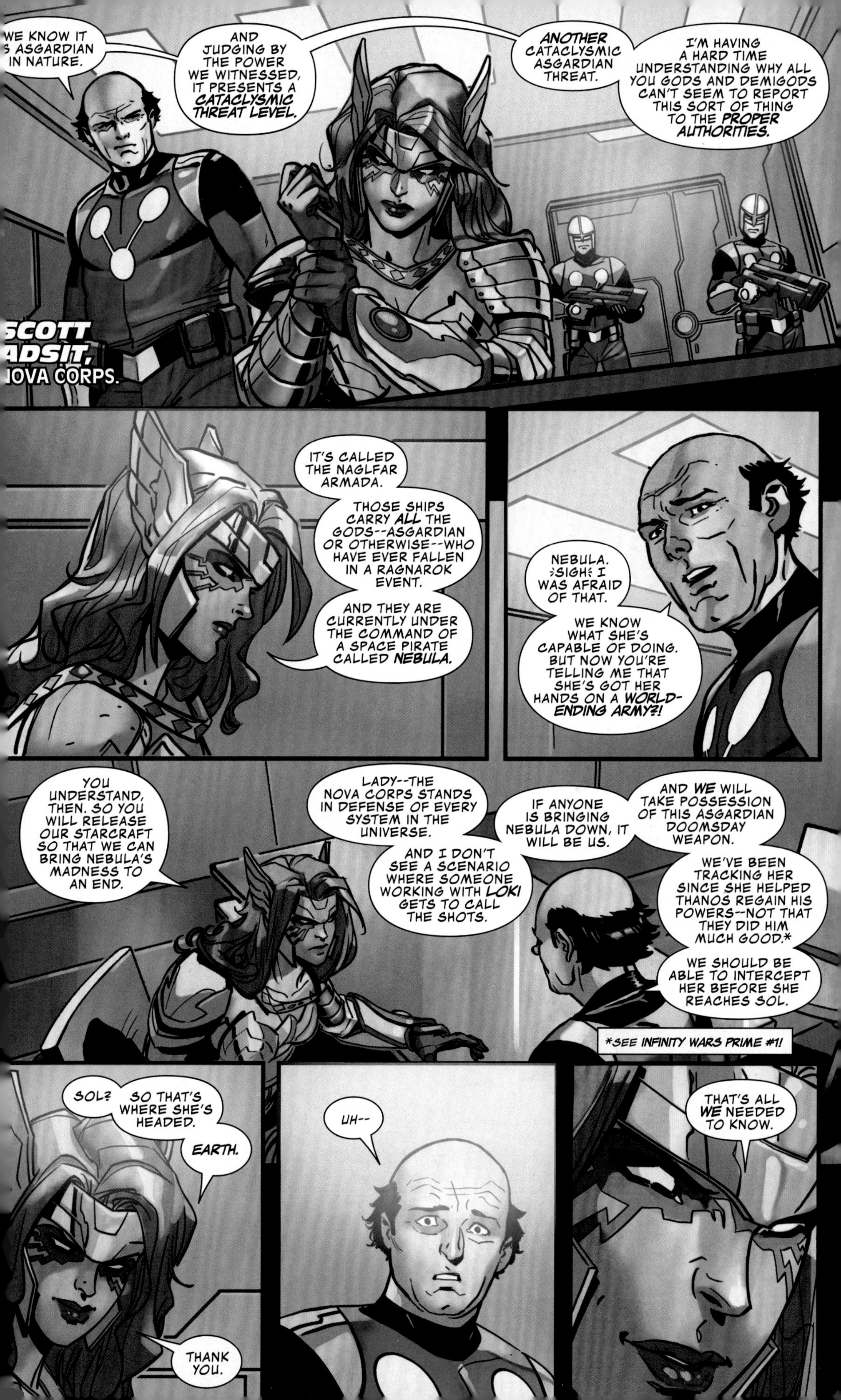
WE KNOW IT S ASGARDIAN IN NATURE.
AND JUDGING BY THE POWER WE WITNESSED, IT PRESENTS A CATACLYSMIC THREAT LEVEL.
ANOTHER CATACLYSMIC ASGARDIAN THREAT.
I'M HAVING A HARD TIME UNDERSTANDING WHY ALL YOU GODS AND DEMIGODS CAN'T SEEM TO REPORT THIS SORT OF THING TO THE PROPER AUTHORITIES.
SCOTT ADSIT, NOVA CORPS.
IT'S CALLED THE NAGLFAR ARMADA.
THOSE SHIPS CARRY ALL THE GODS--ASGARDIAN OR OTHERWISE--WHO HAVE EVER FALLEN IN A RAGNAROK EVENT.
AND THEY ARE CURRENTLY UNDER THE COMMAND OF A SPACE PIRATE CALLED NEBULA.
NEBULA. SIGH I WAS AFRAID OF THAT.
WE KNOW WHAT SHE'S CAPABLE OF DOING. BUT NOW YOU'RE TELLING ME THAT SHE'S GOT HER HANDS ON A WORLD-ENDING ARMY?!
YOU UNDERSTAND, THEN. SO YOU WILL RELEASE OUR STARCRAFT SO THAT WE CAN BRING NEBULA'S MADNESS TO AN END.
LADY--THE NOVA CORPS STANDS IN DEFENSE OF EVERY SYSTEM IN THE UNIVERSE.
AND I DON'T SEE A SCENARIO WHERE SOMEONE WORKING WITH LOKI GETS TO CALL THE SHOTS.
IF ANYONE IS BRINGING NEBULA DOWN, IT WILL BE US.
AND WE WILL TAKE POSSESSION OF THIS ASGARDIAN DOOMSDAY WEAPON.
WE'VE BEEN TRACKING HER SINCE SHE HELPED THANOS REGAIN HIS POWERS--NOT THAT THEY DID HIM MUCH GOOD.*
WE SHOULD BE ABLE TO INTERCEPT HER BEFORE SHE REACHES SOL.
*SEE INFINITY WARS PRIME #1!
SOL? SO THAT'S WHERE SHE'S HEADED.
EARTH.
THANK YOU.
UH--
THAT'S ALL WE NEEDED TO KNOW.

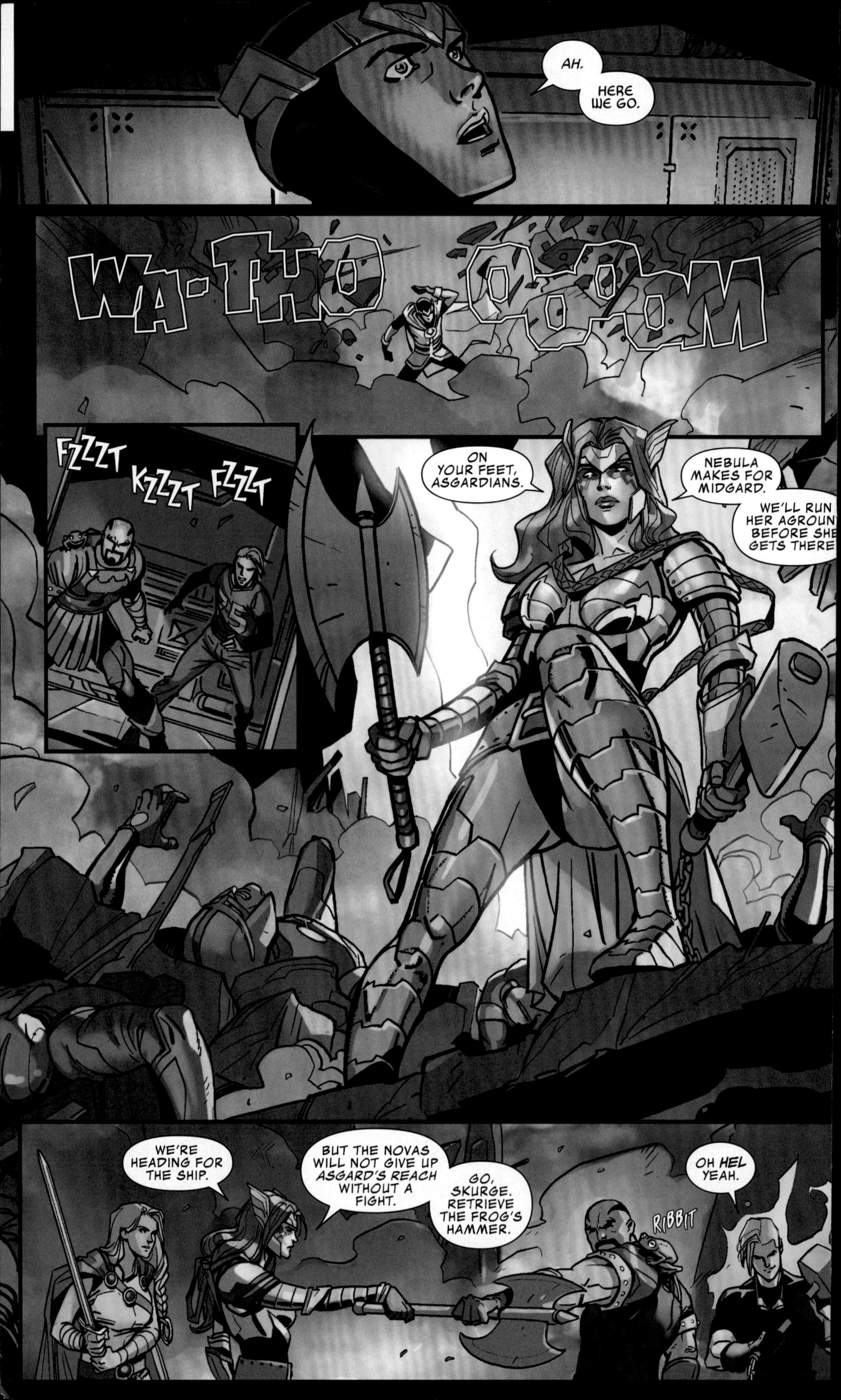
AH.
HERE WE GO.
WA-THOOOOOM
FZZZT KZZZT FZZZT
ON YOUR FEET, ASGARDIANS.
NEBULA MAKES FOR MIDGARD.
WE'LL RUN HER AGROUN BEFORE SHE GETS THERE
WE'RE HEADING FOR THE SHIP.
BUT THE NOVAS WILL NOT GIVE UP ASGARD'S REACH WITHOUT A FIGHT.
GO, SKURGE. RETRIEVE THE FROG'S HAMMER.
RIBBIT
OH HEL YEAH.

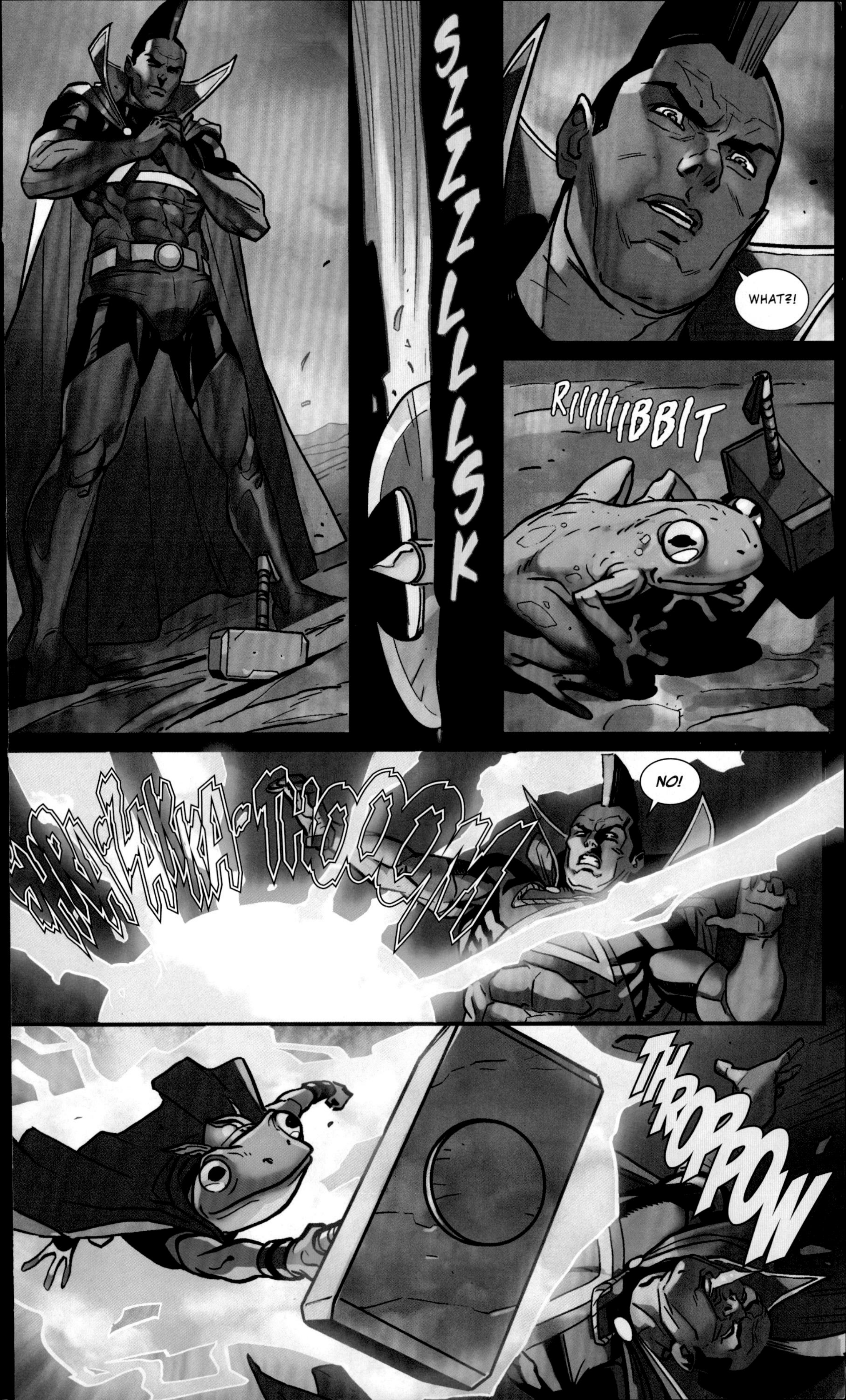
SZZZZLLLLSK
WHAT?!
RIIIIIBBIT
CRAKKA-THOOOM
NO!
THOOPOW

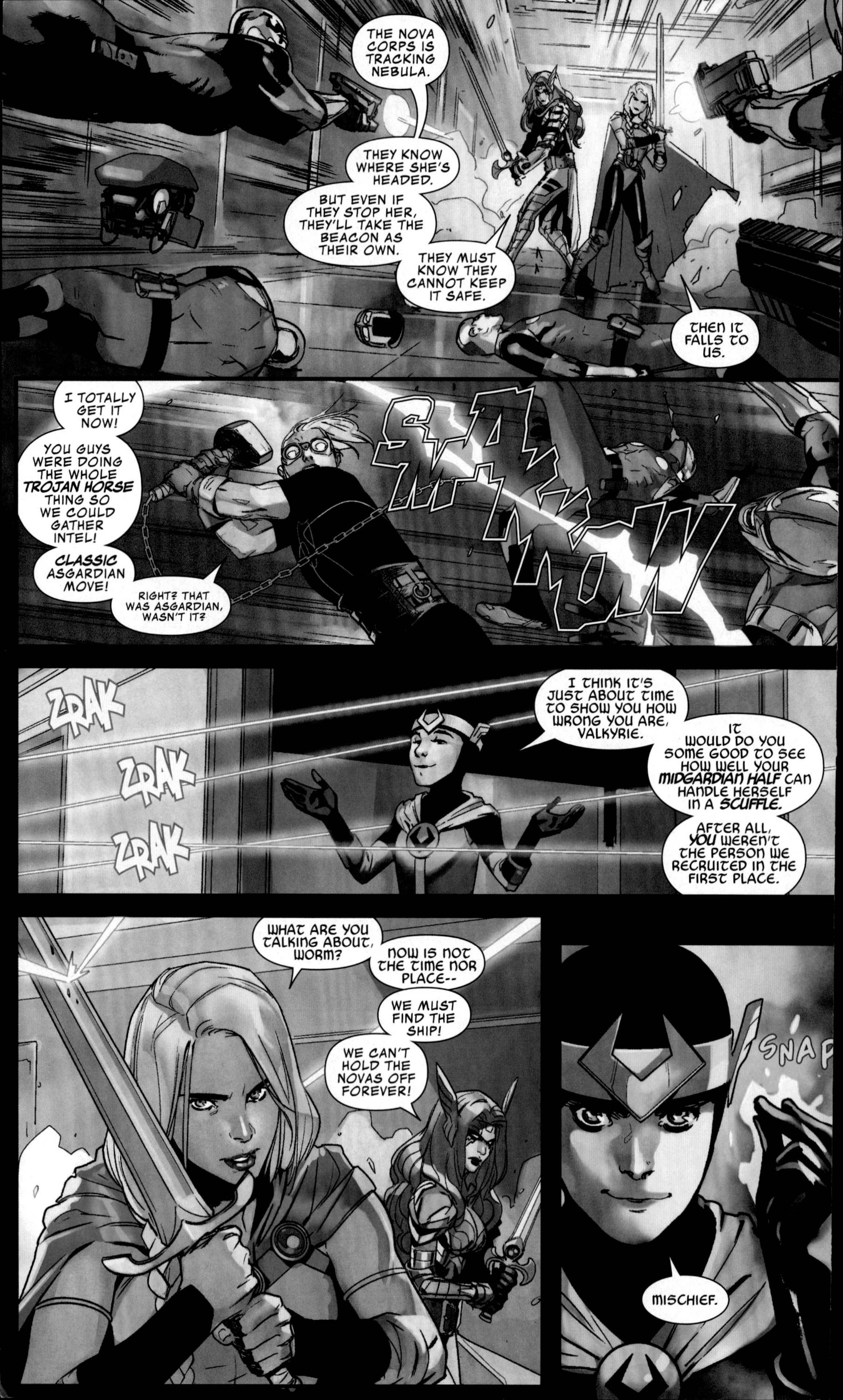
THE NOVA CORPS IS TRACKING NEBULA.
THEY KNOW WHERE SHE'S HEADED.
BUT EVEN IF THEY STOP HER, THEY'LL TAKE THE BEACON AS THEIR OWN.
THEY MUST KNOW THEY CANNOT KEEP IT SAFE.
THEN IT FALLS TO US.
I TOTALLY GET IT NOW!
YOU GUYS WERE DOING THE WHOLE TROJAN HORSE THING SO WE COULD GATHER INTEL!
CLASSIC ASGARDIAN MOVE!
RIGHT? THAT WAS ASGARDIAN, WASN'T IT?
ZRAK
ZRAK
ZRAK
I THINK IT'S JUST ABOUT TIME TO SHOW YOU HOW WRONG YOU ARE, VALKYRIE.
IT WOULD DO YOU SOME GOOD TO SEE HOW WELL YOUR MIDGARDIAN HALF CAN HANDLE HERSELF IN A SCUFFLE.
AFTER ALL, YOU WEREN'T THE PERSON WE RECRUITED IN THE FIRST PLACE.
WHAT ARE YOU TALKING ABOUT, WORM?
NOW IS NOT THE TIME NOR PLACE--
WE MUST FIND THE SHIP!
WE CAN'T HOLD THE NOVAS OFF FOREVER!
MISCHIEF.

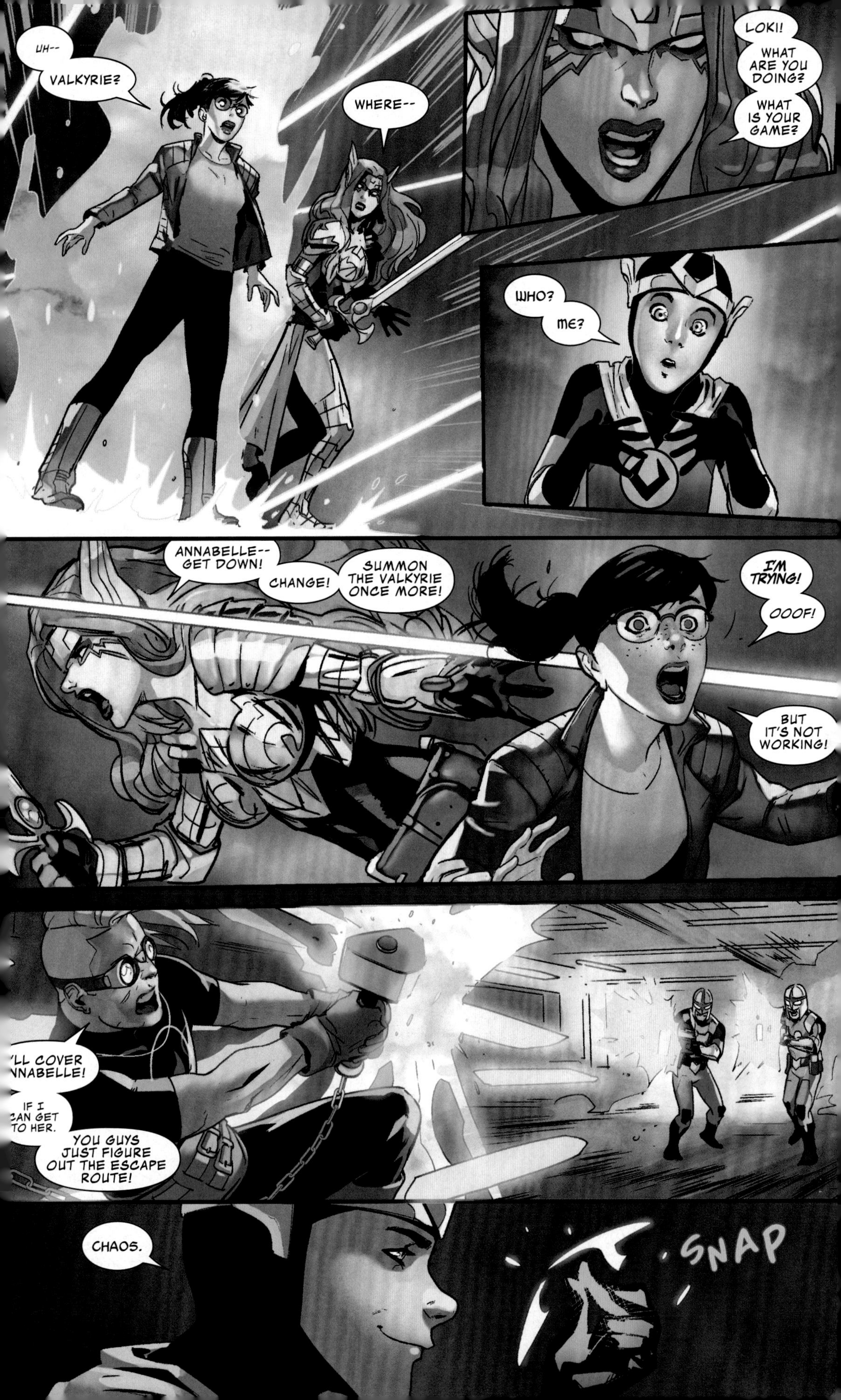
UH--
VALKYRIE?
WHERE--
LOKI!
WHAT ARE YOU DOING?
WHAT IS YOUR GAME?
WHO?
ME?
ANNABELLE-- GET DOWN!
CHANGE!
SUMMON THE VALKYRIE ONCE MORE!
I'M TRYING!
OOOF!
BUT IT'S NOT WORKING!
I'LL COVER ANNABELLE!
IF I CAN GET TO HER.
YOU GUYS JUST FIGURE OUT THE ESCAPE ROUTE!
CHAOS.
SNAP

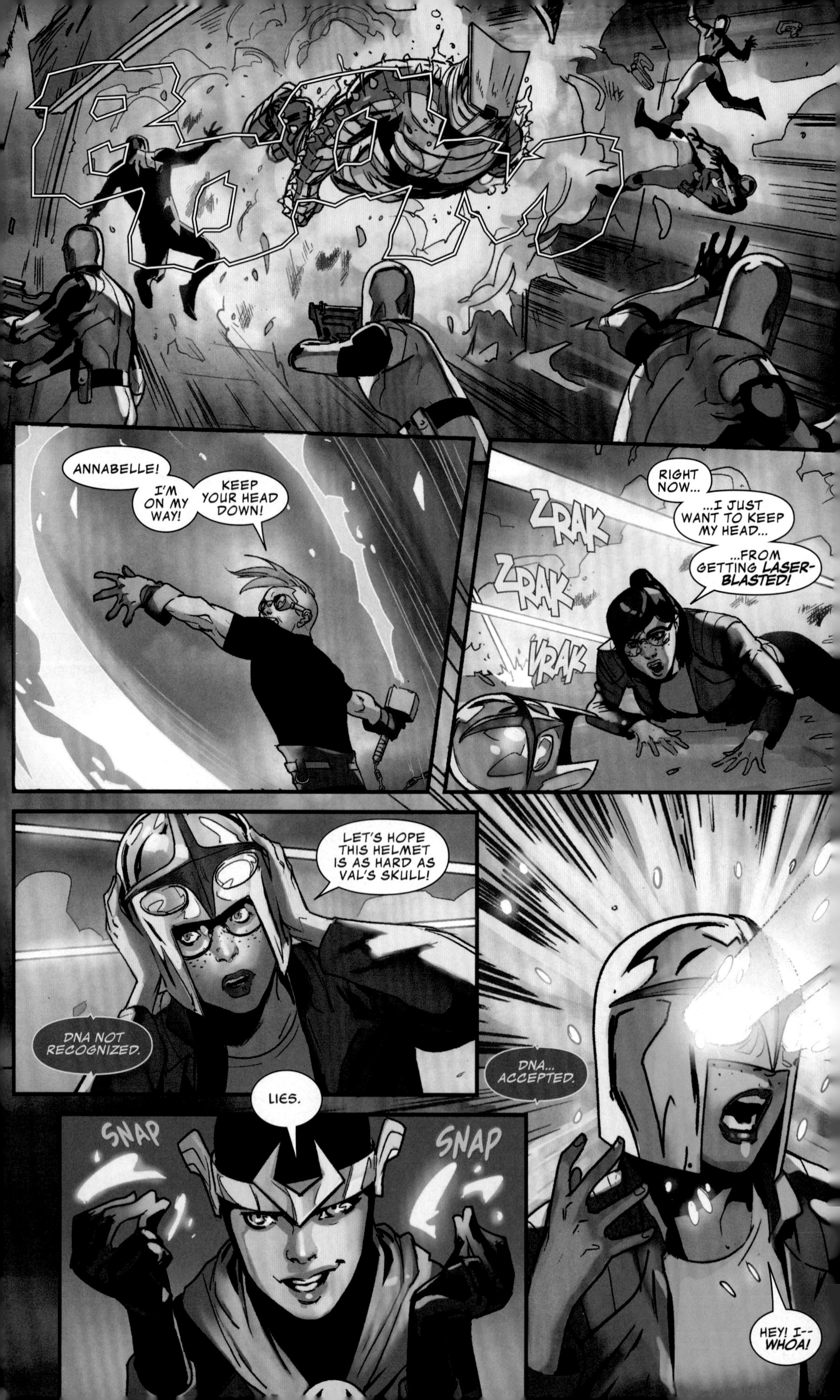
ANNABELLE!
I'M ON MY WAY!
KEEP YOUR HEAD DOWN!
RIGHT NOW...
...I JUST WANT TO KEEP MY HEAD...
...FROM GETTING LASER-BLASTED!
ZRAK
ZRAK
VRAK
LET'S HOPE THIS HELMET IS AS HARD AS VAL'S SKULL!
DNA NOT RECOGNIZED.
DNA... ACCEPTED.
LIES.
SNAP
SNAP
HEY! I-- WHOA!

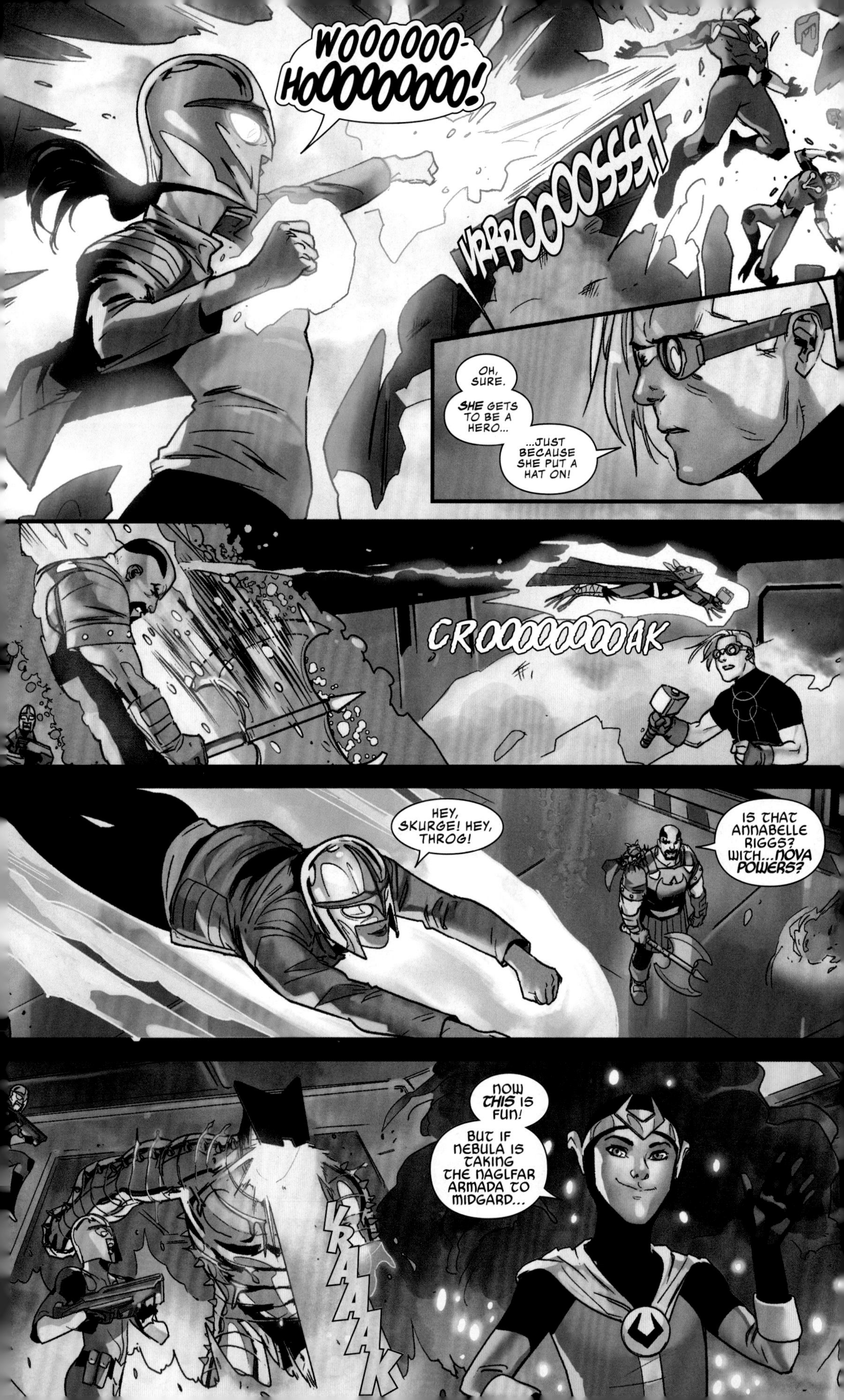
WOOOOOO-HOOOOOOOOO!
VRRROOOOSSSH
OH, SURE.
SHE GETS TO BE A HERO...
...JUST BECAUSE SHE PUT A HAT ON!
CROOOOOOOOOAK
HEY, SKURGE! HEY, THROG!
IS THAT ANNABELLE RIGGS? WITH...NOVA POWERS?
NOW THIS IS FUN!
BUT IF NEBULA IS TAKING THE NAGLFAR ARMADA TO MIDGARD...
KRAAAAK

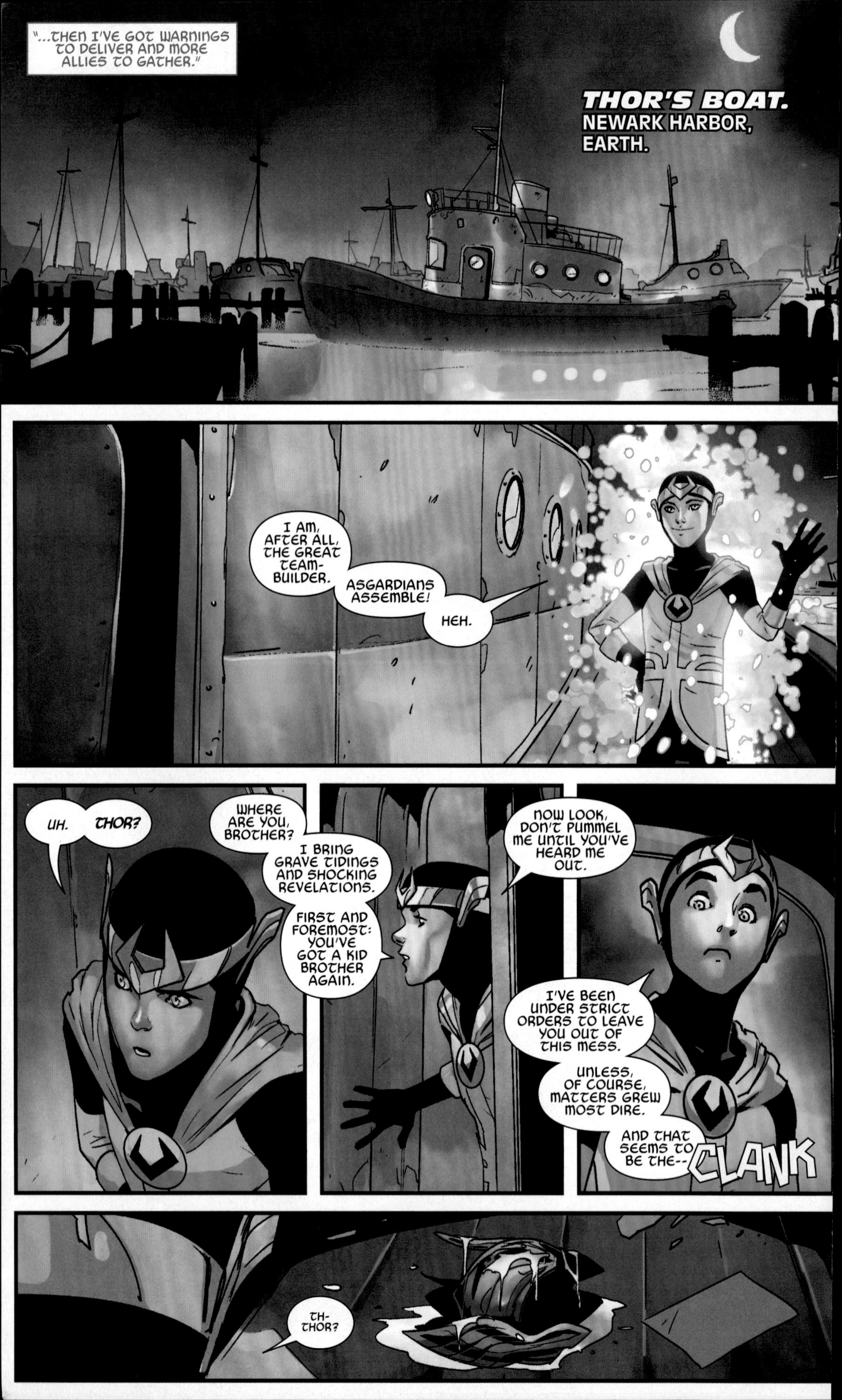
"...THEN I'VE GOT WARNINGS TO DELIVER AND MORE ALLIES TO GATHER."
THOR'S BOAT.
NEWARK HARBOR, EARTH.
I AM, AFTER ALL, THE GREAT TEAM-BUILDER.
ASGARDIANS ASSEMBLE!
HEH.
UH.
THOR?
WHERE ARE YOU, BROTHER?
I BRING GRAVE TIDINGS AND SHOCKING REVELATIONS.
FIRST AND FOREMOST: YOU'VE GOT A KID BROTHER AGAIN.
NOW LOOK, DON'T PUMMEL ME UNTIL YOU'VE HEARD ME OUT.
I'VE BEEN UNDER STRICT ORDERS TO LEAVE YOU OUT OF THIS MESS.
UNLESS, OF COURSE, MATTERS GREW MOST DIRE.
AND THAT SEEMS TO BE THE--
CLANK
TH-THOR?

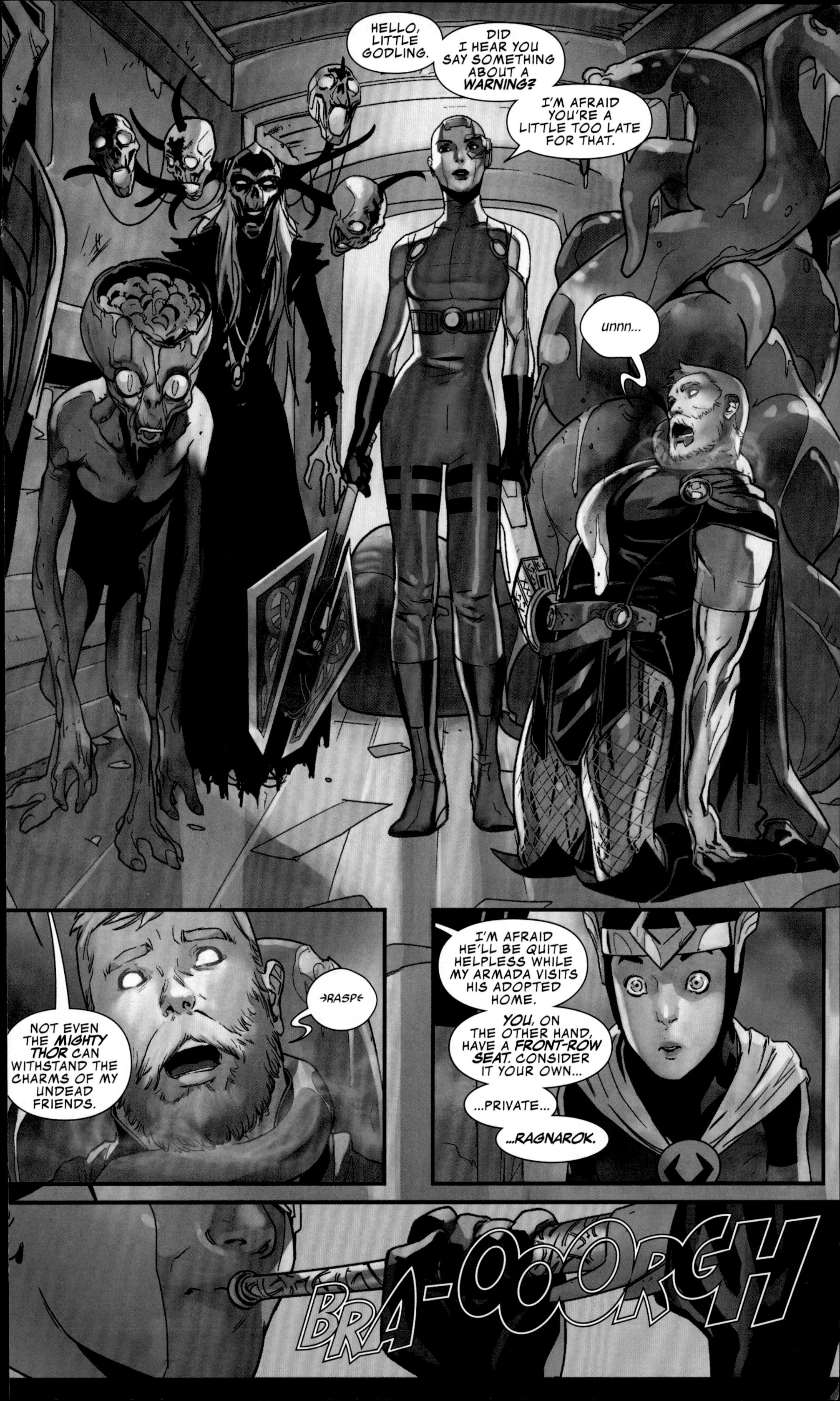

HELLO, LITTLE GODLING.
DID I HEAR YOU SAY SOMETHING ABOUT A *WARNING?*
I'M AFRAID YOU'RE A LITTLE TOO LATE FOR THAT.
unnn...
NOT EVEN THE *MIGHTY THOR* CAN WITHSTAND THE CHARMS OF MY UNDEAD FRIENDS.
RASP
I'M AFRAID HE'LL BE QUITE HELPLESS WHILE MY ARMADA VISITS HIS ADOPTED HOME.
YOU, ON THE OTHER HAND, HAVE A *FRONT-ROW SEAT*. CONSIDER IT YOUR OWN...
...PRIVATE...
...RAGNAROK.
BRA-OOORCH

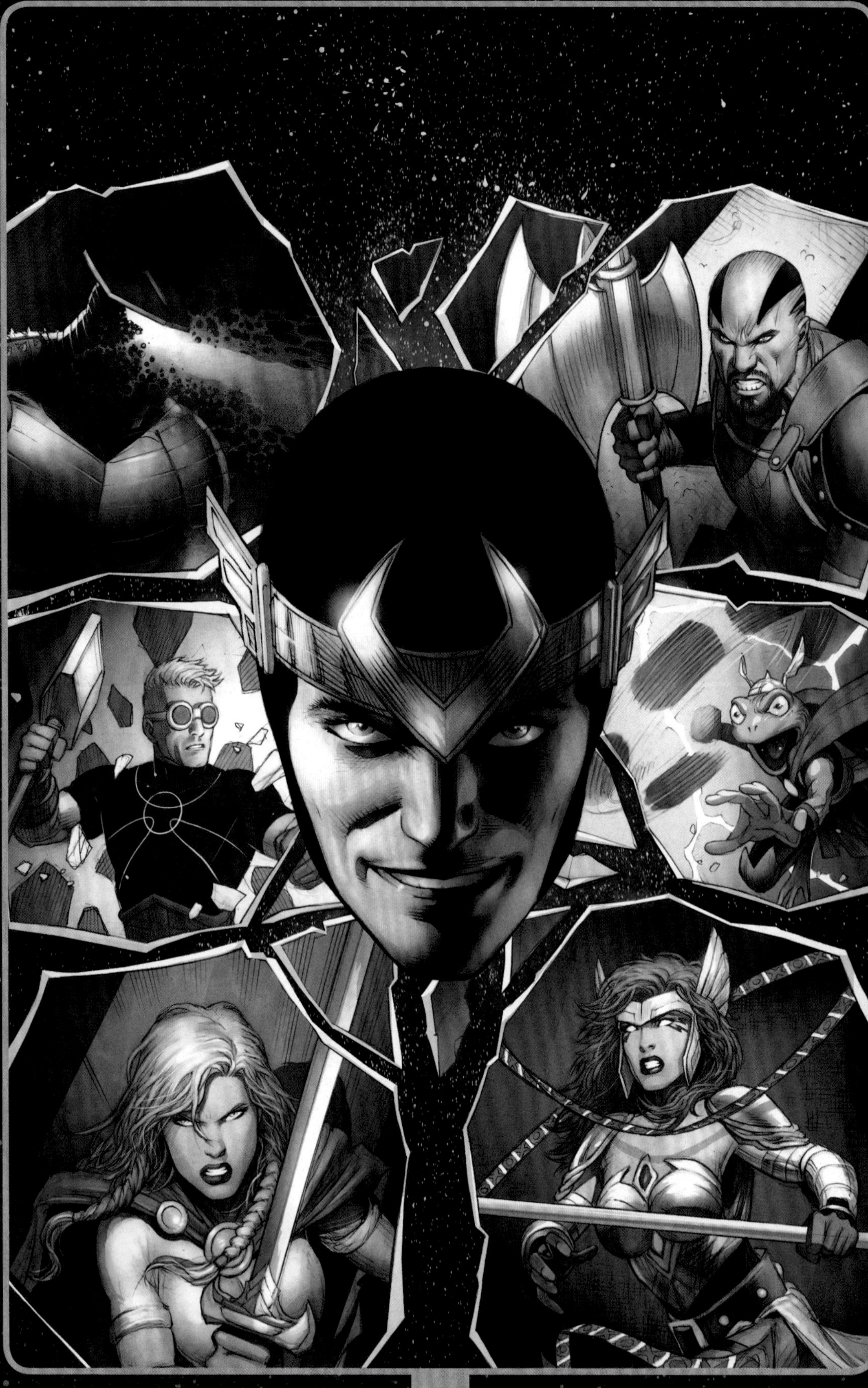

5

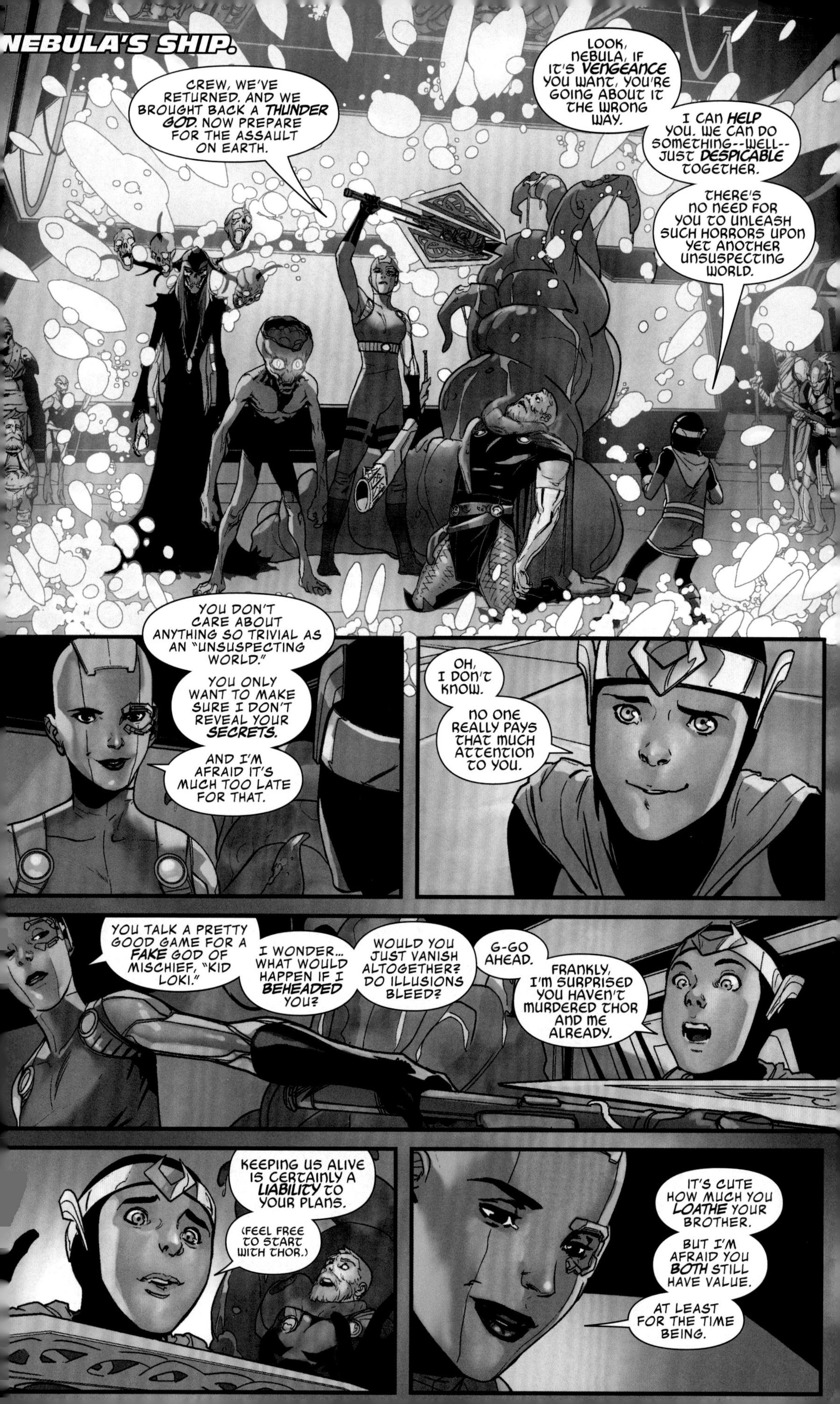
NEBULA'S SHIP.
CREW, WE'VE RETURNED. AND WE BROUGHT BACK A THUNDER GOD. NOW PREPARE FOR THE ASSAULT ON EARTH.
LOOK, NEBULA, IF IT'S VENGEANCE YOU WANT, YOU'RE GOING ABOUT IT THE WRONG WAY.
I CAN HELP YOU. WE CAN DO SOMETHING--WELL--JUST DESPICABLE TOGETHER.
THERE'S NO NEED FOR YOU TO UNLEASH SUCH HORRORS UPON YET ANOTHER UNSUSPECTING WORLD.
YOU DON'T CARE ABOUT ANYTHING SO TRIVIAL AS AN "UNSUSPECTING WORLD."
YOU ONLY WANT TO MAKE SURE I DON'T REVEAL YOUR SECRETS.
AND I'M AFRAID IT'S MUCH TOO LATE FOR THAT.
OH, I DON'T KNOW.
NO ONE REALLY PAYS THAT MUCH ATTENTION TO YOU.
YOU TALK A PRETTY GOOD GAME FOR A FAKE GOD OF MISCHIEF, "KID LOKI."
I WONDER... WHAT WOULD HAPPEN IF I BEHEADED YOU?
WOULD YOU JUST VANISH ALTOGETHER? DO ILLUSIONS BLEED?
G-GO AHEAD.
FRANKLY, I'M SURPRISED YOU HAVEN'T MURDERED THOR AND ME ALREADY.
KEEPING US ALIVE IS CERTAINLY A LIABILITY TO YOUR PLANS.
(FEEL FREE TO START WITH THOR.)
IT'S CUTE HOW MUCH YOU LOATHE YOUR BROTHER.
BUT I'M AFRAID YOU BOTH STILL HAVE VALUE.
AT LEAST FOR THE TIME BEING.

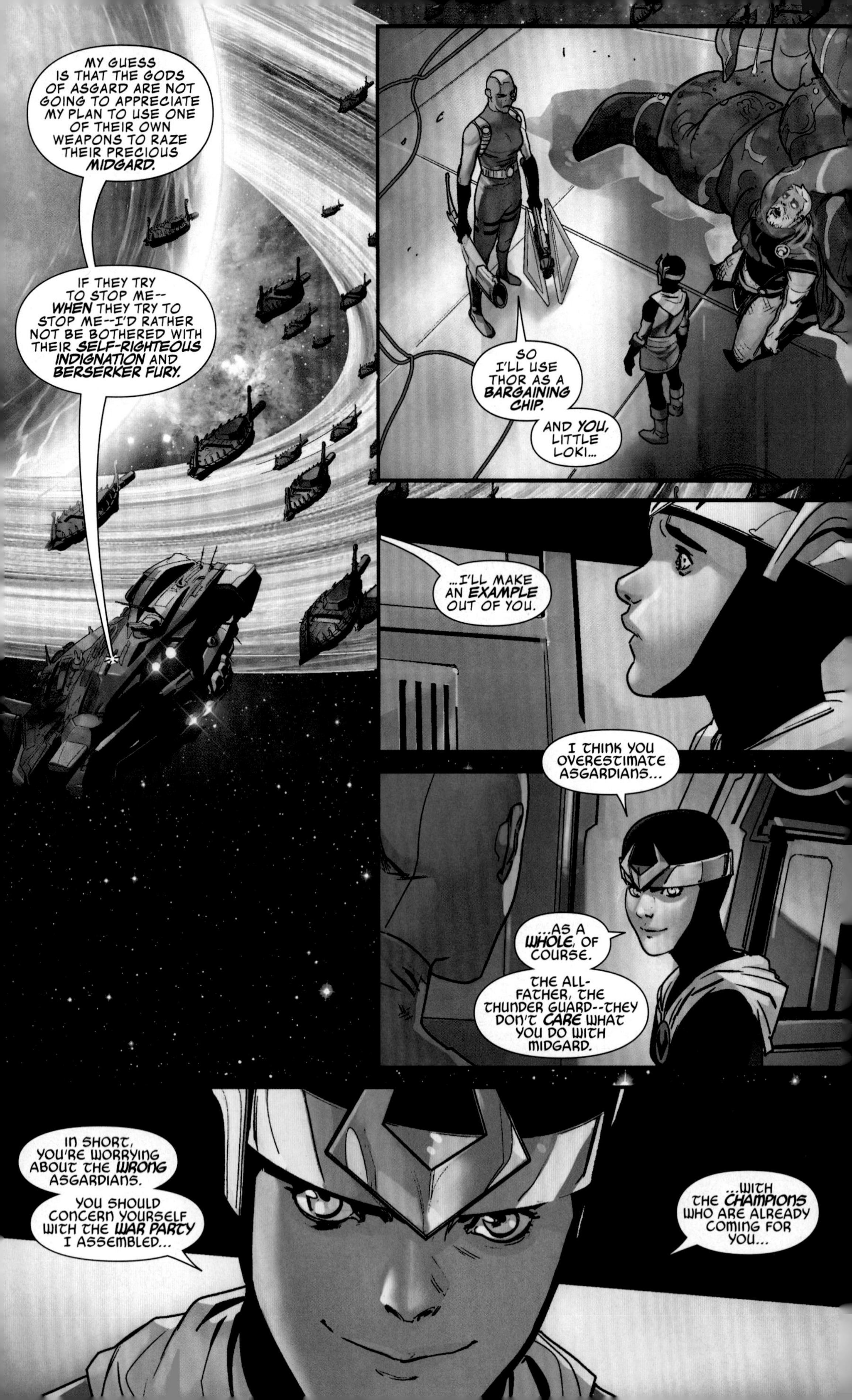
MY GUESS IS THAT THE GODS OF ASGARD ARE NOT GOING TO APPRECIATE MY PLAN TO USE ONE OF THEIR OWN WEAPONS TO RAZE THEIR PRECIOUS MIDGARD.
IF THEY TRY TO STOP ME-- WHEN THEY TRY TO STOP ME--I'D RATHER NOT BE BOTHERED WITH THEIR SELF-RIGHTEOUS INDIGNATION AND BERSERKER FURY.
SO I'LL USE THOR AS A BARGAINING CHIP.
AND YOU, LITTLE LOKI...
...I'LL MAKE AN EXAMPLE OUT OF YOU.
I THINK YOU OVERESTIMATE ASGARDIANS...
...AS A WHOLE, OF COURSE.
THE ALL-FATHER, THE THUNDER GUARD--THEY DON'T CARE WHAT YOU DO WITH MIDGARD.
IN SHORT, YOU'RE WORRYING ABOUT THE WRONG ASGARDIANS.
YOU SHOULD CONCERN YOURSELF WITH THE WAR PARTY I ASSEMBLED...
...WITH THE CHAMPIONS WHO ARE ALREADY COMING FOR YOU...

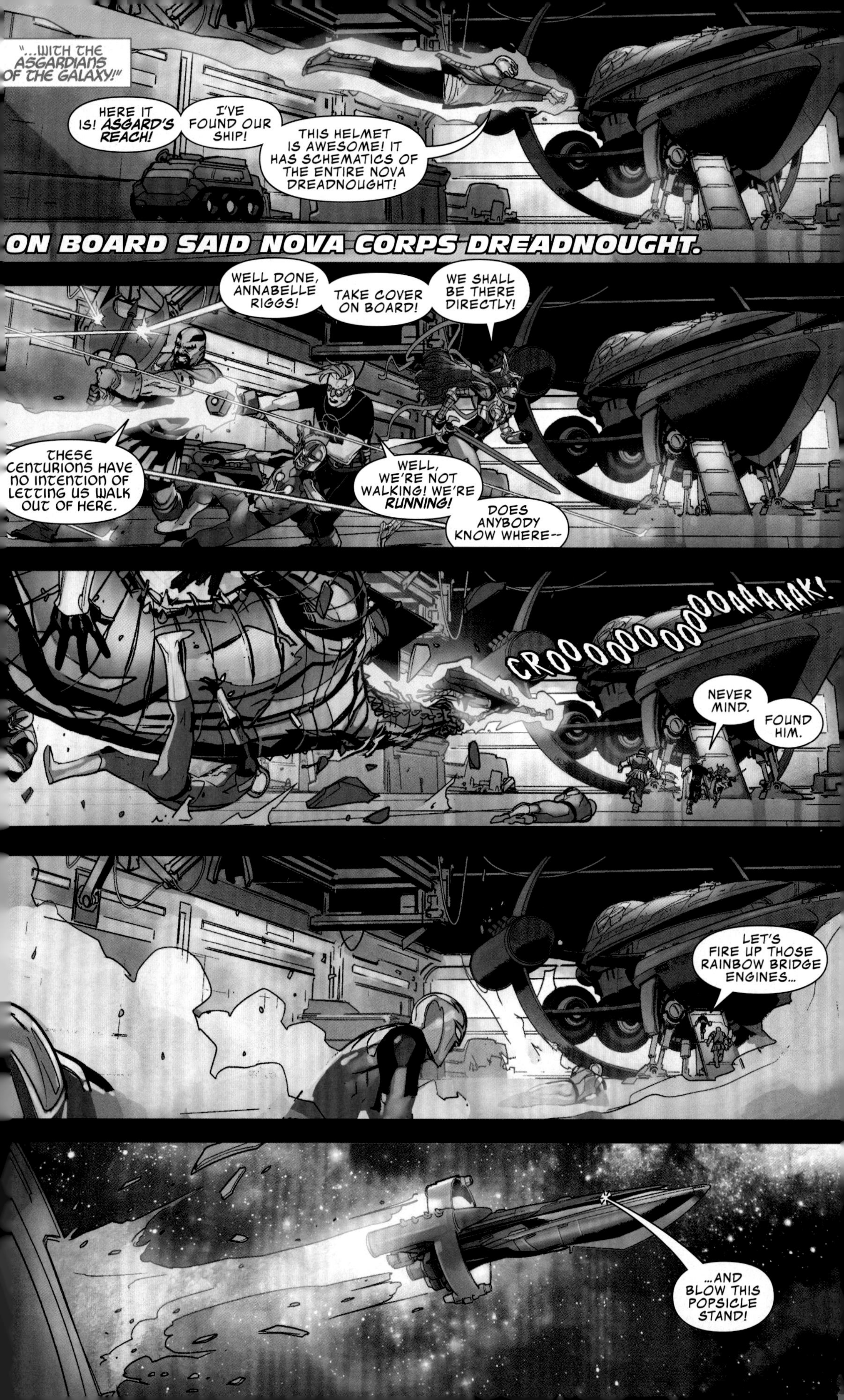
"...WITH THE ASGARDIANS OF THE GALAXY!"
HERE IT IS! ASGARD'S REACH!
I'VE FOUND OUR SHIP!
THIS HELMET IS AWESOME! IT HAS SCHEMATICS OF THE ENTIRE NOVA DREADNOUGHT!
ON BOARD SAID NOVA CORPS DREADNOUGHT.
WELL DONE, ANNABELLE RIGGS!
TAKE COVER ON BOARD!
WE SHALL BE THERE DIRECTLY!
THESE CENTURIONS HAVE NO INTENTION OF LETTING US WALK OUT OF HERE.
WELL, WE'RE NOT WALKING! WE'RE RUNNING!
DOES ANYBODY KNOW WHERE--
CROOOOOOOOOOOAAAAAK!
NEVER MIND.
FOUND HIM.
LET'S FIRE UP THOSE RAINBOW BRIDGE ENGINES...
...AND BLOW THIS POPSICLE STAND!

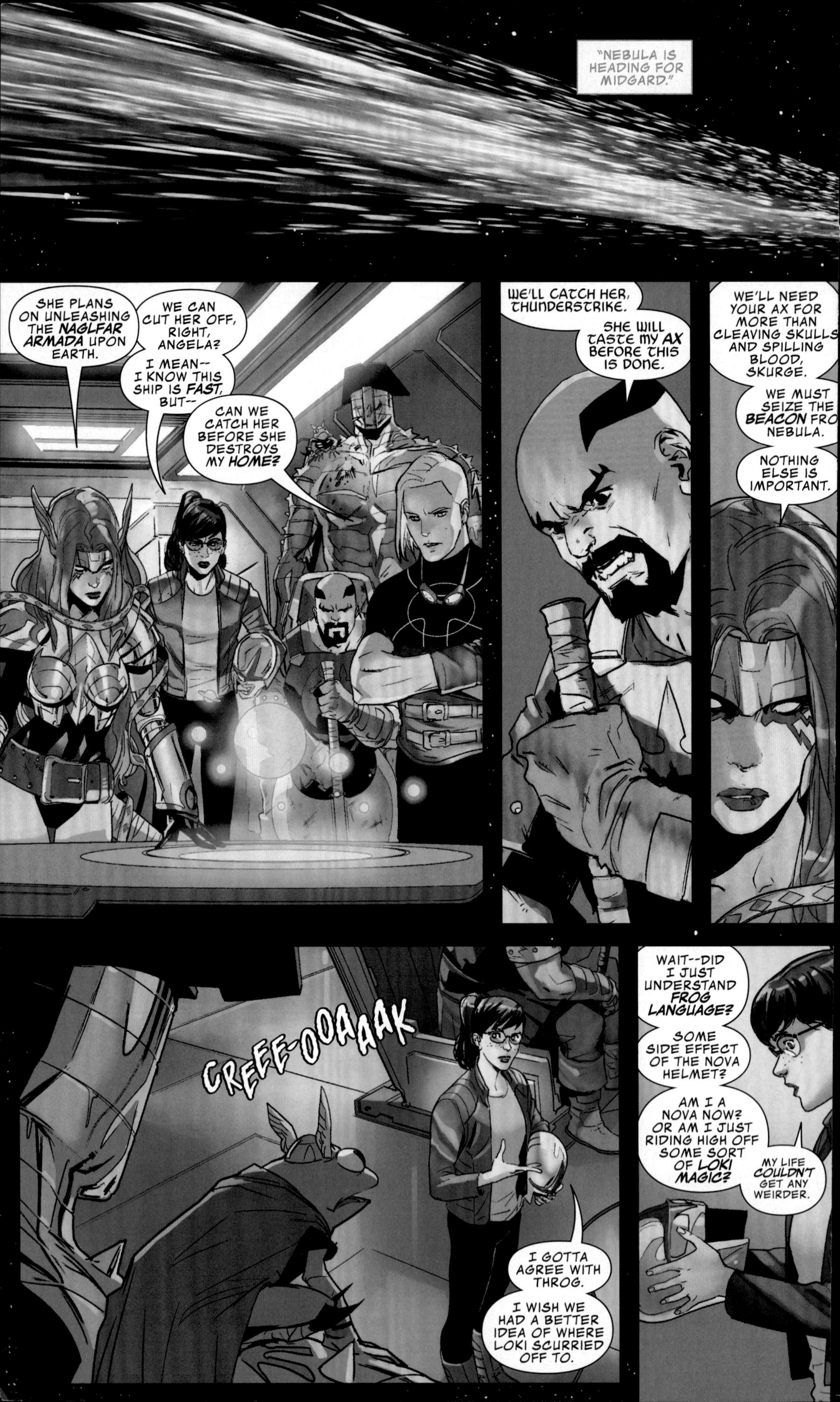

"NEBULA IS HEADING FOR MIDGARD."
SHE PLANS ON UNLEASHING THE NAGLFAR ARMADA UPON EARTH.
WE CAN CUT HER OFF, RIGHT, ANGELA?
I MEAN-- I KNOW THIS SHIP IS FAST, BUT--
CAN WE CATCH HER BEFORE SHE DESTROYS MY HOME?
WE'LL CATCH HER, THUNDERSTRIKE.
SHE WILL TASTE MY AX BEFORE THIS IS DONE.
WE'LL NEED YOUR AX FOR MORE THAN CLEAVING SKULLS AND SPILLING BLOOD, SKURGE.
WE MUST SEIZE THE BEACON FRO NEBULA.
NOTHING ELSE IS IMPORTANT.
CREEE-OOAAAK
I GOTTA AGREE WITH THROG.
I WISH WE HAD A BETTER IDEA OF WHERE LOKI SCURRIED OFF TO.
WAIT--DID I JUST UNDERSTAND FROG LANGUAGE?
SOME SIDE EFFECT OF THE NOVA HELMET?
AM I A NOVA NOW? OR AM I JUST RIDING HIGH OFF SOME SORT OF LOKI MAGIC?
MY LIFE COULDN'T GET ANY WEIRDER.

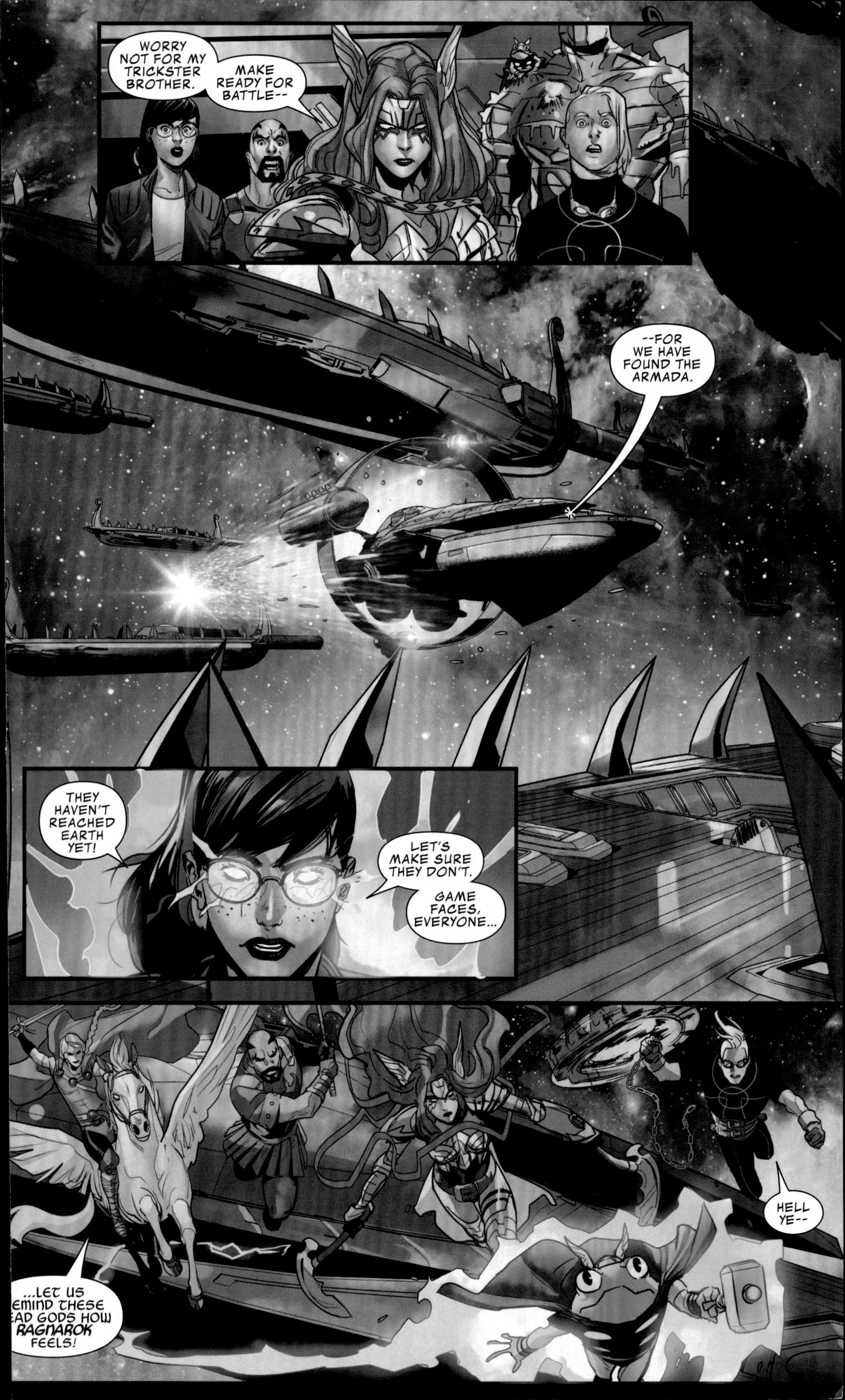
WORRY NOT FOR MY TRICKSTER BROTHER.
MAKE READY FOR BATTLE--
--FOR WE HAVE FOUND THE ARMADA.
THEY HAVEN'T REACHED EARTH YET!
LET'S MAKE SURE THEY DON'T.
GAME FACES, EVERYONE...
...LET US EMIND THESE EAD GODS HOW RAGNAROK FEELS!
HELL YE--

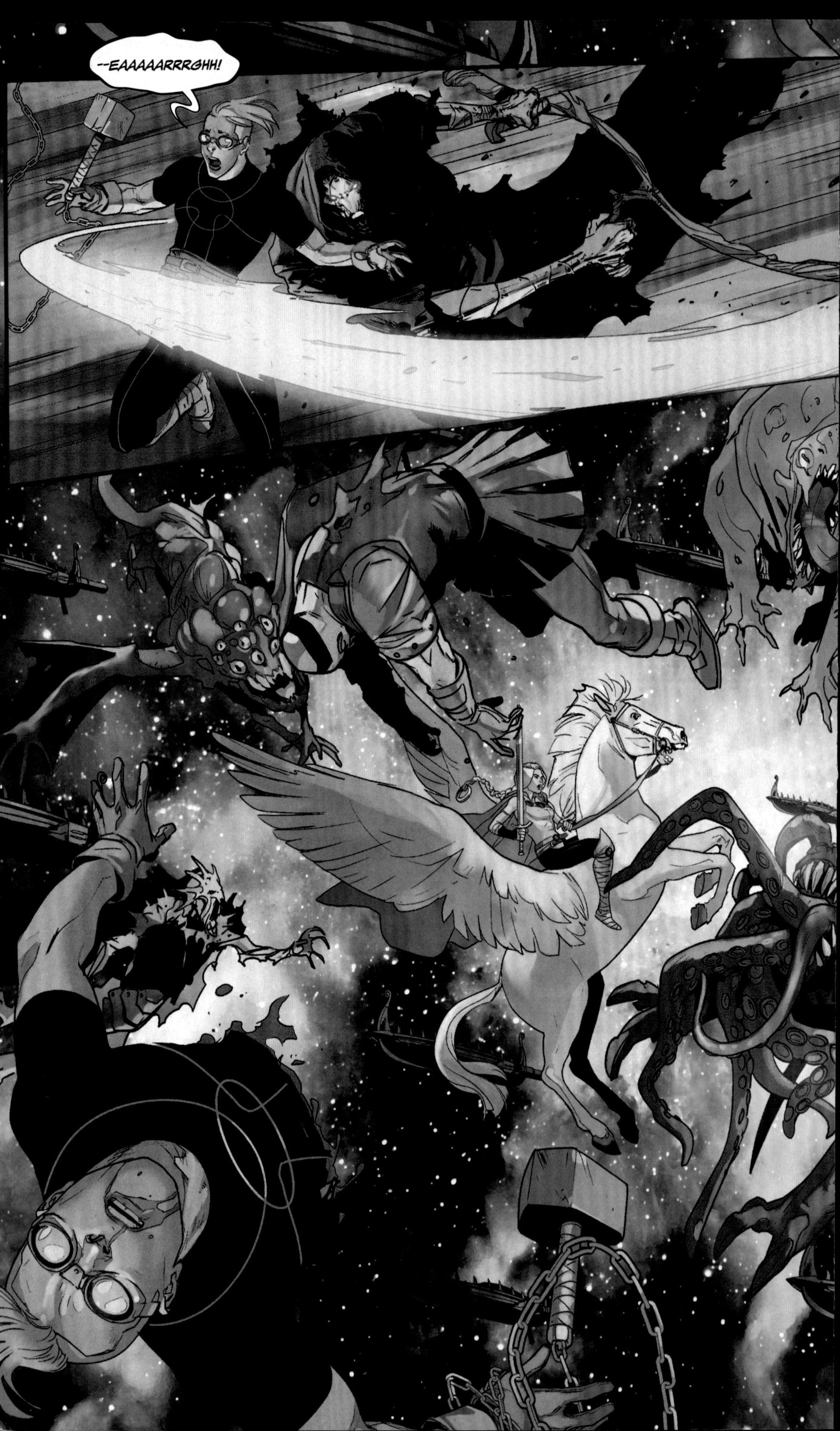
--EAAAAARRRGHH!

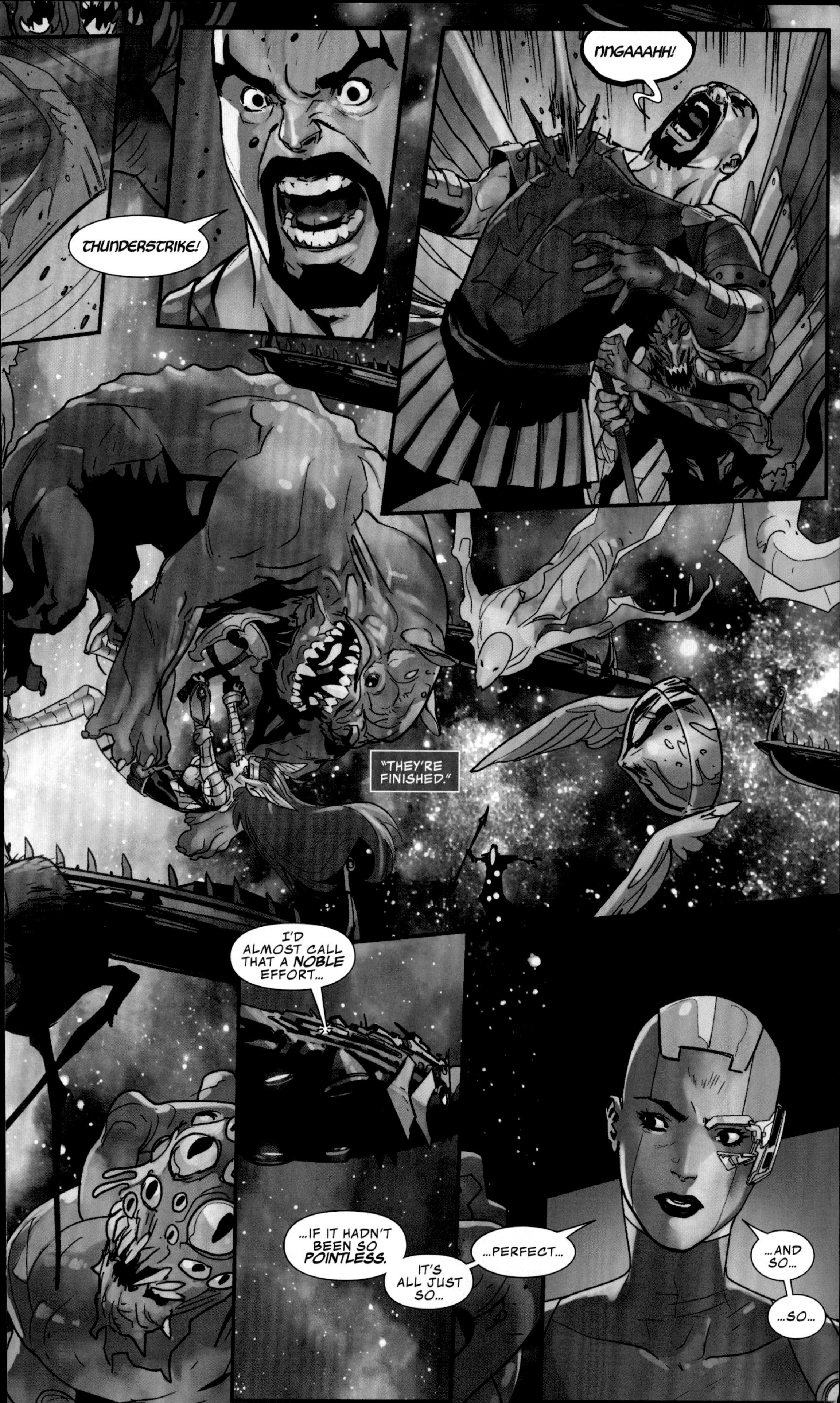
THUNDERSTRIKE!
NNGAAAHH!
"THEY'RE FINISHED."
I'D ALMOST CALL THAT A NOBLE EFFORT...
...IF IT HADN'T BEEN SO POINTLESS.
IT'S ALL JUST SO...
...PERFECT...
...AND SO...
...SO...

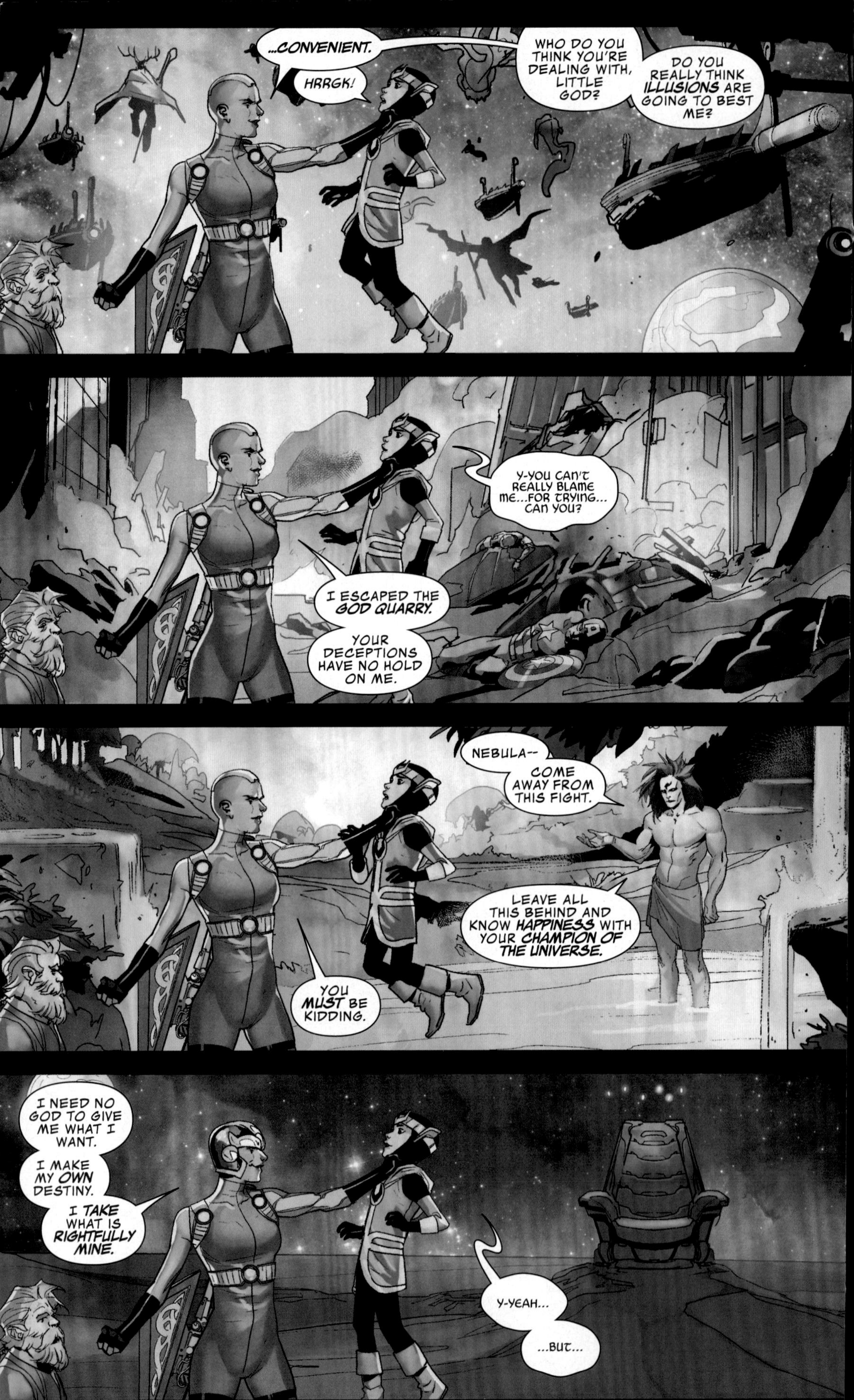
...CONVENIENT.
HRRGK!
WHO DO YOU THINK YOU'RE DEALING WITH, LITTLE GOD?
DO YOU REALLY THINK ILLUSIONS ARE GOING TO BEST ME?
Y-YOU CAN'T REALLY BLAME ME...FOR TRYING... CAN YOU?
I ESCAPED THE GOD QUARRY.
YOUR DECEPTIONS HAVE NO HOLD ON ME.
NEBULA--
COME AWAY FROM THIS FIGHT.
LEAVE ALL THIS BEHIND AND KNOW HAPPINESS WITH YOUR CHAMPION OF THE UNIVERSE.
YOU MUST BE KIDDING.
I NEED NO GOD TO GIVE ME WHAT I WANT.
I MAKE MY OWN DESTINY.
I TAKE WHAT IS RIGHTFULLY MINE.
Y-YEAH...
...BUT...

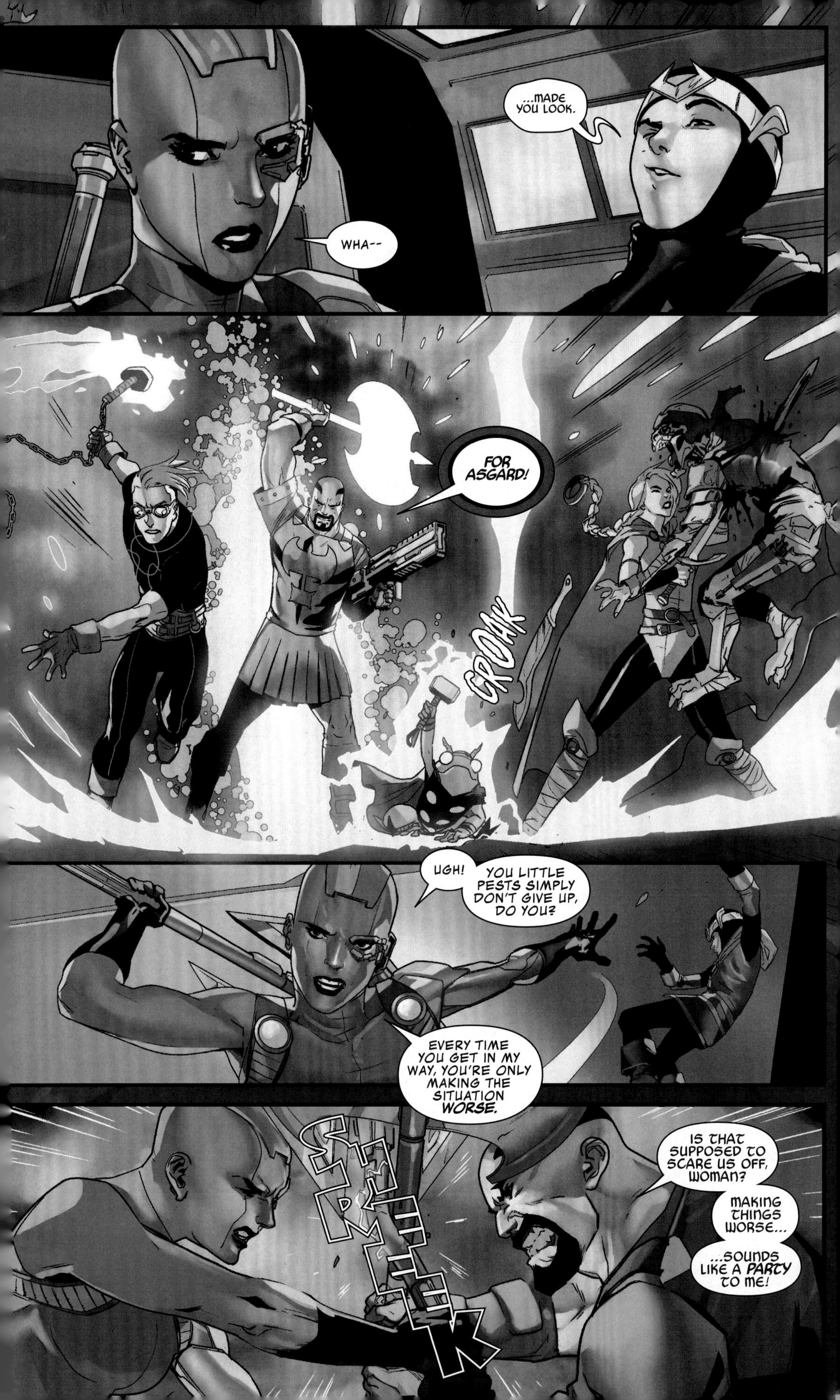

...MADE YOU LOOK.
WHA--
FOR ASGARD!
GROAK
UGH!
YOU LITTLE PESTS SIMPLY DON'T GIVE UP, DO YOU?
EVERY TIME YOU GET IN MY WAY, YOU'RE ONLY MAKING THE SITUATION WORSE.
SHREEK
IS THAT SUPPOSED TO SCARE US OFF, WOMAN?
MAKING THINGS WORSE...
...SOUNDS LIKE A PARTY TO ME!

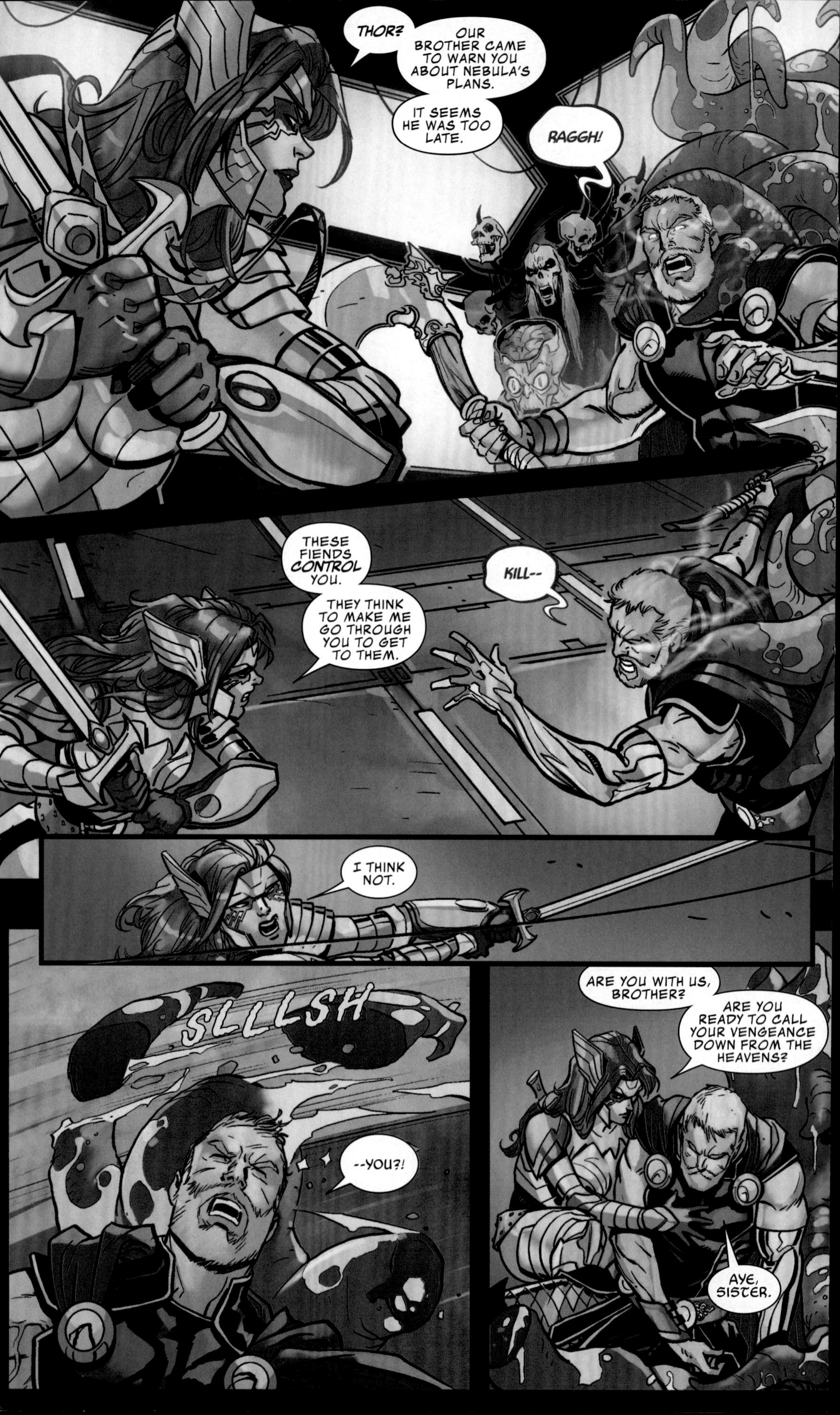
THOR?
OUR BROTHER CAME TO WARN YOU ABOUT NEBULA'S PLANS.
IT SEEMS HE WAS TOO LATE.
RAGGH!
THESE FIENDS CONTROL YOU.
THEY THINK TO MAKE ME GO THROUGH YOU TO GET TO THEM.
KILL--
I THINK NOT.
SLLLSH
--YOU?!
ARE YOU WITH US, BROTHER?
ARE YOU READY TO CALL YOUR VENGEANCE DOWN FROM THE HEAVENS?
AYE, SISTER.

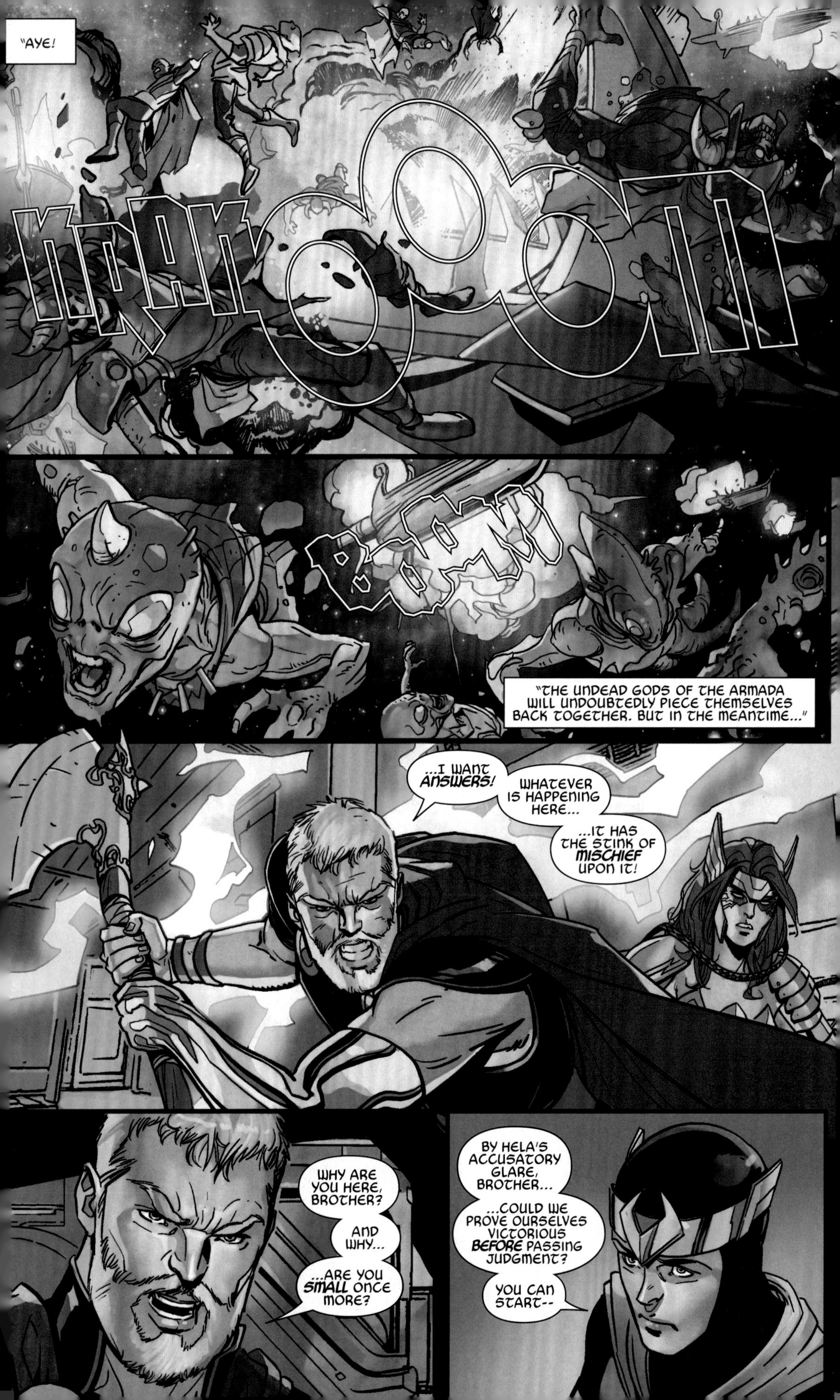

"AYE!
KRAKOOOM
BOOM
"THE UNDEAD GODS OF THE ARMADA WILL UNDOUBTEDLY PIECE THEMSELVES BACK TOGETHER. BUT IN THE MEANTIME..."
...I WANT ANSWERS!
WHATEVER IS HAPPENING HERE...
...IT HAS THE STINK OF MISCHIEF UPON IT!
WHY ARE YOU HERE, BROTHER?
AND WHY...
...ARE YOU SMALL ONCE MORE?
BY HELA'S ACCUSATORY GLARE, BROTHER...
...COULD WE PROVE OURSELVES VICTORIOUS BEFORE PASSING JUDGMENT?
YOU CAN START--

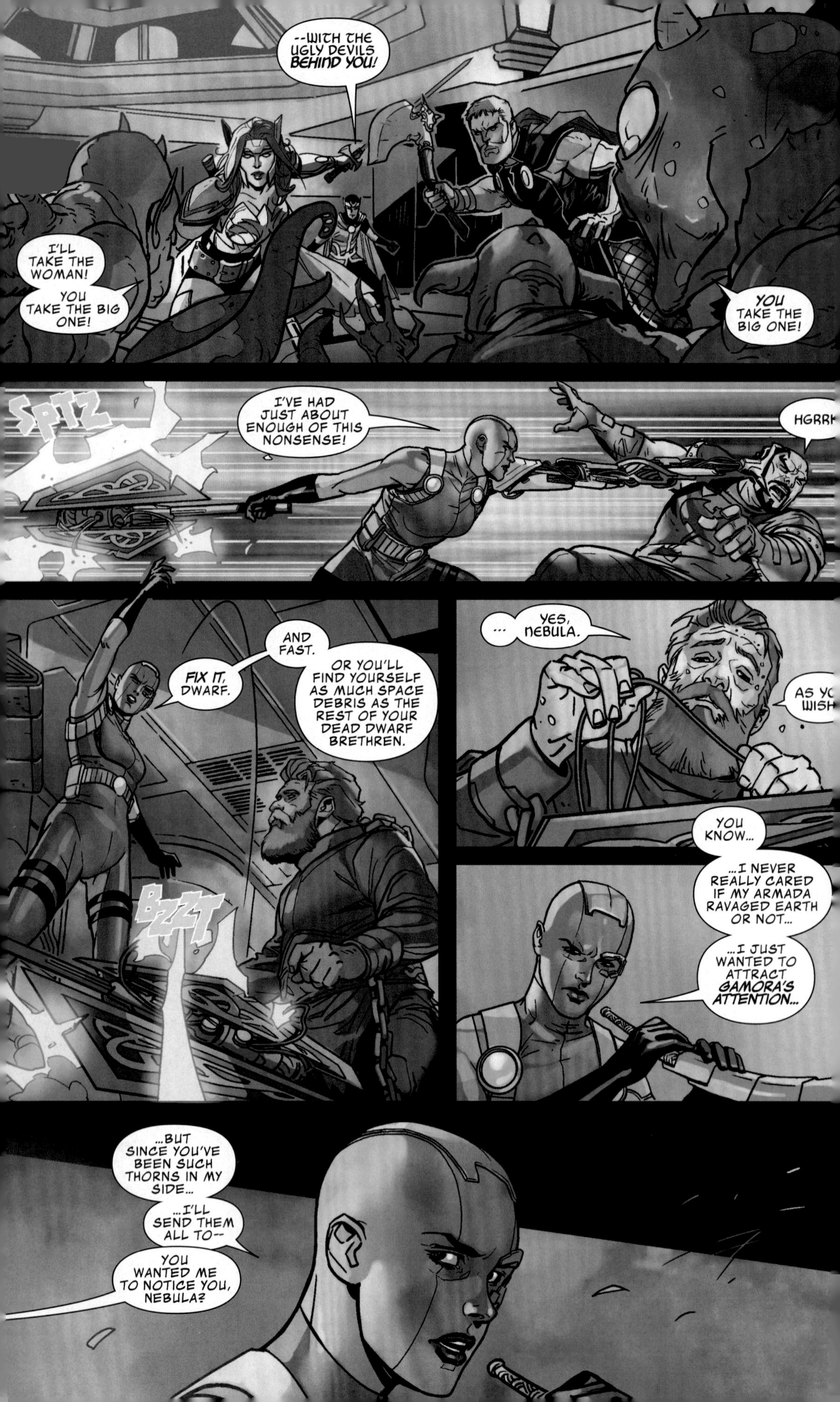
--WITH THE UGLY DEVILS BEHIND YOU!
I'LL TAKE THE WOMAN!
YOU TAKE THE BIG ONE!
YOU TAKE THE BIG ONE!
SPTZ
I'VE HAD JUST ABOUT ENOUGH OF THIS NONSENSE!
HGRRK
FIX IT, DWARF.
AND FAST.
OR YOU'LL FIND YOURSELF AS MUCH SPACE DEBRIS AS THE REST OF YOUR DEAD DWARF BRETHREN.
BZZT
... YES, NEBULA.
AS YO WISH
YOU KNOW...
...I NEVER REALLY CARED IF MY ARMADA RAVAGED EARTH OR NOT...
...I JUST WANTED TO ATTRACT GAMORA'S ATTENTION...
...BUT SINCE YOU'VE BEEN SUCH THORNS IN MY SIDE...
...I'LL SEND THEM ALL TO--
YOU WANTED ME TO NOTICE YOU, NEBULA?

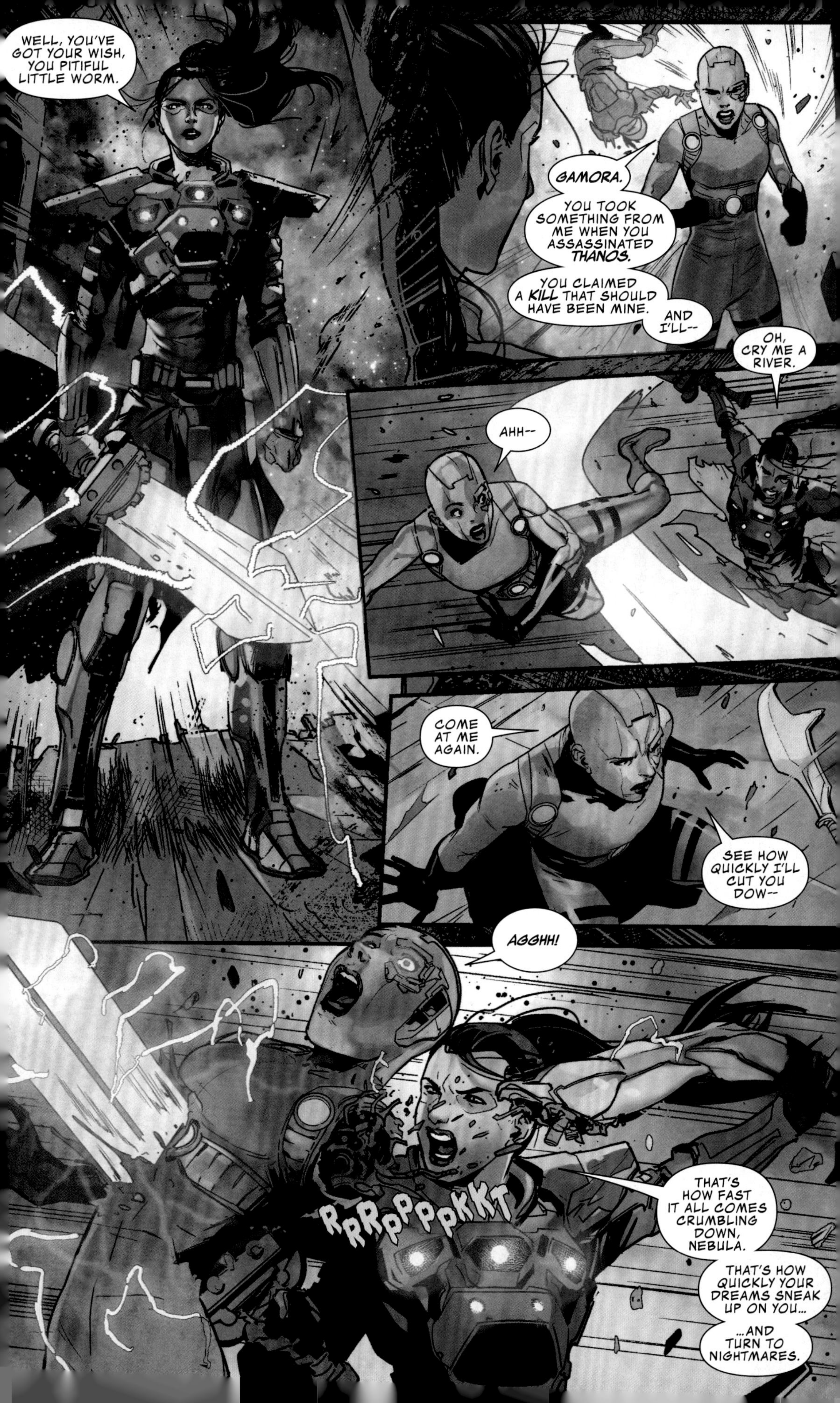

WELL, YOU'VE GOT YOUR WISH, YOU PITIFUL LITTLE WORM.
GAMORA.
YOU TOOK SOMETHING FROM ME WHEN YOU ASSASSINATED THANOS.
YOU CLAIMED A KILL THAT SHOULD HAVE BEEN MINE.
AND I'LL--
OH, CRY ME A RIVER.
AHH--
COME AT ME AGAIN.
SEE HOW QUICKLY I'LL CUT YOU DOW--
AGGHH!
RRRPPPPKKT
THAT'S HOW FAST IT ALL COMES CRUMBLING DOWN, NEBULA.
THAT'S HOW QUICKLY YOUR DREAMS SNEAK UP ON YOU...
...AND TURN TO NIGHTMARES.

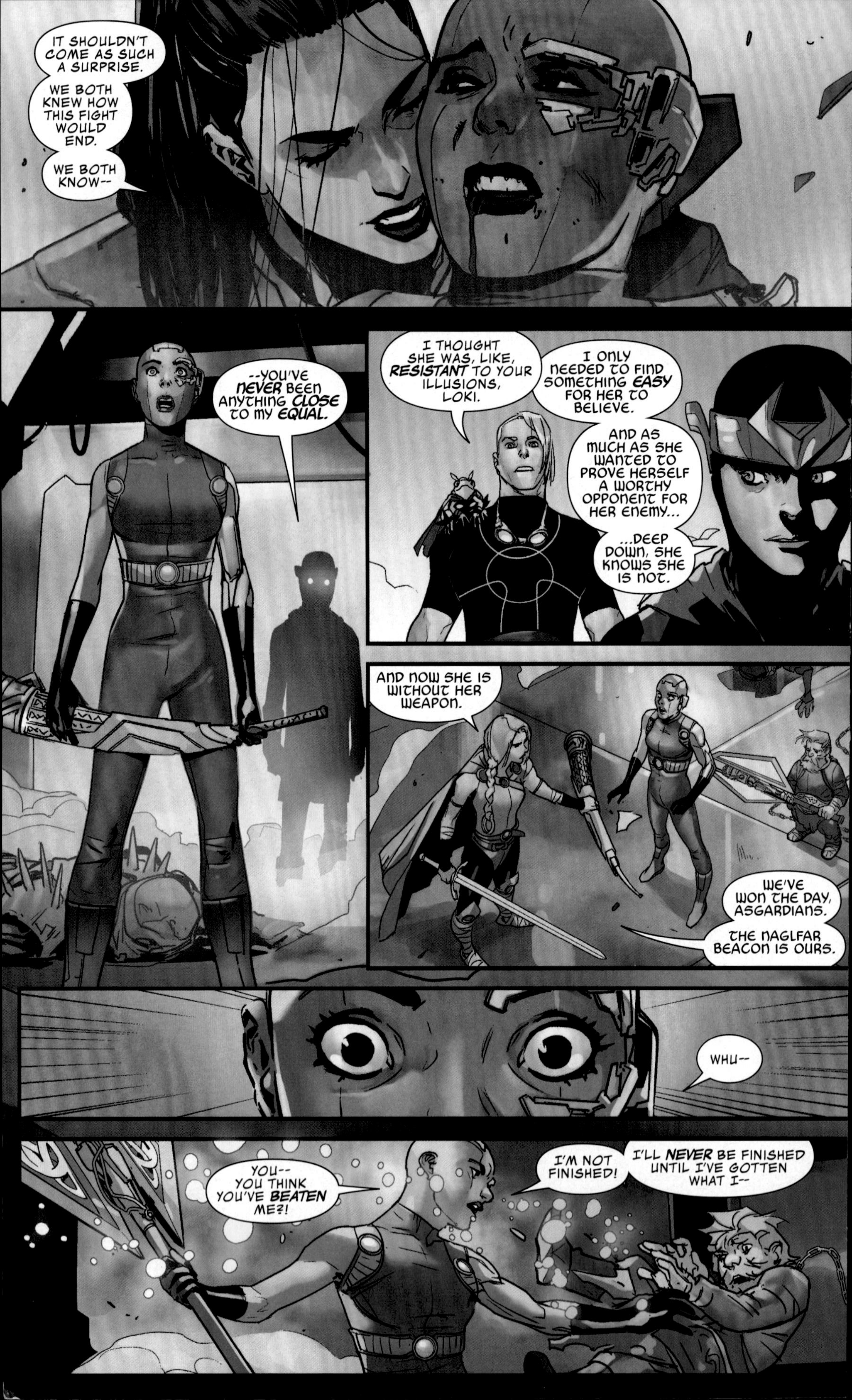
IT SHOULDN'T COME AS SUCH A SURPRISE.
WE BOTH KNEW HOW THIS FIGHT WOULD END.
WE BOTH KNOW--
--YOU'VE NEVER BEEN ANYTHING CLOSE TO MY EQUAL.
I THOUGHT SHE WAS, LIKE, RESISTANT TO YOUR ILLUSIONS, LOKI.
I ONLY NEEDED TO FIND SOMETHING EASY FOR HER TO BELIEVE.
AND AS MUCH AS SHE WANTED TO PROVE HERSELF A WORTHY OPPONENT FOR HER ENEMY...
...DEEP DOWN, SHE KNOWS SHE IS NOT.
AND NOW SHE IS WITHOUT HER WEAPON.
WE'VE WON THE DAY, ASGARDIANS.
THE NAGLFAR BEACON IS OURS.
WHU--
YOU-- YOU THINK YOU'VE BEATEN ME?!
I'M NOT FINISHED!
I'LL NEVER BE FINISHED UNTIL I'VE GOTTEN WHAT I--

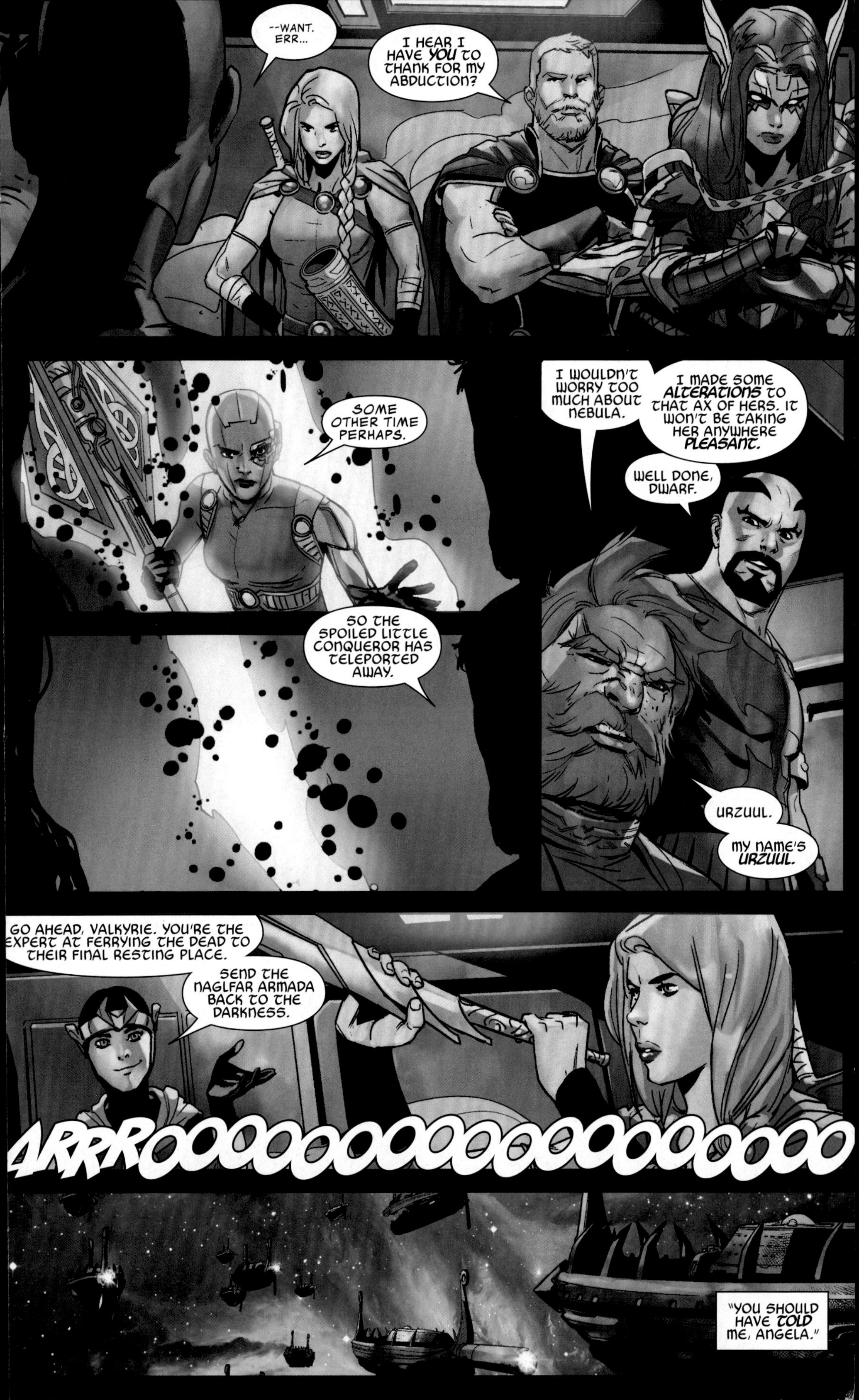
--WANT. ERR...
I HEAR I HAVE YOU TO THANK FOR MY ABDUCTION?
SOME OTHER TIME PERHAPS.
SO THE SPOILED LITTLE CONQUEROR HAS TELEPORTED AWAY.
I WOULDN'T WORRY TOO MUCH ABOUT NEBULA.
I MADE SOME ALTERATIONS TO THAT AX OF HERS. IT WON'T BE TAKING HER ANYWHERE PLEASANT.
WELL DONE, DWARF.
URZUUL.
MY NAME'S URZUUL.
GO AHEAD, VALKYRIE. YOU'RE THE EXPERT AT FERRYING THE DEAD TO THEIR FINAL RESTING PLACE.
SEND THE NAGLFAR ARMADA BACK TO THE DARKNESS.
ARRROOOOOOOOOOOOOOOOOO
"YOU SHOULD HAVE TOLD ME, ANGELA."

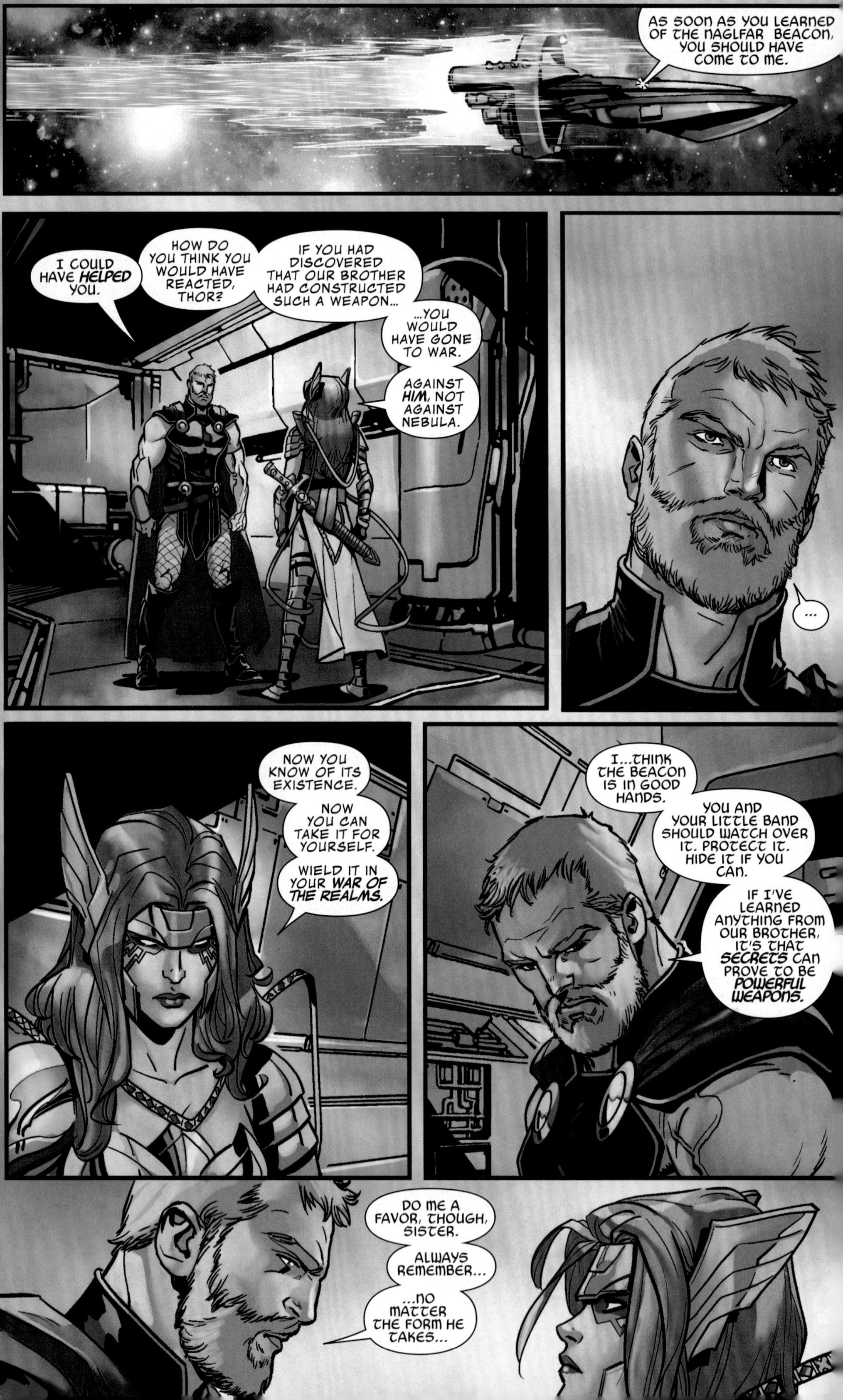

AS SOON AS YOU LEARNED OF THE NAGLFAR BEACON, YOU SHOULD HAVE COME TO ME.
I COULD HAVE HELPED YOU.
HOW DO YOU THINK YOU WOULD HAVE REACTED, THOR?
IF YOU HAD DISCOVERED THAT OUR BROTHER HAD CONSTRUCTED SUCH A WEAPON...
...YOU WOULD HAVE GONE TO WAR.
AGAINST HIM, NOT AGAINST NEBULA.
...
NOW YOU KNOW OF ITS EXISTENCE.
NOW YOU CAN TAKE IT FOR YOURSELF.
WIELD IT IN YOUR WAR OF THE REALMS.
I...THINK THE BEACON IS IN GOOD HANDS.
YOU AND YOUR LITTLE BAND SHOULD WATCH OVER IT. PROTECT IT. HIDE IT IF YOU CAN.
IF I'VE LEARNED ANYTHING FROM OUR BROTHER, IT'S THAT SECRETS CAN PROVE TO BE POWERFUL WEAPONS.
DO ME A FAVOR, THOUGH, SISTER.
ALWAYS REMEMBER...
...NO MATTER THE FORM HE TAKES...

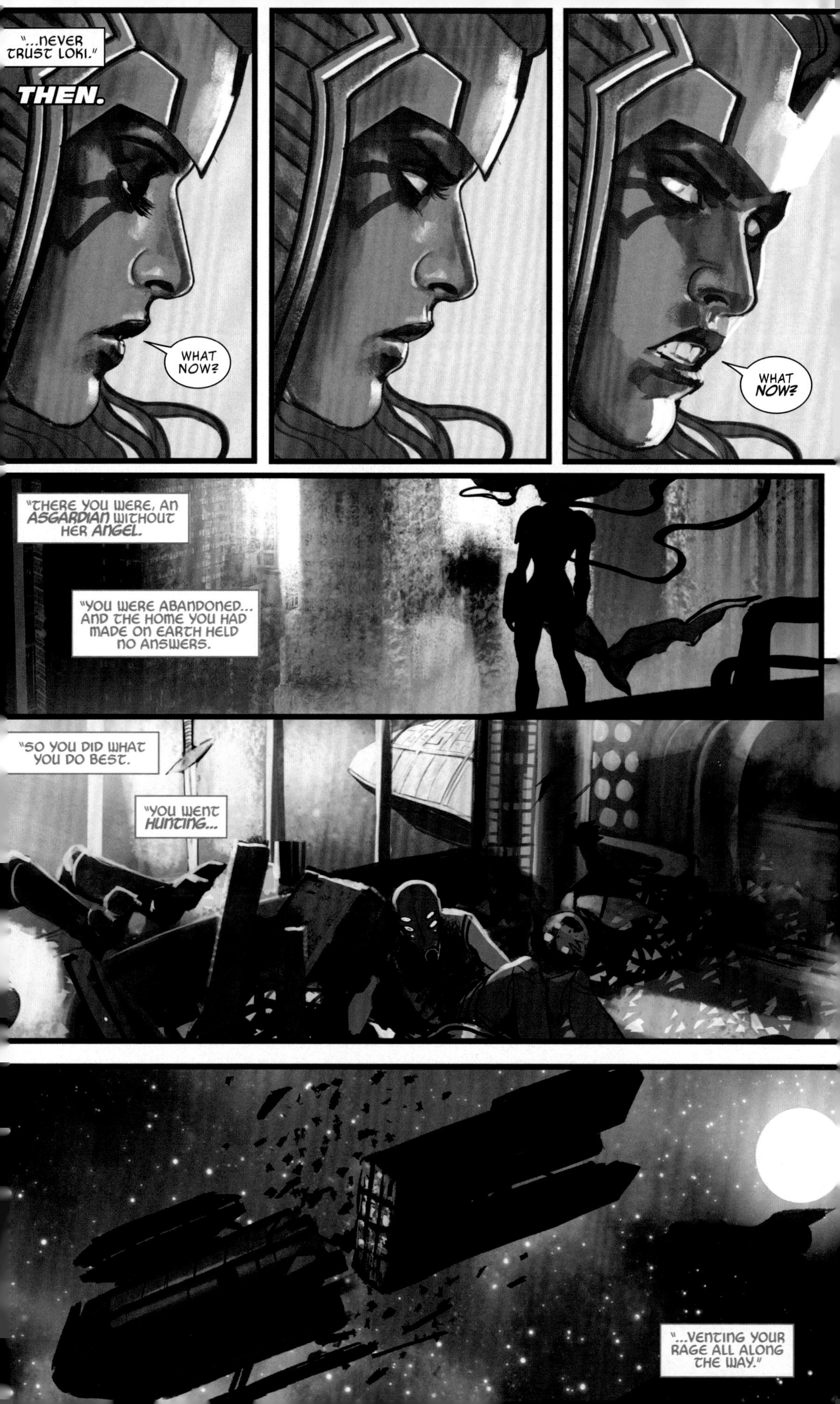
"...NEVER TRUST LOKI."
THEN.
WHAT NOW?
WHAT NOW?
"THERE YOU WERE, AN ASGARDIAN WITHOUT HER ANGEL.
"YOU WERE ABANDONED... AND THE HOME YOU HAD MADE ON EARTH HELD NO ANSWERS.
"SO YOU DID WHAT YOU DO BEST.
"YOU WENT HUNTING...
"...VENTING YOUR RAGE ALL ALONG THE WAY."

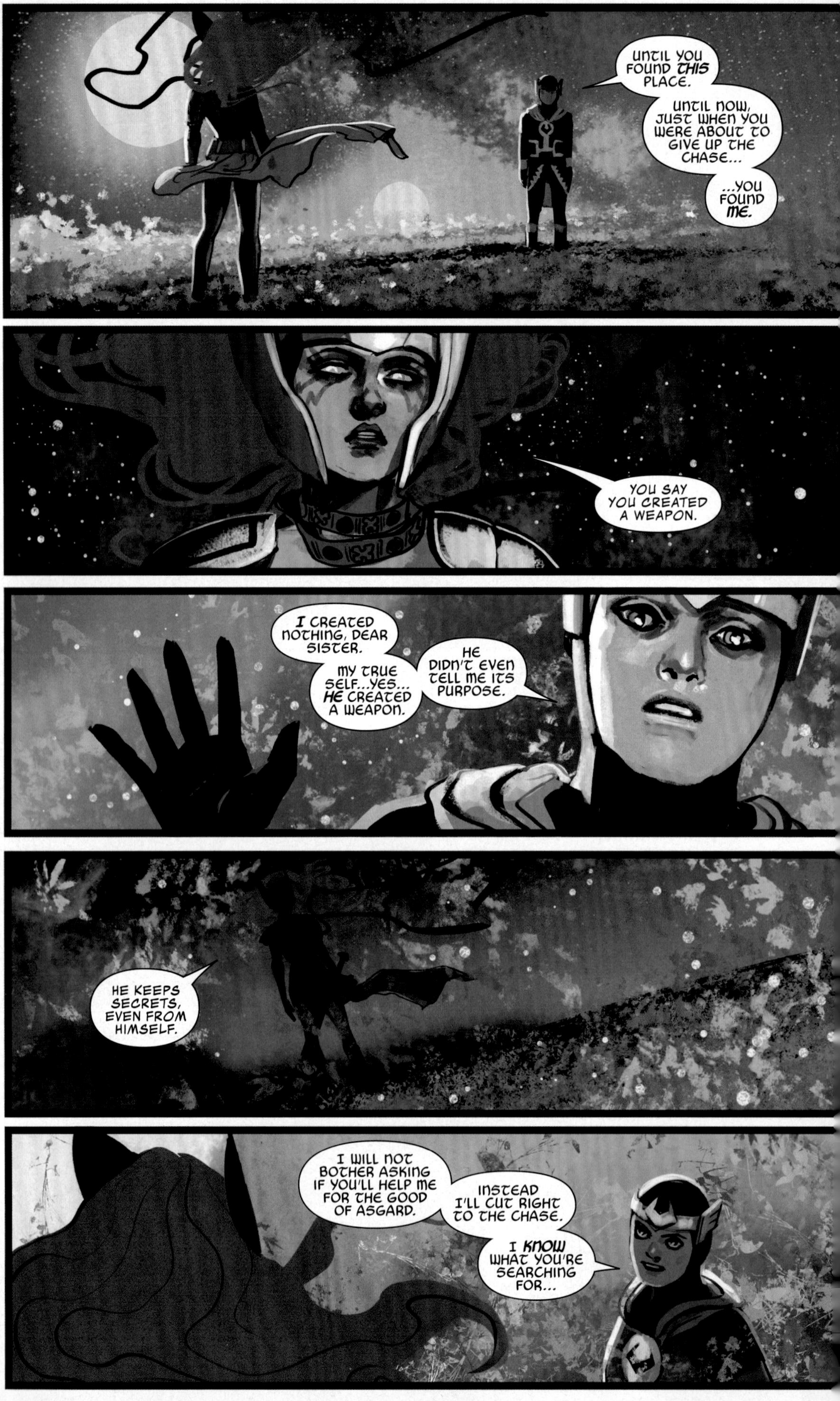

UNTIL YOU FOUND THIS PLACE.
UNTIL NOW, JUST WHEN YOU WERE ABOUT TO GIVE UP THE CHASE...
...YOU FOUND ME.
YOU SAY YOU CREATED A WEAPON.
I CREATED NOTHING, DEAR SISTER.
MY TRUE SELF...YES... HE CREATED A WEAPON.
HE DIDN'T EVEN TELL ME ITS PURPOSE.
HE KEEPS SECRETS, EVEN FROM HIMSELF.
I WILL NOT BOTHER ASKING IF YOU'LL HELP ME FOR THE GOOD OF ASGARD.
INSTEAD I'LL CUT RIGHT TO THE CHASE.
I KNOW WHAT YOU'RE SEARCHING FOR...

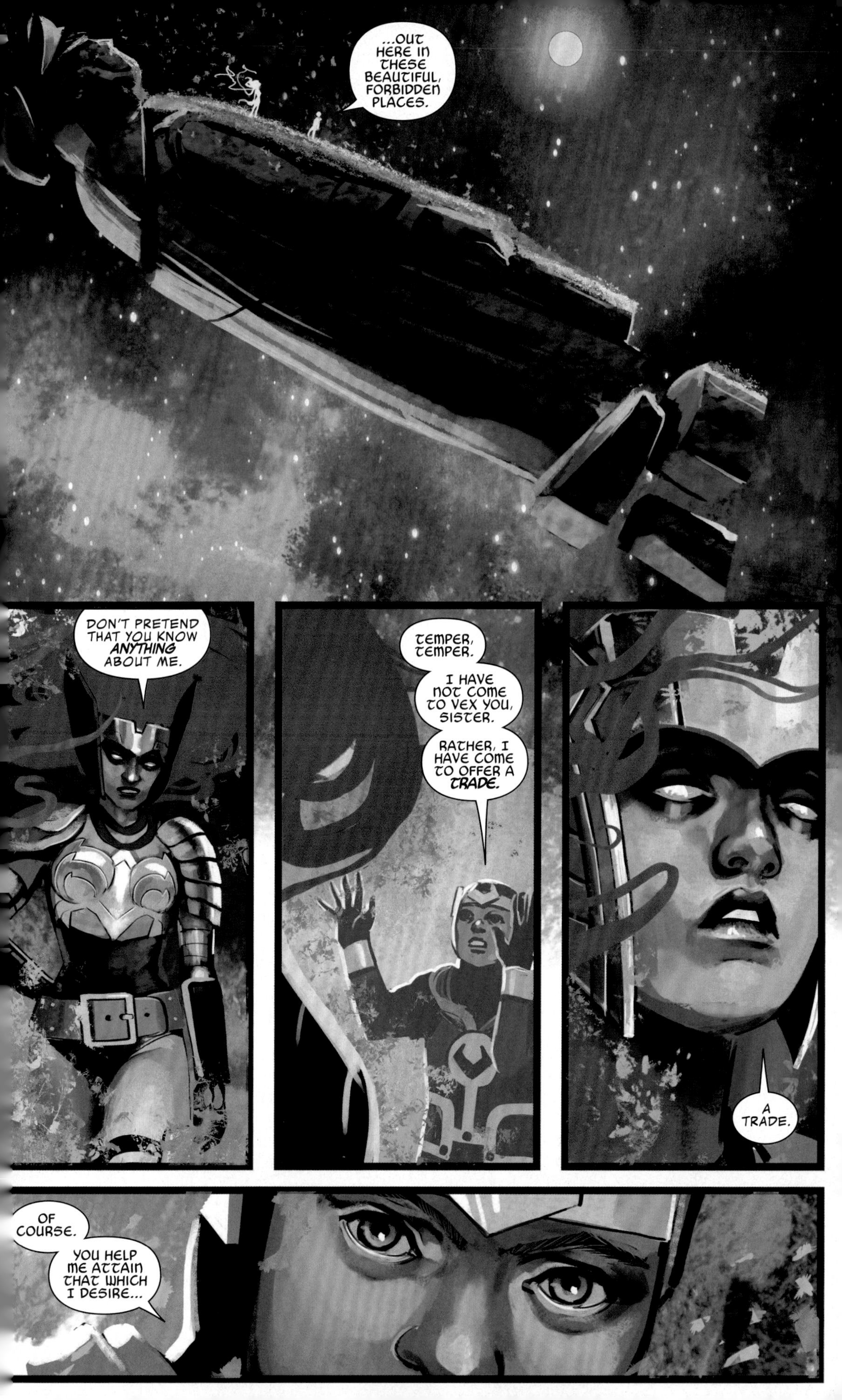
...OUT HERE IN THESE BEAUTIFUL, FORBIDDEN PLACES.
DON'T PRETEND THAT YOU KNOW ANYTHING ABOUT ME.
TEMPER, TEMPER.
I HAVE NOT COME TO VEX YOU, SISTER.
RATHER, I HAVE COME TO OFFER A TRADE.
A TRADE.
OF COURSE.
YOU HELP ME ATTAIN THAT WHICH I DESIRE...

"...AND I'LL DO THE SAME FOR YOU."

NOW.

ALL RIGHT. NAV COMPUTERS ARE FIRED UP.

WHERE TO?

Y'KNOW... WE'RE PRETTY CLOSE TO EARTH.

NOW THAT THE FIGHT'S OVER, DO YOU THINK YOU COULD JUST DROP ME OFF?

I KINDA HAVE SOMEONE WAITING FOR ME.

THE BATTLE MAY BE WON, ANNABELLE, BUT WE STILL HAVE A DIRE TASK AHEAD OF US.

THE SECRET OF THE NAGLFAR ARMADA HAS BEEN REVEALED.

WE MUST HIDE THE WEAPON SO THAT NO OTHER SHOULD DISCOVER IT.

AND WE'LL NEED ALL THE HELP WE CAN GET--ESPECIALLY NOW THAT THOR HAS TAKEN THE DESTROYER ARMOR BACK TO ASGARD WITH HIM.

I'LL STAY WITH YOU--AS PENANCE FOR HELPING NEBULA FIND THE BEACON.

AS PENANCE FOR LIVING WHILE MY BROTHERS DIED.

OH, PLEASE. PENANCE, SCHMENANCE.

YOU LIVED THERE'S NO SHAME IN THAT.

YOU LIVED SO YOU MIGHT DIE FOR SOME GREATER GOOD, PERHAPS IN THIS TERRIBLE WAR THAT BREWING

AND LUCKILY, I KNOW JUST THE PLACE TO STASH THE NAGLFAR BEACON...AND PONY UP ON SOME OF MY BARGAINS WHILE I'M AT IT

LET'S GO FIND ANGELA'S EX.

LET'S GO FIND SERA.

TO BE CONTINUED.

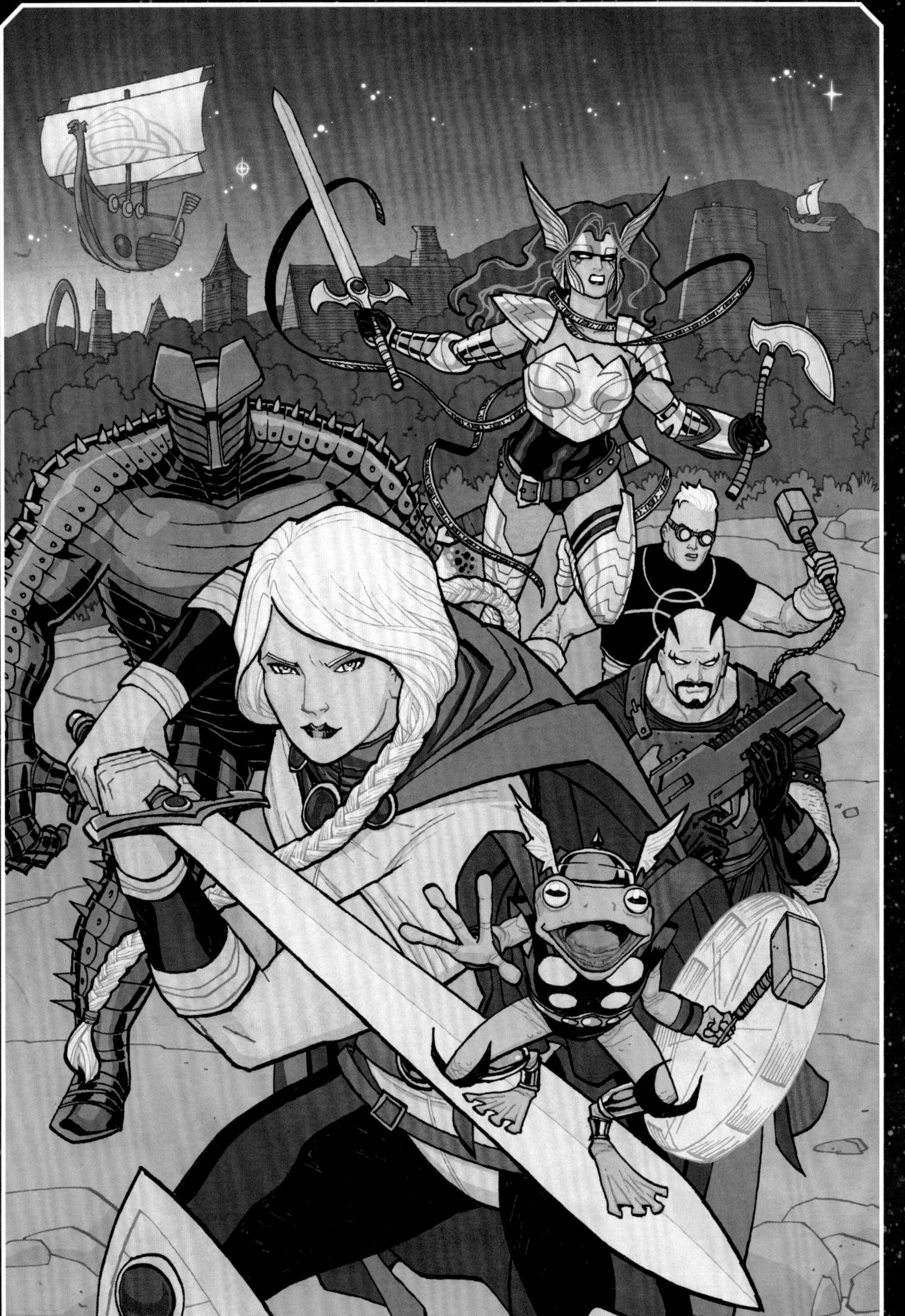
CLIFF CHIANG 2018

CLIFF CHIANG
#1 VARIANT

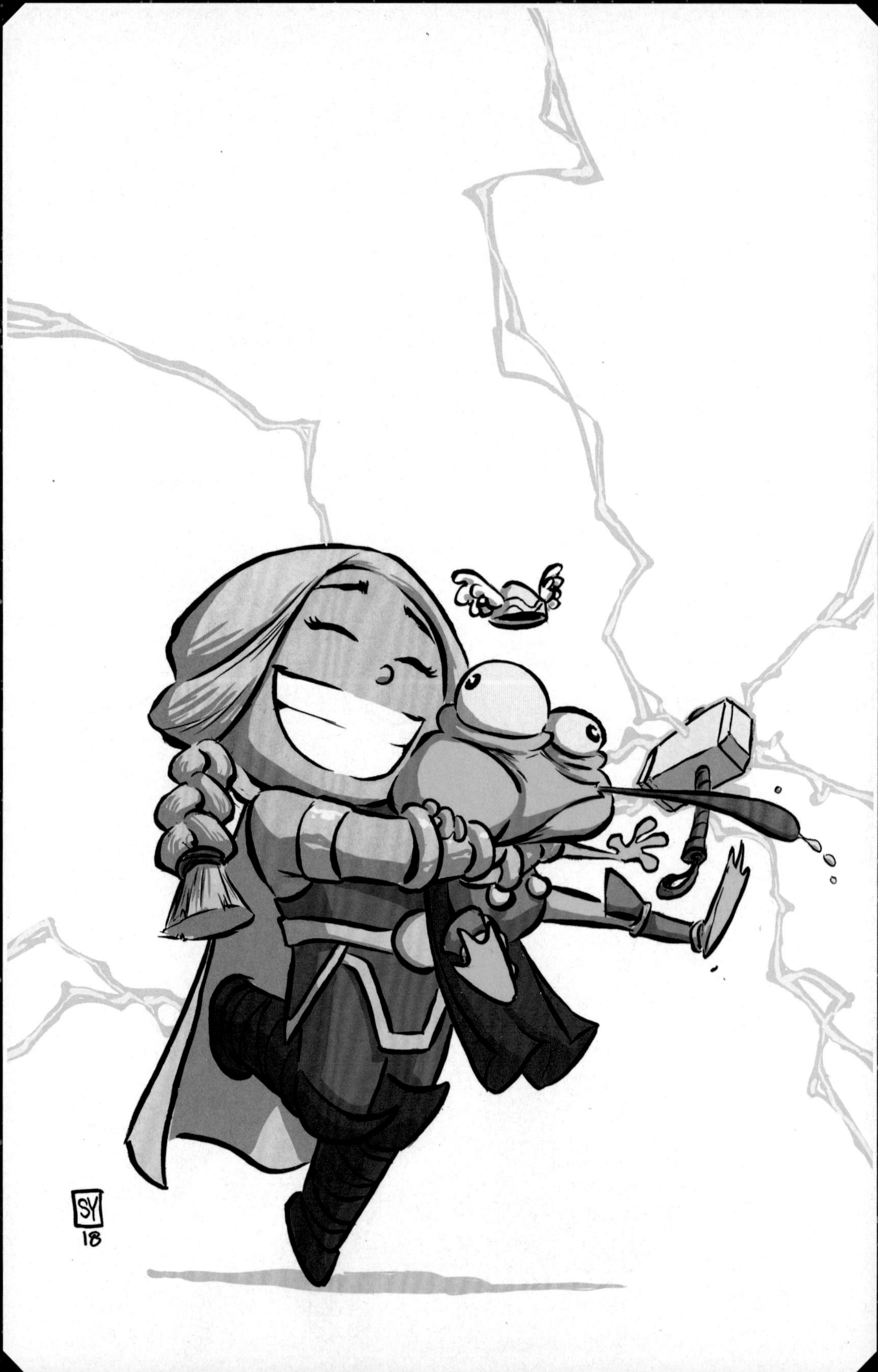

SKOTTIE YOUNG
#1 VARIANT